STUDY GUIDE

Contemporary Financial Management

Eighth Edition

R. Charles Moyer

Babcock Graduate School of Management, Wake Forest University

James R. McGuigan

JRM Investments

William J. Kretlow

University of Houston

Prepared by
Steve A. Johnson

South-Western College Publishing
Thomson Learning™

Australia • Canada • Mexico • Singapore • Spain • United Kingdom • United States

Study Guide to accompany *Contemporary Financial Management, Eighth Edition* by R. Charles Moyer, James R. McGuigan, and William J. Kretlow

Vice President/Publisher: Jack W. Calhoun
Acquisitions Editor: Michael B. Mercier
Senior Developmental Editor: Susanna C. Smart
Marketing Manager: Julie Lindsay
Media Technology Editor: Kurt Gerdenich
Media Development Editor: Vicky True
Production Editor: Amy S. Gabriel
Manufacturing Coordinator: Charlene Taylor
Printer: Phoenix Color

Printed in the United States of America
1 2 3 4 5 03 02 01 00

For more information contact South-Western College Publishing, 5101 Madison Road, Cincinnati, Ohio, 45227 or find us on the Internet at http://www.swcollege.com

For permission to use material from this text or product, contact us by
• telephone: 1-800-730-2214
• fax: 1-800-730-2215
• web: http://www.thomsonrights.com

Library of Congress Cataloging-in-Publication Data
0-324-05258-8

This book is printed on acid-free paper.

Contents

Preface

This Study Guide is a supplement to the 8th edition of *Contemporary Financial Management* by Moyer, McGuigan and Kretlow. Students should use this Study Guide as an ancillary learning aid to the textbook. The guide is designed to help students master the material in the textbook by reinforcing key concepts and by providing additional exercises to test their understanding of the qualitative and quantitative material in the text. Each chapter of the Study Guide consists of the following:

1. Detailed outline of the key concepts developed in the textbook. It is suggested that the student use the outline before and after reading the main textbook. Prior reading would help students appreciate the major concepts of each chapter. A second reading would further reinforce the student's understanding of the material's key issues.

2. True-false statements with solutions. The true-false questions test the student's understanding of the conceptual material presented in the chapter.

3. Multiple choice questions with answers. These questions are presented to further assess the student's comprehension of the material presented in the chapter.

4. Quantitative problems with solutions. These problems test the student's understanding of the analytical material presented in each chapter. This section of the supplement is designed as a self-test, and for optimal results, the student should treat it as such. That is, attempt the problem without consulting the solution. The problem section also contains specific problems supported by the Excel templates accompanying the text.

Chapter

1

The Role and Objective of Financial Management

This introductory chapter provides an overview of corporate finance. Included in this chapter are discussions of the types of business organizations, the objective of financial management and that of the corporation, and the decision areas of the financial manager. Also discussed in Chapter One are the major elements of the financial decision making process, the interrelationship between finance and other functional areas of business, and possible careers in finance.

I.   Finance is concerned with several important questions that confront all business firms. Examples of financial management questions include:

   A.   The assets that a firm should acquire;

   B.   The acquisition of assets to be financed; i.e., what are the costs and sources of funds?

   C.   The proper mix of the various sources of funds used to finance a firm's activities; i.e. what is the optimal capital structure?

   D.   The distribution of the profits from an enterprise; i.e., what is the optimal dividend policy?

   E.   The nature of the trade-offs between risk and expected return that have to be made in financial management decisions;

   F.   The level of inventory that a firm should hold;

   G.   Determination of a firm's credit policy;

   H.   Is a merger or acquisition advisable?

   I.   How much cash, or access to cash, does the firm need to meet its daily operating needs?

II.   The three principal forms of business organization are the sole proprietorship, partnership, and corporation.

    A.   A sole proprietorship is simply a business owned by one person.

        1.   Ease of formation is an advantage of sole proprietorships.

        2.   The primary disadvantages are unlimited personal liability and difficulty raising funds to finance growth.

        3.   About 75% of all businesses in the United States are sole proprietorships accounting for less than 6% of total U.S. business revenues.

    B.   A partnership is a business organization of two or more persons.

        1.   Partnerships may be classified as either general or limited partnerships. In a general partnership, each partner has unlimited liability for all the obligations of the business. In a limited partnership, the one or more general partners have unlimited liability and the one or more limited partners have limited liability (the extent to which is spelled out in the partnership agreement). Approximately 90% of all partnerships in the U.S. are classified as general partnerships. Overall, partnerships account for 7% of all U.S. businesses and less than 5% of total U.S. business revenues.

        2.   When one partner dies or quits, the partnership is dissolved and another one must be formed.

    C.   A corporation is a "legal person" composed of one or more natural persons and is separate and distinct from these persons. As a "legal person," a corporation can purchase and own assets, borrow money, sue, and be sued.

        1.   The owners of a corporation are called shareholders or stockholders. The money shareholders invest in the corporation is called capital stock.

        2.   The corporate form of organization has four major advantages.

            a.   The stockholders have limited liability. The most they can lose is their investment in the shares of the company.

            b.   The corporation continues in existence even if shareholders die or sell their shares giving the company the benefit of continuity.

            c.   It is very easy to change ownership (compared to partnerships)--just sell your shares to someone else.

            d.   A major advantage of the corporate form of organization is the ability to raise large amounts of capital. This is due to limited liability of owners and the easy marketability of shares of ownership.

        3.   In theory the board of directors are responsible for managing the corporation. The board of directors is elected by the shareholders. The board in turn hires officers who do the actual managing of the company on a day to day basis. The officers are considered to be *agents* of the corporation who act on behalf of the owners (shareholders) of the company. The officers might include a president, one or more vice presidents, a treasurer, and a secretary.

4. Corporations issue debt and equity securities to fund corporate operations.

    a. Debt securities promise periodic interest payments as well as the return of the principal amount of the debt.
    b. Preferred stockholders have priority over common stockholders with regard to the earnings and assets of the corporation. Creditors have priority over preferred stockholders.
    c. Common stockholders are the true residual owners of the corporation. Their claims on earnings and assets of the firm are considered only after all other claims have been met.

5. Common stockholders possess several specific rights including dividend rights, asset rights, voting rights, and preemptive rights.

III. To understand the content of this book as well as the real world practice of finance, it is crucial to understand the objective of financial management.

A. The most widely accepted objective of the firm is to maximize the value of the firm for its owners; that is, to *maximize shareholders' wealth*. Shareholder wealth is represented by the market price of the firm's common stock. Stock prices reflect the magnitude, timing, and risk associated with the expected future benefits accruing to stockholders. Profit maximization is inadequate for handling many finance decisions.

B. The advantages of shareholder wealth maximization are that it is a conceptually clear guide for decisions, that it does consider risk, and that it is impersonal.

C. Wealth maximization does not deny the existence of social objectives and obligations. In many respects, these other objectives are consistent with shareholder wealth maximization and, in addition, the government may place regulations and laws on businesses (as well as individuals) whenever it feels that private and public goals are in conflict. Many corporations recognize their responsibilities to various constituencies, including stockholders, customers, employees, the community, and the environment.

D. Due to a separation of ownership and control in many corporations, a divergence frequently exists between the owners' goals (shareholder wealth maximization) and the managers' goals (such as job security). For example, managers may be more concerned with long run survival (job security) causing them to minimize (or limit) the amount of risk incurred by the firm.

E. Agency relationships occur when one or more individuals (the *principals*) hire another individual (the *agent*) to perform a service on behalf of the principals. In an agency relationship, decision-making authority is often delegated to the agent.

    1. An important agency relationship in corporate finance is between stockholders (the principals) and managers (the agents).
    2. Inefficiencies that arise in agency relationships are called *agency problems*. Agency problems occur when managers maximize their own welfare instead of that of the principals. Examples of agency problems can include a preoccupation by management with their job security, excessive perquisite (perk) consumption, and managerial shirking.

3.   Shareholders incur *agency costs* to minimize agency problems.   Agency costs include:

    a.   the cost of management incentives designed to induce managers to act in the shareholders' interests;

    b.   expenditures to monitor management's actions and performance;

    c.   bonding expenditures to protect shareholders from managerial fraud; and

    d.   the opportunity cost of lost profits arising from complex organizational structures that prevent timely responses to opportunities.

4.   Another agency conflict is between stockholders and creditors. If the firm engages in high-risk activities, the creditors (because they have fixed claims against the firm) may not share the rewards if the risky venture works out well, but the creditors are left holding the bag if things don't work out well. In order to protect their interests creditors often insist on certain protective covenants in their contracts with the firm.

5.   Agency problems and agency costs can be reduced when financial markets operate efficiently.   For example, the existence of an efficient takeover market ensures that managers act in the best interest of shareholders; if they do not, managers face the prospect of their firm being taken over by an outsider and losing their jobs.

IV.   How do managers maximize shareholder wealth?

A.   One misconception is that managers maximize shareholder wealth by maximizing profits. Unfortunately, profit maximization has too many shortcomings to provide consistent guidance to the practicing manager.

1.   The profit maximization rule is that an economic action should be continued up to the point where marginal revenue (benefit) equals marginal costs.

2.   While the rule offers excellent insights, it frequently fails because (1) it is static, ignoring the time value of money, (2) it is vague with many different definitions, and (3) it ignores risk.

B.   Maximization of shareholder wealth is a market concept. Managers should attempt to maximize the market value of the company's shares, not accounting or book value per share.

C.   The three major factors that determine the market value of a company's stock are:

(1) the amount of the cash flows expected to be generated for the benefit of stockholders;
(2) the timing of these cash flows; and,
(3) the risk of the cash flows.

Management decisions affect these three factors. In addition, economic environment factors and conditions in financial markets outside of management control affect the amount, timing, and risk of expected cash flows and, hence, the market price of the company's stock.

Examples of decisions under management control, economic environment factors, and conditions in financial markets that affect stock prices are summarized in the figure on the next page.

V.   The *cash flow concept* is one of the central elements of financial analysis, planning, and resource allocation decisions. Firms need cash flows to pay creditors, employees, suppliers, and owners. Cash, not net income, can be spent.

   A.   A firm raises firms externally by selling shares to owners (equity) and by borrowing from creditors (debt). It may raise firms internally from cash flows from operations or by selling assets. These funds are used to acquire assets that, in turn, are used to produce and sell products or services. After paying for the cost of producing these products or services, any remaining cash flow can be used for reinvestment or distributed to owners and creditors.

   B.   The valuation of debt and equity securities is based on the present value of the cash flows that these securities are expected to provide to investors.

   C.   By emphasizing cash flows rather than accounting-based measures of performance when making decisions, a manager is more likely to achieve the objective of shareholder wealth maximization.

   D.   The *net present value (NPV)* of an investment is equal to the present value of the expected future cash flows generated by the investment minus the initial investment of cash, or

NPV = Present value of future cash flows *minus* initial outlay.

The net present value of an investment represents the contribution of that investment to the value of the firm and, accordingly, to the wealth of shareholders. The net present value concept is the bridge between cash flows and the goal of shareholder wealth maximization.

VI.   The ethical dimensions of business practice do much more than provide explosive news stories. Ethical issues will confront financial managers as they make important financial decisions.

   A.   Ethics is the "discipline dealing with what is good or bad, right or wrong, or with moral duty and obligation," according to *Webster's*.

   B.   Business ethics involves hardheaded thought, not just sentimentality. Several managerial approaches to addressing ethical dimensions of a business problem exist. These techniques include:

   • Clarify the parameters of the problem,
   • Involve the right team of participants,
   • Collect all facts bearing on the problem,
   • Articulate the benefits and harms from the proposed actions,
   • Weigh the consequences of alternatives, and
   • Seek equity for those who may be affected.

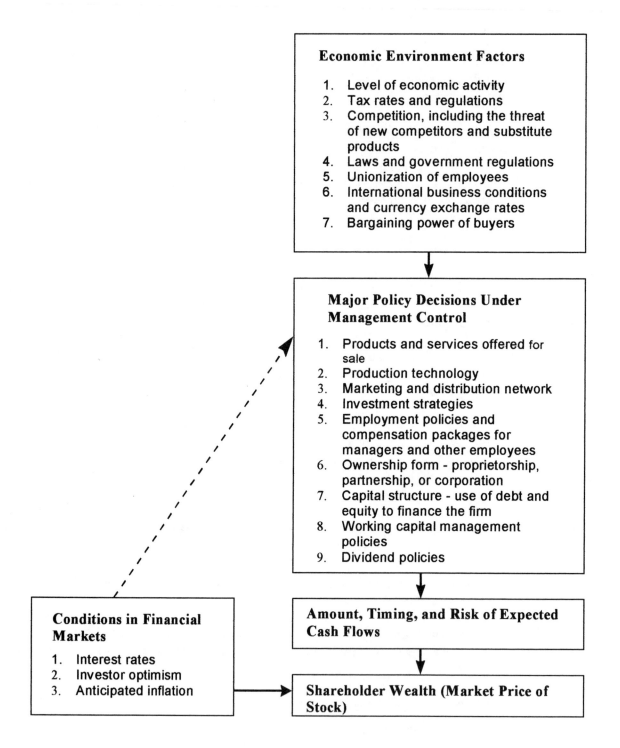

Economic Environment Factors

1. Level of economic activity
2. Tax rates and regulations
3. Competition, including the threat of new competitors and substitute products
4. Laws and government regulations
5. Unionization of employees
6. International business conditions and currency exchange rates
7. Bargaining power of buyers

Major Policy Decisions Under Management Control

1. Products and services offered for sale
2. Production technology
3. Marketing and distribution network
4. Investment strategies
5. Employment policies and compensation packages for managers and other employees
6. Ownership form - proprietorship, partnership, or corporation
7. Capital structure - use of debt and equity to finance the firm
8. Working capital management policies
9. Dividend policies

Conditions in Financial Markets

1. Interest rates
2. Investor optimism
3. Anticipated inflation

Amount, Timing, and Risk of Expected Cash Flows

Shareholder Wealth (Market Price of Stock)

C.   Some good ethical guidelines for managers include:

- Avoid personal conflicts with business decisions.
- Maintain the confidentiality of information given to you.
- Make decisions on an objective business basis rather than on inappropriate factors such as race, sex, or religion.
- Act fairly in dealing with customers while maintaining the legitimate interests of the business.

VII.   Entrepreneurial finance deals with the financing issues facing small businesses.

A.   Small businesses generally are not the dominant firm in the industries in which they compete. They tend to grow more rapidly than larger firms. They have limited access to financial markets. They do not have the depth of specialized managerial resources available to larger firms. And they often have a high failure rate.

B.   For many entrepreneurial firms that are corporations, their stock is not publicly traded and current stock prices are not good signals of performance. Other entrepreneurial firms are proprietorships and partnerships. The owners of these firms are often poorly diversified because so much of their wealth is invested in the firm.

C.   The owners and managers are frequently the same persons, thus, the agency conflict between owners and managers is not as severe as in large corporations. Other agency conflicts, such as between owners and lenders, still remain, however.

D.   The fundamental concepts are the same for large and small businesses. However, expensive, sophisticated analysis is often not justified in a small firm because it lacks the economies of scale that large firms possess. Small firms also may lack the depth of managerial talent to apply sophisticated financial techniques.

VIII.   In a large corporation, the finance area is headed by a person normally titled the financial vice president or chief financial officer.

A.   The financial vice president or chief financial officer reports directly to the president.

B.   The chief financial officer might divide financial management responsibility between the controller and the treasurer.

C.   The controller normally has responsibility for accounting-related activities. These activities include:

1.   Financial accounting - the preparation of financial statements,

2.   Cost accounting - preparing operating budgets and monitoring the performance of units within the firm,

3.   Taxes - preparing local, state, and federal tax reports, and

4.   Data processing.

D.   The treasurer is normally concerned with the acquisition, custody, and expenditure of funds. Treasury activities include:

1.   Cash and marketable securities management - forecasting cash needs, obtaining short-term funds and investing short-term funds,

2.   Capital budgeting analysis - evaluating the purchase of long-term assets,

3.   Financial planning - analyzing long-term sources of funds (issuing bonds or stocks),

4.   Credit analysis - evaluating the credit-worthiness of credit customers,

5.   Investor relations - working with institutional investors, bond-rating agencies, and the general financial community, and

6.   Pension fund management - managing the investment of employee pension fund contributions.

IX.   Finance has drawn heavily from other disciplines, most notably economics and accounting, and financial managers must learn from and communicate with persons from many disciplines.

A.   Accountants develop financial statements such as balance sheets, income statements, and statements of cash flows.

1.   These financial statements assist in evaluating past performance and in making decisions about the future direction of the firm.

2.   The payment of taxes is based on the accounting system.

B.   Finance also draws heavily on economics.

1.   Several macroeconomics topics are relevant to finance, such as the banking system and operation of money and capital markets.

2.   Finance evolved from the theory of the firm in microeconomics.

C.   Marketing, production, and quantitative methods are frequently related to the day-to-day decisions of financial managers.

X.   The finance profession offers a number of exciting career opportunities. In addition to careers in corporate finance, opportunities are available in the financial services sector. The financial services sector includes businesses such as commercial banks, securities brokers, investment banks, mutual funds, pension funds, real estate companies, and insurance companies.

XI.   There are several professional organizations for practicing financial management.

    A.   These include the Financial Executives Institute, the Institute of Chartered Financial Analysts, and the Financial Management Association.

    B.   The FMA (Financial Management Association) sponsors student chapters at many universities as well as the FMA National Honor Society. For membership information, contact your professor or the Financial Management Association, c/o College of Business Administration, The University of South Florida, Tampa, FL 33620.

TRUE AND FALSE QUESTIONS

Agree with each of the statements or **reject** it and modify it so that it is acceptable.

1.   When a partner dies or quits, the partnership is dissolved and a new one must be formed.

2.   Corporate stockholders have unlimited liability.

3.   Shareholders are the true residual owners of the corporation.

4.   Stockholders can require the payment of dividends by exercising their dividend rights.

5.   The most widely accepted objective of the firm is to maximize profitability.

6.   Agency problems arise whenever the principal and the agent are the same.

7.   Profit maximization and shareholder wealth maximization are equivalent.

8.   The Net Present Value of an investment made by a firm represents the contribution of that investment to the value of the firm.

9.   The finance function in a corporation is charged with the primary responsibility of developing financial statements such as the balance sheet, income statement, and the statement of cash flows.

Answers to True and False Questions

1.   True.
2.   Stockholders have limited liability.
3.   True.
4.   If dividends are paid, the dividend right means that shareholders will share equally on a per share basis.
5.   The primary objective should be to maximize shareholder wealth. Profit maximization is not always consistent with shareholder wealth maximization.
6.   Agency problems arise when the principal (manager) is different from the agent (owner or shareholders).
7.   Profit maximization and shareholder wealth maximization are different. Profit maximization is based on an accounting definition subject to different interpretations, it lacks a time dimension and it does not capture the risk element. Shareholder wealth maximization, on the other hand, refers to maximizing the present value of all future cash flows to shareholders.

8.   True.
9.   The accounting function is charged with the responsibility of developing the financial statements.

MULTIPLE CHOICE QUESTIONS

1.   _____ are "legal persons" composed of one or more natural persons and is separate and distinct from these persons. The owners of these business entities have limited liability.
   A.   Sole proprietorships
   B.   General partnerships
   C.   Limited partnerships
   D.   Corporations
   E.   Boards of directors

2.   The most widely accepted objective of the firm is to maximize _____.
   A.   the firm's after-tax income.
   B.   shareholder wealth.
   C.   shareholder cash flow.
   D.   shareholder expected utility.
   E.   direct and indirect employee compensation.

3.   Which of the following are not examples of agency costs?
   A.   The cost of management incentives designed to induce managers to act in the shareholders' interests.
   B.   Bonding expenditures to protect shareholders from managerial fraud.
   C.   Litigation expenses arising from the introduction of poorly designed and produced products.
   D.   The opportunity costs of lost profits arising from complex organizational structures preventing timely responses to opportunities.
   E.   Expenditures to monitor management's action and performance.

4.   The three major factors (within the control of management) that determine the market value of a company's stock are (1) the amount of the expected cash flows to shareholders, (2) the timing of these cash flows, and (3):
   A.   The risk of these cash flows.
   B.   The conditions in financial markets.
   C.   The tax rates and legal regulations under which the firm operates.
   D.   The excellence of the managerial team.
   E.   The size and nature of the firm's agency costs.

5.   Which of the following is not considered a "good ethical guideline" for managers?
   A.   Avoid personal conflicts with business decisions.
   B.   Maintain the confidentiality of information given to you.
   C.   Act fairly in dealing with customers while maintaining the legitimate interests of the business.
   D.   Use objective business criteria to make decisions.
   E.   Include factors such as race, sex and religion in making decisions pertaining to employment and customer relations.

6. The ultimate responsibility of managing a corporation lies with:
    A. The shareholders.
    B. The Chief Executive Officer (CEO).
    C. The Board of Directors.
    D. The Chief Operating Officer (COO).
    E. The President of the company.

7. Which of the following is not a specific right of a firm's common shareholders?
    A. Rights to dividends or other distributions of income.
    B. Rights to participate in the managerial decision making process.
    C. Preemptive rights to maintain their specific percentage of ownership.
    D. Residual ownership rights—what remains after asset liquidation.

8. The primary advantage of a sole proprietorship is:
    A. Limited liability.
    B. Easy access to funding for additional growth.
    C. Unlimited life.
    D. Relative ease of changing ownership.
    E. Ease of formation.

9. The Net Present Value (NPV) of an investment:
    A. Represents the contribution that the investment makes to the value of the firm.
    B. Is defined as the present value of future cash inflows.
    C. Violates the basic firm objective of wealth maximization.
    D. Ignores the initial cost of the investment.

10. Select the following sentence completion that is incorrect. Small business tend to:
    A. Grow more rapidly than do larger firms.
    B. Have limited access to financial markets.
    C. Lack specialized managerial resources.
    D. Lack agency problems evident in larger firms.
    E. Experience a lower failure rate than larger firms.

Answers to Multiple Choice Questions

1.	D	5.	E	9.	A
2.	B	6.	C	10.	E
3.	C	7.	B		
4.	A	8.	E		

Chapter

2

The Domestic and International Financial Marketplace

Chapter 2 provides a look at the domestic and international marketplaces in which firms operate. The role of the financial marketplace is to allocate scarce resources from savers to investors. This chapter provides an overview of the U.S. financial system and how funds are transferred between savers and investors. The major financial intermediaries and the operation and structure of secondary security markets are discussed. Aspects of international financial markets also are covered. Efficient markets concepts, the calculation of holding period returns, and the role of taxes are discussed as well.

I.   Corporate and personal income taxes have important implications for financial managers. Because so many financial decisions are based on after-tax cash flows, finance and business professionals must have a basic understanding of tax matters. Specific provisions of the Federal income tax laws applicable to corporations are discussed in Appendix 2A at the end of the chapter.

    A.   Several financial decisions that are affected by income taxes are previewed in this chapter.

        1.   Capital structure policy. Because interest payments on debt financing are deductible expenses when computing the income tax liability and because dividends paid on common or preferred stock are not deductible, there is a tax advantage to debt financing over equity financing.

        2.   Dividend policy. When dividend are paid to common stockholders, these dividends are taxed immediately as income. If, instead, the firm retains and reinvests the earnings, the price of the common stock should increase. Personal taxes on the stock price appreciation are deferred until the stock is sold. Thus, some stockholders prefer capital gains to dividend income, which would affect dividend policy.

        3.   Capital budgeting. Capital expenditure decisions are based on after-tax cash flows. Changes in depreciation schedules will affect the cash flows and net present value of capital investments.

4.   Leasing. Tax effects can motivate leasing (rather than buying) if the tax rates of the lessee (asset user) and the lessor (asset owner) are different.

B.   Corporate tax rates are progressive - the larger the income, the higher the tax rate. In this text, we will use an assumed marginal tax rate of 40 percent rather than the actual rate of 35%. This simplifies calculations, and the combined effect of state and federal income taxes might be close to 40 percent in many cases.

II.   The U.S. financial system serves an important function by channeling funds from saving units to investing units.

A.   For the economy as a whole, the savings for a given period of time must equal the investments in that period of time. This phenomenon is called the savings-investment cycle. The savings-investment cycle depends on net savers, or *surplus spending units*, and net investors, or *deficit spending units*. The cycle is completed when the surplus spending units transfer funds to the deficit spending units. The main purpose of the U.S. financial system is to facilitate this transfer of funds.

B.   The funds flow through financial middlemen and financial intermediaries.

1.   Financial middlemen include brokers (who buy securities for investors), dealers (who sell securities to investors from their own inventory of securities), and investment bankers (who help corporations sell their securities).

2.   Financial intermediaries sell claims against themselves (called secondary claims) to surplus spending units in order to get the funds to buy the obligations of the deficit spending units (called primary claims). Secondary claims frequently possess more liquidity, safety, and divisibility than primary claims.

C.   Debt and equity securities are the assets of investors who own them and, at the same time, the liabilities of corporations that issue them. Liabilities and stockholders' equity appear on the issuing company's balance sheet.

D.   Financial markets are classified as money or capital markets and as primary or secondary markets.

1.   Money markets deal in securities with a maturity of one year or less. Capital markets deal in securities with maturities exceeding one year.

2.   The market for newly issued securities is the primary market. The market for reselling outstanding securities is the secondary market.

E.   A variety of financial intermediaries exist to facilitate the flow of funds between spending surplus units and deficit spending units.

1.   Commercial Banks. They are major suppliers of short-term and intermediate-term loans to businesses for a variety of purposes. Commercial Banks accept time deposits and demand deposits. These funds are loaned to individuals, businesses and governments.

2.   Thrift institutions—include savings and loan associations and mutual savings banks. They accept demand and time deposits and invest these funds in home mortgages and consumer loans.

3.   Investment companies—mutual funds and real estate investment trusts (REITs). They pool funds from many savers and invest the funds in a various types of assets.

4.   Pension funds. They pool pension contributions from employers and their employees and invest the funds in a variety of financial assets.

5.   Insurance companies—life insurance and property and casualty companies. The premiums received by insurance companies are invested in variety of assets. The proceeds from these assets are used to pay claims against insured events/losses such as death, disability, accident, fire, etc.

6.   Finance companies. They obtain funds by issuing their own debt or by borrowing from commercial banks. These funds are loaned out to individuals and businesses.

F.   The primary suppliers of capital in U.S. capital markets are private U.S. investors, insurance companies and pension funds, and foreign banks and investors.

III.   A smoothly functioning secondary market aids the primary market, improves liquidity, and lowers the cost of capital to the firm.

A.   Secondary markets can be classified as listed security exchanges or over-the-counter (OTC) markets. Listed exchanges operate at designated places of business and have requirements governing the types of securities they will list or trade. The OTC security markets do not have centralized places of business, but are networks connected by communications systems that allow dealers to post the prices at which they are willing to buy and sell various securities.

1.   By far, the largest listed security exchange is the New York Stock Exchange (NYSE).

a.   The NYSE (also called the Big Board) tends to list the stocks of large firms. Over 2,000 common and preferred stocks and 800 bonds are listed on the NYSE.

b.   The American Stock Exchange (ASE or AMEX) is the other major listed exchange. It is also located in New York and companies listed on the AMEX are smaller on average than those on the NYSE.

c.   There are several regional exchanges around the country. The largest of these are the Chicago, the Pacific, the Philadelphia, the Boston, and the Cincinnati Stock Exchanges. The regional exchanges primarily trade stocks of companies in their geographical areas, but many NYSE stocks are traded on both the NYSE and regional exchanges.

2.   Stocks not listed on exchanges are traded "over-the-counter" (OTC).

a.   OTC trading includes trading in the stocks of small and relatively unknown companies, many bank and insurance company stocks, most corporate bonds and preferred stocks, and most U.S. Treasury and municipal bonds.

    b.   Price quotations on OTC stocks are available from NASDAQ, the automated quotation system of the National Association of Security Dealers.

3.   Stock market indexes give an indication of how the stock market, or some segment of it, is performing.

    a.   The most frequently quoted stock market index is the Dow Jones Industrial Average (DJIA), which is based on the prices of thirty, large, well-established stocks. The DJIA is based on the prices of these 30 stocks, which are divided by a number reflecting prior stock dividends and splits.

    b.   The Dow Jones Transportation Average is based on twenty major railroad, airline, and trucking stocks, and the Dow Jones Utility Average is derived from the prices of fifteen major utility stocks. The DJIA Composite Average is based on a combination of the DJIA, Dow Jones Transportation Average, and the Dow Jones Utility Average.

    c.   The Standard and Poor's 500 Stock Price Index (S&P 500) is a broader index than the DJIA. It is derived from the prices of 400 leading industrial firms, 20 transportation firms, 40 utilities, and 40 financial institutions. The S&P 500 is a market value-weighted index, which means that a stock whose total market value is $100 million influences the index twice as much as a stock whose total market value is $50 million.

B.   Both individual states and the federal government regulate the securities business.

1.   Because of many abuses such as incomplete and fraudulent information, states enacted the so-called blue sky laws. The term blue sky came about because many risky securities were called nothing more than "pieces of blue sky."

2.   Following the 1929 stock market crash, the federal government enacted its two principal pieces of security regulation, the Securities Act of 1933 and the Securities Exchange Act of 1934. Federal legislation has been aimed primarily at ensuring full disclosure of security information.

3.   The Securities and Exchange Commission (SEC) regulates the disclosure of information in new security offerings and sets disclosure requirements for nearly all firms trading publicly.

4.   The SEC also regulates "insider" trading, which includes trading done by directors, officers, and major shareholders of a corporation. All trading by insiders must be reported to the SEC. In addition, the SEC attempts to prevent insiders from secretly trading securities on the basis of private information that outside shareholders do not possess.

IV.   All firms engaged in international business transactions face unique problems and risks not encountered by firms that operate in only one country.

A.   Business enterprises participate in the global marketplace in a wide variety of ways.

  1.   The simplest case would be firms that only import or export finished products or raw materials.

  2.   At the other extreme are multinational corporations, which have direct investments in manufacturing and/or distribution facilities in more than one country.

B.   Firms that are engaged in international financial transactions face the following problems:

  1.   Firms doing business in different currencies are concerned with fluctuations in the exchange rates between currencies.

  2.   Firms doing business in foreign countries face different governmental regulations, tax laws, business practices, and political environments.

V.   The *exchange rate* is the number of units of one currency which may be exchanged for another currency. If a U.S. company buys materials from a foreign supplier, the foreign company usually prefers payment in its own currency. In order to pay for these goods, or to invest or repay loans, companies will have to exchange dollars for the foreign currency at some exchange rate. (For example, the exchange rate could be 2.4080 dollars per pound, or reciprocally, 0.4153 pounds per dollar.)

A.   A *Eurocurrency* is a currency that is deposited in a bank located outside of the country of origin. For example, Eurodollars are dollars deposited in a bank outside of the United States.

  1.   An example is dollars deposited in a German bank or a German branch of a U.S. bank.

  2.   The Eurocurrency market is an important alternative to domestic sources of funds for multinational funds. The interest rate in the Eurodollar market is usually related to the London interbank offer rate, or LIBOR.

B.   The *Euro* is a new composite currency created in 1999 by the member countries of the European Union. Its value is based on a market basket of the participating countries' currencies.

C.   Exchange rates can be expressed either as direct quotes or indirect quotes.

  1.   A *direct quote* is the home currency price of one unit of foreign currency. An example would be a quote of $1.48 per British pound.

  2.   An *indirect quote* is the foreign currency price of one unit of the home currency. An example would be a quote of 0.6757 pounds per dollar.

  3.   Direct and indirect quotes are the reciprocal of each other. In this example, 1/1.48 = 0.6757.

D.   The spot rate is the exchange rate for currencies being bought and sold for immediate delivery.

E.   Forward exchange rates are exchange rates for currencies being bought and sold for delivery at some future date, usually 30, 90, or 180 days from today.

    1.   A forward contract is a contract for delivery of a specified amount of foreign currency at a future point in time at a price set at the present time.

    2.   If the forward rate is higher than the spot rate, the higher rates are termed premiums. Premiums arise when the spot rate is expected to rise in the future. Discounts (the forward rate is below the spot rate) occur when the spot rate is expected to decline in the future.

    3.   The premium between the spot rate and the forward rate can be expressed on an annual percentage basis using this equation:

$$\begin{array}{c} \textit{Annualized} \\ \textit{forward premium} \\ \textit{or discount} \end{array} = \left(\frac{F - S_0}{S_0}\right)\left(\frac{12}{n}\right)(100\%)$$

where:
    S_0 = spot rate
    F = forward rate, and
    n = number of months forward.
In this formula, F and S_0 are expressed as direct quotes ($ per unit of foreign currency).

F.   A foreign currency *futures* contract is similar to a forward contract. Both call for delivery of a specified amount of foreign currency at a future point in time at a price set at the present time.

    1.   *Forward* contracts are contracts between individuals who are known to each other, but performance of the contract depends on the character and capacity of the two individuals. Hence, forward contracts are not liquid; that is, it is difficult for either party to sell its interest to another party.

    2.   A *futures* contract is an exchange traded agreement that calls for the delivery of a standardized amount of currency at a standardized maturity date. An example would be foreign currency futures contracts traded on the Chicago Mercantile Exchange (CME). These contracts are standardized, the two parties to the contract post collateral, gains and losses are realized daily ("marked to market"), and the exchange makes it very difficult for parties to the contract to default on their promises.

G.   Foreign currency options are contracts that give the buyer the right, but not the obligation, to buy or sell a fixed amount of foreign currency at a fixed price up to, or at, the expiration date of the option.

   1.   A *call* option is an option to buy something, such as a foreign currency, and a *put* option is an option to sell.

   2.   An *American option* gives the holder the right to buy (with a call) or sell (with a put) the underlying currency at any time prior to expiration. A *European option* gives the holder the right to buy or sell only at expiration.

VI.   Market efficiency is one of the most important concepts in finance. In an efficient capital market, stock prices provide an unbiased estimate of the true value of an enterprise (or the securities issued by the firm).

A.   Capital markets are efficient if prices instantaneously and fully reflect in an unbiased manner all economically relevant information about a security's prospective returns and the risk of those returns.

B.   Three degrees of market efficiency have been defined, depending on the information set under consideration.

   1.   Weak-form efficiency: No investor can expect to earn excess returns based on an investment strategy using information such as historical prices or historical returns information. This information is fully reflected in the current price of a stock.

   2.   Semistrong-form efficiency: No investor can expect to earn excess returns based on an investment strategy using any publicly available information.

   3.   Strong-form efficiency: Security prices fully reflect all information, both public and private.

C.   Capital markets have been shown to be quite efficient. Market efficiency has very important implications for financial managers.

   1.   Timing or gambling. Since there is no predictable pattern of stock prices and interest rate movements over time, financing decisions based on market timing are not likely to be profitable, on average.

   2.   Security investments have a zero NPV. The purchase and sale of securities in an efficient market represents a zero NPV transaction. Investments in real assets will have positive and negative NPVs because the real markets are not as efficient as security markets.

   3.   Corporate diversification is expensive and unnecessary. Since investors can diversify their own portfolios, it is unnecessary for corporate managers to diversify the firm's investments. (Corporate diversification probably benefits managers even when it doesn't benefit stockholders.)

4.   Capital markets are rarely fooled. In an efficient market, security prices reflect expected cash flows and the risk of those cash flows. Also, cosmetic accounting or other non-substantive transactions do not fool investors.

5.   Security prices tell a story. Prices in an efficient market change in response to new information.

D.   Extensive empirical testing of the efficiency of security markets in the U.S. has led researchers to the conclusions that these markets are quite efficient.

E.   Large capital markets outside the U.S. are also highly efficient. Some international markets are not very efficient, however. Some of the barriers that contribute to market inefficiency include:

1.   Legal restrictions on the amount of investment by foreign investors,

2.   High transactions costs,

3.   Taxation policies that discourage capital flows,

4.   Political risks of expropriation and limits on flows of profits and assets, and

5.   Foreign exchange risks.

Market inefficiencies (such as those listed above) may lead to segmented international capital markets. To the extent that international markets are not fully integrated, aggressive multinational firms are able to exploit market inefficiencies in managing their investment and capital raising functions.

VII.   The concept of a holding period rate of return is extremely useful.

A.   The rate of return during a period of time is:

$$\begin{matrix} Holding \\ period \\ return\ (\%) \end{matrix} = \frac{\begin{matrix} Ending \\ price \end{matrix} - \begin{matrix} Beginning \\ price \end{matrix} + \begin{matrix} Distributions \\ received \end{matrix}}{\begin{matrix} Beginning \\ price \end{matrix}} \times 100\%$$

where distributions include interest on debt or cash dividends on stock.

B.   A return computed with this equation is called a realized, or *ex post* (after the fact), return. Expected, or *ex ante* (before the fact) returns also may be calculated where the distributions and ending prices are estimated values.

TRUE AND FALSE QUESTIONS

Agree with each of the statements or **reject** it and modify it so that it is acceptable.

1.   The S&P 500 Stock Price Index is a broader index than the Dow Jones Industrial Average, which is based on the prices of 30 large stocks.

2.   Pension funds are an example of a thrift institution.

3.   Financial intermediaries purchase primary securities from surplus spending units and sell secondary securities to deficit spending units.

4.   A private placement is the sale of new securities directly to a few large investors instead of to the public.

5.   Primary securities are not sold on secondary markets.

6.   A direct quote refers to the foreign currency price of one unit of the home currency.

7.   The exchange rate of 4.0000 pralines per dollar is equivalent to .2500 dollars per praline.

8.   Because of the time value of money, forward exchange rates are always higher than spot rates.

9.   Euro-currency is a currency that is deposited in a European bank.

10.   Futures contract is another term for Forward contract.

11.   Foreign currency option contracts require that the option buyer must either buy or sell a fixed amount of foreign currency at a fixed price, at any time up to and including the expiration date of the option.

12.   The net present value of an investment is equal to the present value of the investment's future returns minus the initial outlay.

13.   Weak-form efficiency requires that security prices reflect all information both public and private.

14.   Because of market efficiency, stockholders react favorably to news that the firm is diversifying its investments.

15.   High transactions costs could limit the degree of market efficiency.

Answers to True and False Questions

1.   True.
2.   Savings and loan associations, mutual savings banks, and credit unions are classed as thrift institutions.
3.   Financial intermediaries purchase primary securities from <u>deficit</u> spending units and sell secondary securities to <u>surplus</u> spending units.
4.   True.

5.   Outstanding primary securities are sold on secondary markets.
6.   Direct quote is the home currency price of one unit of foreign currency.
7.   True.
8.   Forward rates may have either premiums or discounts over the spot rate.
9.   Euro-currency is a currency that is deposited in a bank located outside of the country of origin.
10.   Futures contracts and forward contracts are similar but not identical. The futures contract, in contrast to forward contracts, are exchange traded agreements with standardized amounts and standardized maturity dates.
11.   The options contract does not require that you "must" exercise it; it gives you the "right" but not the obligation to buy or sell a fixed amount of foreign currency at a fixed price on or before the expiration date.
12.   True.
13.   Weak-form efficiency says that prices reflect historical security prices and returns.
14.   Stockholders do not react favorably to attempts at corporate diversification because they are already diversified.
15.   True.

MULTIPLE CHOICE QUESTIONS

1.   _____ are major suppliers of short-term and intermediate-term loans to businesses for a variety. These financial services firms also accept time deposits and demand deposits.
      A.   Investment companies
      B.   Pension funds
      C.   Insurance companies
      D.   Commercial banks
      E.   Finance companies

2.   _____ markets do not have centralized places of business, but are networks connected by communication systems.
      A.   Primary
      B.   Listed
      C.   U.S. capital
      D.   Secondary
      E.   Over-the-counter

3.   The Dow Jones Industrial Average (DJIA), the most frequently quoted stock market index, is based on the prices of _____ large, well-established stocks.
      A.   Five hundred
      B.   Thirty
      C.   Four hundred
      D.   Two thousand
      E.   Forty

4. The _____ regulates the disclosure of information in new security offerings and sets disclosure requirements for nearly all firms that are traded publicly.
    A. New York Stock Exchange
    B. Securities and Exchange Commission
    C. Federal Reserve System
    D. U.S. Treasury Department
    E. Internal Revenue Service

5. Firms engaged in international financial transactions face all of the following problems and risks except:
    A. Fluctuations in exchange rates
    B. Unique customs and business practices
    C. Different political environments
    D. Distinct government regulations
    E. Firms engaged in international financial transactions face all of the above problems.

6. _____ are standardized traded agreements that calls for delivery of a commodity such as foreign exchange at a standardized maturity date.
    A. Forward contracts
    B. Futures contracts
    C. Call options
    D. Put options
    E. Spot rates

7. If the directly stated exchange rate between the U.S. dollar and the Swiss franc is $0.50 per Swiss franc, what is the exchange rate between these two currencies stated indirectly?
    A. Sf 1.0 per US dollar
    B. Sf 1.5 per US dollar
    C. Sf 5.0 per US dollar
    D. Sf 2.5 per US dollar
    E. Sf 2.0 per US dollar

8. If capital markets are efficient, then:
    A. Stock prices and interest rates have predictable patterns over time.
    B. Corporate diversification is unnecessary.
    C. Cosmetic accounting changes can influence asset prices.
    D. Security investments have a zero NPV.

9. Financial markets are _____ efficient if security prices fully reflect all information, both public and private.
    A. Weak-form
    B. Semistrong-form
    C. Strong-form
    D. Allocationally
    E. Pricing

10.   Which of the following is not a barrier that contributes to financial market inefficiency?
A.   Complete access to financial information
B.   High transactions costs
C.   Political risks
D.   Foreign exchange risks
E.   Tax on capital flows

Answers to Multiple Choice Questions:

1.	D	5.	E	9.	C
2.	E	6.	B	10.	A
3.	B	7.	E		
4.	B	8.	B		

PROBLEMS

1.   Calculate the premium between the forward rate and spot rate (on an annual basis) for the following currencies.

Currency	Spot Rate	90-Day Forward Rate
British Pound	1.4665	1.4510
Canadian Dollar	.7201	.7156
Japanese Yen	.006399	.006416
Swiss Franc	.5895	.5920
German Mark	.4787	.4806

All the exchange rates are given in U.S. dollars per unit of the foreign currency.

Solution:

Use this forward premium equation for each currency:

$$\begin{matrix} Annualized \\ forward\ premium \\ or\ discount \end{matrix} = \left(\frac{F - S_0}{S_0}\right)\left(\frac{12}{n}\right)(100\%)$$

Ninety days is three months.

British Pound:

$$Premium = \left(\frac{1.4510 - 1.4665}{1.4665}\right)\left(\frac{12}{3}\right)(100\%) = -4.23\%$$

Canadian Dollar:

$$Premium = \left(\frac{.7156-.7201}{.7201}\right)\left(\frac{12}{3}\right)(100\%) = -2.50\%$$

Japanese Yen:

$$Premium = \left(\frac{.006416-.006399}{.006399}\right)\left(\frac{12}{3}\right)(100\%) = 1.06\%$$

Swiss Franc:

$$Premium = \left(\frac{.5920-.5895}{.5895}\right)\left(\frac{12}{3}\right)(100\%) = 1.70\%$$

German Mark:

$$Premium = \left(\frac{.4806-.4787}{.4787}\right)\left(\frac{12}{3}\right)(100\%) = 1.59\%$$

2.   One year ago, Frank Mueller bought shares of International Merchandising for $73.00 per share. If Frank received dividends of $2.75 per share and sold the stock today for $86.50, what is her percentage rate of return?

Solution:

$$\begin{array}{c} Holding \\ period \\ return\ (\%) \end{array} = \frac{\begin{array}{c}Ending \\ price\end{array} - \begin{array}{c}Beginning \\ price\end{array} + Distributions}{\begin{array}{c}Beginning \\ price\end{array}} \times 100\%$$

$$\begin{array}{c} Holding \\ period \\ return \end{array} = \frac{86.50-73.00+2.75}{73.00} = \frac{10.25}{73.00} = 22.26\%$$

3.   Juan Sanchez bought a £1000, 8.5% bond one year ago for £950. If Juan receives two £42.50 coupon payments and sells the bond today for £960, what has been his percentage rate of return?

Solution:

$$\begin{array}{c} Holding \\ period \\ return \end{array} = \frac{960-950+85}{950} = \frac{95}{950} = 10.0\%$$

4.   An outlay of $1,000 is expected to produce a cash flow of $1,150 in one year.

    a.   What is the present value of the expected future return if the required rate of return is 10%? What is the net present value?

    b.   What is the present value and net present value if the required return is 20%?

Solution:

    a.   Net present value = Present value - Outlay

$$\frac{Present}{value} = cashflow \times \frac{1}{1+i} = 1150 \times \frac{1}{1+.10} = 1045$$

NPV = 1045 - 1000 = $45

This investment has a positive NPV.

    b.   Net present value = Present value - Outlay

$$\frac{Present}{value} = 1150 \frac{1}{1+.20} = 1150 \frac{1}{1.20} = 958$$

NPV = 958 - 1000 = -$42

At a higher required rate of return, the present value of the future cash flow decreases, and this project now has a negative NPV.

Chapter 3

Evaluation of Financial Performance

This chapter deals with the evaluation of financial performance using financial statement analysis. It is useful in assessing firm performance and in identifying the major strengths and weaknesses of the business.

I.   Financial ratio analysis is used to measure the relative performance and creditworthiness of a business entity. Some specific uses for ratio analysis include:

      A.   Ratios are used internally by management for planning and for evaluating performance.

      B.   Ratios are used by credit managers to estimate the riskiness of potential borrowers.

      C.   Ratios are used by investors to evaluate the stocks and bonds of various corporations.

      D.   Ratios are used by managers to identify and assess potential merger candidates.

II.   A *financial ratio* is a relationship that indicates something about a firm's activities, such as the ratio between the firm's current assets and current liabilities or between its accounts receivable and annual sales. Financial ratios are frequently grouped into six types of ratios.

      A.   *Liquidity ratios* indicate the ability of the firm to meet short-term financial obligations.

      B.   *Asset management ratios* indicate how efficiently the firm is utilizing its resources.

      C.   *Financial leverage management ratios* indicate the firm's capacity to meet its debt obligations, both short-term and long-term.

      D.   *Profitability ratios* measure the total effectiveness of management in generating profits on sales, assets, and owners' investment.

      E.   *Market-based ratios* measure the financial market's assessment of a company's performance.

F. *Dividend policy ratios* indicate the dividend practices of the firm.

G. The firm's major financial statements are published quarterly and annually.

1. The Balance Sheet contains information on a firm's assets, liabilities, and stockholders' equity at the end of each period.

2. The Income Statement presents the firm's net sales, cost of sales, other operating expenses, interest expenses, taxes, and net income for the period.

3. The Statement of Cash Flows lists how a firm generated cash flows from its operations, how it used cash in investing activities, and how it obtained cash from financing activities.

H. Common-size statements are also helpful in financial analysis.

1. A common-size balance sheet shows the firm's assets and liabilities as a percentage of total assets (rather than as dollar amounts).

2. A common-size income statement shows the firm's income and expense items as a percentage of net sales (rather than as dollar amounts).

III. The data for constructing ratios generally comes from a firm's balance sheet, income statement, and statement of cash flows.

A. Liquidity ratios:

$$Current\ ratio\ =\ \frac{Current\ assets}{Current\ liabilities}$$

$$Quick\ (Acid\ test)\ ratio\ =\ \frac{Current\ assets - Inventories}{Current\ liabilities}$$

The quick ratio can also be adjusted downward by removing accounts receivable over 90 days old from the numerator of the quick ratio.

An aging schedule shows the liquidity of the firm's accounts receivable. The aging schedule, for example, might show the amount and percentage of total accounts receivable in several age categories, such as less than 30 days old, 30 to 60 days old, 60 to 90 days old, and over 90 days old.

B.   Asset Management Ratios:

$$Average\ collection\ period = \frac{Accounts\ receivable}{Annual\ credit\ sales\ /\ 365}$$

$$Inventory\ turnover = \frac{Cost\ of\ sales}{Average\ inventory}$$

$$Fixed\text{-}asset\ turnover = \frac{Sales}{Net\ fixed\ assets}$$

$$Total\ asset\ turnover = \frac{Sales}{Total\ assets}$$

C.   Financial Leverage Management Ratios:

$$Debt\ ratio = \frac{Total\ debt}{Total\ assets}$$

$$Debt\text{-}to\text{-}equity\ ratio = \frac{Total\ debt}{Total\ equity}$$

$$Times\ interest\ earned = \frac{Earnings\ before\ interest\ and\ taxes\ (EBIT)}{Interest\ charges}$$

$$Fixed\ charge\ coverage =$$

$$\frac{EBIT + Lease\ payments}{Interest + Lease\ payments + \frac{Preferred\ dividends}{before\ tax} + \frac{Before\ tax}{sinking\ fund}}$$

D.   Profitability Ratios:

$$Gross\ profit\ margin\ =\ \frac{Sales\ -\ Cost\ of\ sales}{Sales}$$

$$Net\ profit\ margin\ =\ \frac{Earnings\ after\ taxes\ (EAT)}{Sales}$$

$$Return\ on\ investment\ (ROI)\ =\ \frac{Earnings\ after\ taxes\ (EAT)}{Total\ assets}$$

$$Return\ on\ stockholders\ equity\ =\ \frac{Earnings\ after\ taxes\ (EAT)}{Stockholders\ equity}$$

E.   Market-Based Ratios

$$Market\ to\ book\ Ratio\ =\ P\ /\ B\ =\ \frac{Market\ price\ per\ share}{Book\ value\ per\ share}$$

$$Price\ to\ earnings\ ratio\ =\ P\ /\ E\ =\ \frac{Market\ price\ per\ share}{Current\ earnings\ per\ share}$$

F.   Dividend Policy Ratios:

$$Payout\ ratio\ =\ \frac{Dividends\ per\ share}{Earnings\ per\ share}$$

$$Dividend\ yield\ =\ \frac{Expected\ dividend\ per\ share}{Stock\ price}$$

IV.   The effective use of financial ratio analysis requires some experience and effort. There are some basic approaches to financial ratio analysis, some basic interrelationships among ratios, and sources of information that can enhance the analyst's effectiveness.

A.   Two common types of ratio analysis are time-series and cross-sectional analysis.

1.   *Trend or time-series analysis*--This requires the analyst to examine the ratios of a firm for several periods. This shows whether the firm's financial condition is improving or deteriorating over time.

2.   *Cross-sectional analysis*--The analyst compares the ratios of the firm to the industry norms or other individual firms in the industry.

3.   Frequently, time-series and cross-sectional analyses are pooled and performed simultaneously.

B.   There are logical relationships among many of the ratios.

1.   Return on Investment = Net Profit Margin x Total Asset Turnover.

$$ROI = \frac{EAT}{Sales} \times \frac{Sales}{Total\ assets} = \frac{EAT}{Total\ assets}$$

2.   Return on Stockholders' Equity = Return on Investment x Equity Multiplier. (The equity multiplier is the ratio of assets to equity).

$$\frac{Return\ on}{stockholders\ equity} = \frac{EAT}{Total\ assets} \times \frac{Total\ assets}{Stockholders\ equity}$$

$$\frac{Return\ on}{stockholders\ equity} = \frac{Net\ profit}{margin} \times \frac{Total\ asset}{turnover} \times \frac{Equity}{multiplier}$$

3.   *Dupont analysis*--Dupont charts, such as the one in the textbook, present the major ratios in a logical, organized fashion. This Dupont Chart provides a good starting point for analyzing the firm. For example, suppose a firm's return on stockholders' equity is considered low. Is this because of a low ROI or a low equity multiplier (or both)? If the ROI is too low, is this due to a low net profit margin or low total asset turnover (or both)? If the net profit margin is low, which expenses are out of line?

C.   Sources of comparative financial information--The most popular sources of financial information for businesses and industries are:

- *Industry Norms and Key Business Ratios* published by Dun and Bradstreet (D&B)
- *Statement Studies* from Robert Morris Associates
- Reports of the Federal Trade Commission (FTC) and the Securities and Exchange Commission (SEC)
- Prentice-Hall's *Almanac of Business and Industrial Financial Ratios*
- *Financial Studies of Small Business* from Financial Research Associates
- Moody's or Standard and Poor's Industrial, Financial, Transportation, and Over-the-Counter manuals
- Annual reports and 10K's from corporations
- Trade associations and trade journals
- Publications of some commercial banks.

D.   Computerized data bases are available to assist in financial statement analysis. Standard and Poors provides the *Compustat* data base containing balance sheet, income statement, stock price and dividend information. *Value Line* provides financial information on a large number of firms. The *Disclosure* database is available for microcomputers. Additional financial data may be accessed via the Internet.

V.   Even though ratios can provide valuable information, they can be misleading for a number of reasons.

A.   Ratios are only as reliable as the accounting data on which they are based.

B.   Industry "average" ratios may not be very meaningful if there is significant dispersion in the ratio for the industry.

C.   Industry classifications may be defined too broadly to make reliable comparative analysis between a firm and a particular industry average.

D.   Financial ratios provide a historical assessment of performance which may or may not be a useful basis for making future projections.

E.   A comparison of a firm's ratios with industry norms provides a relative measure of performance, not an absolute measure. For example, a firm's profitability ratios may be relatively better than its industry average, but on an absolute basis it may be poor compared to the universe of firms.

VI.   The final assessment of the firm's financial condition depends on its quality of earnings and quality of the balance sheet.

A.   The "quality" of a firm's earnings is positively related to the proportion of cash earnings to total earnings and to the proportion of recurring income to total income. Poor quality of earnings is signaled by the following:

1.   Large non-cash component in the earnings.

2.   Significant non-recurring transactions in the income figure.

B.   The "quality" of a firm's balance sheet is positively related to the ratio of the market value of the firm's assets to the book value of assets and inversely related to the amount of its hidden liabilities. Poor balance sheet quality is indicated by the following:

1.   Presence of hidden liabilities.
2.   Presence of obsolete inventory.
3.   Assets have market values significantly below book values.

VII.   Traditional financial analysis focuses on a set of financial ratios, primarily derived from accounting information. There are important new measures based on the market value of the firm.

A.   Market Value Added (MVA) is defined as the market value of debt, preferred equity, and common equity capitalization less capital. Capital is a measure of the cash raised from investors or retained from earnings to fund new investments in the business since the company's inception.
MVA is the capital market's assessment of the accumulated Net Present Value (NPV) of all of the firm's past and projected investment projects.

$$MVA = Market\ value - Capital$$

B.   Economic Value Added (EVA) is a measure of operating performance that indicates how successful the firm has been at increasing its MVA in a given year. EVA is defined as:

$$EVA = \left[\begin{array}{cc} Return\ on & Cost\ of \\ total\ capital & capital \end{array} \right] \times Capital = [r - k] \times Capital$$

where
r = net operating profits after tax divided by beginning-of-year capital,
k = weighted after-tax cost of capital.

C.   EVA can be thought of as the incremental contribution of a firm's operations to the creation of MVA. Managers find the MVA and EVA concepts to be a useful complement to traditional financial analysis.

VIII.   Inflation can make it difficult to assess performance over time or across firms.

A.   During inflation, the last-in, first-out (LIFO) inventory valuation method results in lower reported profits and lower taxes than the first-in, first-out (FIFO) method.

B.   If inflation causes a rise in interest rates, the value of long-term debt will decline.

C.   Inflation can have an impact on a firm's reported earnings. For example, inventory valuation methods or cost accounting systems will influence earnings.

IX.   Many key performance measures rely on accounting income measures. Financially, accounting income is not the relevant source of value for a firm -- cash flow is.

A.   A firm's after-tax cash flow (ATCF) is its net income (EAT) plus noncash charges: The depreciation expense recorded for a particular year is an allocation of an asset's original cost and does not represent a current cash outlay. Deferred taxes occur when the tax amount reported to stockholders exceeds the cash actually paid. This arises oftentimes because firms use accelerated depreciation for tax purposes and straight-line depreciation for financial reporting purposes. A firm's reported taxes include a current portion (which is paid in cash) and a deferred portion (which is a future liability of the firm). Since depreciation and deferred taxes are not cash outflows, they are added back to the firm's net income to get ATCF.

$$ATCF = EAT + Noncash\ charges$$

$$ATCF = EAT + Depreciation + Deferred\ taxes$$

B.   The Statement of Cash Flows is a major portion of the firm's financial statements, along with the balance sheet and income statement.

    1.   The Statement of Cash Flows shows the effects of the firm's operating, investing, and financing activities on its cash balance:

Net cash
increase (decrease)   = Net cash provided (used) by operating activities
        + Net cash provided (used) by investing activities
        + Net cash provided (used) by financing activities

    2.   Two ways that the Statement of Cash Flows may be prepared are the direct method and the indirect method.

        a.   In the direct method, all actual cash flows are grouped into the three categories above in order to present the net cash provided by operating, investing, or financing.

        b.   In the indirect method, several adjustments are made to the firm's income statement to create the Statement. The indirect method is the one that virtually all companies use in their public financial reports. While the details in the direct and indirect method will differ, the final results will be identical.

X.   The dollar amount of foreign earnings will depend on the exchange rate for the countries where foreign income is earned. In addition, exchange rate fluctuations will give rise to accounts such as "cumulative foreign exchange translation adjustment" or "translation adjustments" in the stockholders' equity portion of the balance sheet.

XI.   Auditing firms as well as government agencies and financial statement users (such as investors, lenders, or banks) want financial statements to present a complete, fair, and accurate picture of the firm's financial position. An important ethical concern is the possibility of manipulation or fraud in the presentation of a firm's financial position.

TRUE AND FALSE QUESTIONS

Agree with each of the statements or **reject** it and modify it so that it is acceptable.

1.   The current ratio will never exceed the quick ratio.

2.   Assuming a current ratio greater than one, the purchase of raw materials on credit decreases the current ratio.

3.   The gross profit margin is greater than the net profit margin.

4.   The average collection period is found by dividing a firm's year-end accounts receivable by its average daily credit sales.

5.   Because total assets exceed net fixed assets, the total asset turnover must exceed the fixed asset turnover.

6.   A short average collection period is a sign of efficient accounts receivable management.

7.   The return on total equity equals the net profit margin times the total asset turnover.

8.   The dividend yield ratio tells you what proportion of the firm's earnings is paid out as dividends.

9.   A change in inflation would have no effect on a firm's current ratio since the current ratio is based on short-term accounts.

10.   Firms with a current ratio below 2.0 are having liquidity problems.

Answers to True and False Questions

1.   The current ratio exceeds the quick ratio for all firms with an inventory.
2.   True.
3.   True.
4.   True.
5.   Because total assets exceed net fixed assets, the total asset turnover must <u>be less than</u> the fixed asset turnover.
6.   A short average collection period is not necessarily a sign of efficient accounts receivable management. It could also result from overly strict credit terms that can reduce the firm's sales and profitability.
7.   The return on total assets equals the net profit margin times the total asset turnover.
8.   Dividend yield is the ratio of expected dividends per share to the market price of the stock.
9.   Inventory could be affected by the use of LIFO or FIFO.
10.   The appropriate current ratio for a given firm can be substantially above <u>or</u> below 2.0 depending on the industry and circumstances relevant to the specific firm.

MULTIPLE CHOICE QUESTIONS

1.   _____ ratios measure the total effectiveness of management in generating profits on sales, assets, and owners' investment.
        A.   Liquidity
        B.   Asset management
        C.   Financial leverage management
        D.   Profitability
        E.   Market-based ratios

2.   A common-size balance sheet shows a firm's assets and liabilities, and shareholders' equity as a percentage of _____.
A.   total sales
B.   net income
C.   total shareholders' equity
D.   total assets
E.   total liabilities

3.   In cross-sectional analysis, the financial analyst compares the ratios of the firm:
A.   For several reporting periods.
B.   To industry norms or other firms in the industry.
C.   To the firm's ratios under ideal operating conditions.
D.   To the industry leader's ratios.
E.   To governmental standards of acceptable accounting performance.

4.   To assess the ability of the firm to meet current financial obligations, a potential lender would most likely be most concerned with the firm's _____:
A.   Payout ratio.
B.   Price to earnings ratio.
C.   Average collection period.
D.   Fixed charge coverage ratio.
F.   Total asset turnover.

5.   If a firm's net profit margin declines and the CEO wants to maintain the return on shareholder equity, he must:
A.   increase the firm's utilization of assets.
B.   reduce the amount of debt in the firm's capital structure.
C.   increase the firm's total sales.
D.   increase the firm's total shareholder equity.
F.   increase the firm's average collection period.

6.   The "quality" of a firm's earnings is positively related to the proportion of _____ and to the proportion of _____.
A.   non-cash earnings to total earnings; nonrecurring income to total income
B.   cash earnings to total earnings; nonrecurring expenses to total income
C.   non-cash earnings to total earnings; recurring income to total income
D.   cash earnings to total earnings; recurring expenses to total income
E.   cash earnings to total earnings; recurring income to total income

7.   _____ is a measure of operating performance that indicates how successful the firm has been at increasing its MVA in a given year.
A.   Economic value added (EVA)
B.   After-tax cash flow (ATCF)
C.   Earnings after taxes (EAT)
D.   Market value added (MVA)
E.   Earnings before interest and taxes (EBIT)

8.   During inflation, the _____ inventory valuation method is preferred because it yields lower reported profits and lower taxes than other inventory valuation methods.
       A.   FIFO
       B.   LIFO
       C.   Weighted Average
       D.   Base stock
       E.   Simple average

9.   Depreciation is the most common example of a non-cash charge that should be added to after-tax income (EAT) to compute after-tax cash flow (ATCF). Which of the following is a second non-cash charge?
       A.   Accrued interest
       B.   Accrued liabilities
       C.   Deferred taxes
       D.   Accelerated depreciation
       E.   Sales discount allowances

10.   _____ returns on an investment are computed using the beginning prices, the actual ending prices and any received distributions from the investment.
       A.   Ex ante
       B.   Effective
       C.   Ex post
       D.   Pro forma
       E.   Efficient

Answers to Multiple Choice Questions

1.	D	5.	A	9.	C
2.	D	6.	E	10.	C
3.	B	7.	A		
4.	D	8.	B		

CHAPTER 3 PROBLEMS

1.   Please supply the missing figures:

	Net Profit Margin	Total Asset Turnover	Return on Investment	Equity Multiplier	Return on Stockholders' Equity
a.	20.0%	0.75	--	1.00	--
b.	--	2.00	8.0%	1.50	--
d.	2.5%	4.00	--	--	25.0%
d.	6.0%	--	9.0%	--	14.4%

Solution:

a.   ROI = NPM x TAT = 20.0%(.75) = 15.0%
        Return on Equity = ROI x Equity Multiplier = 15.0%(1.00) = 15.0%

b.   NPM = ROI/TAT = 8.0%/2.00 = 4%
        Return on Equity = ROI x Equity Multiplier = 8%(1.5) = 12.0%

c.   ROI = NPM x TAT = 2.5%(4.00) = 10%
        Equity Multiplier = Return on Equity/ROI = 25%/10% = 2.50

d.   TAT = ROI/NPM = 9%/6% = 1.50
        Equity Multiplier = Return on Equity/ROI = 14.4%/9% = 1.60

2.   Find the sales of the Franklin Company using the following information:

Current ratio	2.0
Quick ratio	1.6
Current liabilities	$200,000
Inventory turnover	8.0
Gross profit margin	10%

   Solution:

Current assets = 2.0(200,000) = $400,000
Current assets minus inventory = 1.6(200,000) = $320,000
Inventory = 400,000 - 320,000 = $80,000
Inventory Turnover = Sales / Inventory = 8.0 = sales/$80,000
Sales = $640,000

3.   Minor Motors has a net profit margin of 3%, a total asset turnover of 2.2, and an equity multiplier of 2.5. What is Minor's return on investment and return on stockholders' equity?

Solution:

Return on investment = Net profit margin x Total asset turnover
Return on investment = 3% x 2.2 = 6.6%
Return on stockholders' equity = Return on investment x Equity multiplier
Return on stockholders' equity = 6.6 % x 2.5 = 16.5%

4.   Tom Putnam forecasts sales of $4,000,000 for his firm next year. If the firm maintains its average collection period at 40 days and its inventory turnover at 8, what should be the firm's receivables and inventory levels? The gross profit margin is 22%.

Solution:

Accounts receivable = (40/365) 4,000,000 = $444,444
Cost of sales = (100%-gross profit margin) Sales

Cost of sales = 78% (4,000,000) = $3,120,000
Inventory = $3,120,000/8 = $390,000

5.   Joyce Tilleman is planning for a small distributing firm she will operate after graduation. Her best
      guesses about several relevant financial variables are:

Sales	$100,000
Gross profit margin	40%
Average collection period (365 day year)	97 days
Inventory turnover	4.0
Minimum cash balance	$5,000
Investment in fixtures and equipment	$10,000
Long-term bank loan	$15,000
Current ratio	2.76
All other required assets are to be leased	
All sales are credit sales	

Complete the following pro forma balance sheet and indicate how much equity capital Joyce must
invest in her firm.

BALANCE SHEET

Cash	$	Accounts payable	$
Accounts receivable	$	Bank loan	$____
Inventory	$____		
TOTAL CURRENT		TOTAL LIABILITIES	$
ASSETS	$	Stockholders' equity	$____
Long-term assets	$____	TOTAL LIABILITIES	
TOTAL ASSETS	$	& EQUITY	$

Solution:

Cash = $5,000
Long-term assets = $10,000
Bank loan = $15,000
Accounts receivable = 100,000(97/365) = $26,575
Cost of sales = (100% - 40%)sales = (60%)100,000 = $60,000
Inventory = 60,000/4.0 = $15,000
Total current assets = 5,000 + 26,575 + 15,000 = $46,575
Total assets = 46,575 + 10,000 = $56,575
Current assets/current liabilities = 2.76
Accounts payable = current assets/2.76 = 46,575/2.76 = $16,875
Total liabilities = 16,875 + 15,000 = $31,875
Stockholders' equity = total assets - total liabilities = 56,575 - 31,875 = $24,700

BALANCE SHEET

Cash	$ 5,000	Accounts payable	$ 16,875
Accounts receivable	26,575	Bank loan	15,000
Inventory	15,000		
TOTAL		TOTAL	
CURRENT ASSETS	$ 46,575	LIABILITIES	$ 31,875
Long-term assets	10,000	Stockholders' equity	24,700
TOTAL		TOTAL LIABILITIES	
ASSETS	$ 56,575	& EQUITY	$ 56,575

Joyce must invest $24,700 of equity capital in her business.

6.   From the financial statements of the Jackson Products Company, please provide a common-size balance sheet and common-size income statement.

JACKSON PRODUCTS COMPANY
Balance Sheet
December 31, 19X1

Cash and securities	$ 240,000	Accounts payable	$ 380,000
Accounts receivable	320,000	Notes payable	420,000
Inventory	1,040,000	Other current liabilities	50,000
Total current assets	$1,600,000	Total current liabilities	$ 850,000
Net plant & equipment	800,000	L-T debt (10%)	$ 800,000
Total assets	$ 2,400,000	Common stock	400,000
		Retained earnings	350,000
		Total liabilities and equity	$ 2,400,000

INCOME STATEMENT
for the Year Ended December 31, 19X1

Net sales (all on credit)		$ 3,000,000
Cost of sales		1,800,000
Gross profit		$ 1,200,000
Selling, general, and administrative expenses		860,000
Earnings before interest and taxes		$ 340,000
Interest: Notes	$ 37,800	
Long-term debt	80,000	
Total interest charges		117,800
Earnings before tax		$ 222,200
Federal income tax (40%)		88,880
Earnings after tax		$ 133,320

Solution:

JACKSON PRODUCTS COMPANY
Common-Size Balance Sheet
December 31, 19X1

Cash and Securities	10.00%	Accounts payable	15.83%
Accounts Receivable	13.33	Notes payable	17.50
Inventory	43.33	Other current liabilities	2.08
Total current assets	66.67	Total current liabilities	35.42%
Net plant and		Long-term debt	33.33
equipment	33.33	Common stock	16.67
Total assets	100.00%	Retained earnings	14.58
		Total liabilities and	
		stockholders' equity	100.00%

JACKSON PRODUCTS COMPANY
Common-Size Income Statement

Net sales	100.00%
Cost of sales	60.00
Gross profit	40.00%
Selling, general, and administration expenses	28.67
Earnings before interest and taxes	11.33%
Total interest charges	3.93
Earnings before tax	7.40%
Federal income tax	2.96
Earnings after tax	4.44%

7.   Input the balance sheet data and income statement data for Jackson Products Company in problem 6 into the Excel template for financial statement analysis (Finstmta) to do a ratio analysis. The input values and results should look as follows:

Financial Statement Analysis	
Start In What Year?	199X
Balance Sheet	199X
Assets	
Current Assets	
Cash	$240,000
Marketable Securities	0
Accounts Receivable	320,000
Inventories	1,040,000
Prepaid Expenses	0
Other Current Assets	0
Total Current Assets	$1,600,000
Fixed Assets	

Plant, Property, and Equipment	0
Accumulated Depreciation	0
Other Fixed Assets	0
Net Fixed Assets	$800,000
Other Assets	0
Total Assets	$2,400,000

Liabilities & Net Worth

Current Liabilities

Accounts Payable	$380,000
Wages Payable	0
Notes Payable	420,000
Taxes Payable	0
Other Current Liabilities	50,000
Current Portion of L-T Debt	0
Total Current Liabilities	$850,000

Long-Term Debt

Bonds and Debentures	$800,000
Notes Payable	0
Other Long-Term Debt	0
Total Long-Term Debt	$800,000
Deferred Taxes	0
Other Liabilities	0
Total Liabilities	$1,650,000

Net Worth

Common Stock	$400,000
Paid in Capital in Excess of Par	0
Preferred Stock	0
Retained Earnings	350,000
Total Net Worth	$750,000
Total Liabilities and Net Worth	$2,400,000

Income Statement	199X
Sales	
Net Cash Sales	$3,000,000
Net Credit Sales	0
Total Net Sales	$3,000,000
Cost Of Goods Sold	1,800,000
Gross Margin	$1,200,000
Operating Expense	
Labor And Materials	$0

Depreciation	0
Selling	860,000
General & Administrative	0
Utilities	0
Lease Payments	0
Other Operating Expense	0
Total Expense	$860,000
Net Operating Income	$340,000
Less Interest Expense:	
Interest On Notes Payable	$37,800
Interest On Bonds	80,000
Interest On Debentures	0
Total Interest Expense	$117,800
Other Income	$0
Earnings Before Tax	$222,200
Taxes	
Federal Income Tax	$88,880
State Income Tax	0
Other Taxes	0
Total Taxes	$88,880
Net Income	$133,320
Preferred Dividends	$0
Earnings Available To Common	133,320
Common Stock Dividends	$0
Addition To Retained Earnings	$133,320
Earnings Per Share (EPS)	#DIV/0!
Price To Earnings Ratio	#DIV/0!
General Information	
Number Of Common Shares	0
Number Of Preferred Shares	0
Market Price - Common Stock	$0.00
Average Federal Income Tax Rate	40.00%

Industry Financial Ratios	199X
Liquidity Ratios	
Current Ratio	0.00
Quick Ratio	0.00
Activity Ratios	
Average Collection Period	0.00
Inventory Turnover	0.00
Fixed Asset Turnover	0.00
Total Asset Turnover	0.00
Financial Leverage Ratios	
Debt Ratio	0.00%

Debt-To-Equity Ratio	0.00%
Interest Coverage	0.00

Profitability
Ratios

Gross Profit Margin	0.00%
Operating Profit Margin	0.00%
Net Profit Margin	0.00%
Return On Investment (Assets)	0.00%
Return On Equity	0.00%
Earnings Per Share	$0.00
Price-Earnings Ratio	0.00
Market To Book Ratio	0.00

Industry Growth Rates

Sales	0.00%
Net Income	0.00%
Earnings Per Share	0.00%
Dividends Per Share	0.00%

Company Financial Ratios

Liquidity Ratios

Current Ratio	1.88
Quick Ratio	0.66

Activity Ratios

Average Collection Period	#DIV/0!
Inventory Turnover	N/A
Fixed Asset Turnover	3.75
Total Asset Turnover	1.25

Financial Leverage Ratios

Debt Ratio	68.75%
Debt-To-Equity Ratio	220.00%
Interest Coverage	2.89

Profitability
Ratios

Gross Profit Margin	40.00%
Operating Profit Margin	11.33%
Net Profit Margin	4.44%
Return On Investment (Assets)	5.56%
Return On Equity	17.78%
Earnings Per Share	#DIV/0!
Price-Earnings Ratio	#DIV/0!
Market To Book Ratio	#DIV/0!

Company Growth Rates

Sales	N/A
Net Income	N/A
Earnings Per Share	N/A
Dividends Per Share	N/A

Chapter
4
The Time Value of Money

Business and personal financial decisions that involve cash flows occur at different points in time require an understanding of the time value of money. This crucial topic is the most valuable and enduring that you will cover in your introduction to Corporation Finance. The concepts introduced here are important for solving business financial problems as well as personal financial problems. Mastering this topic is a prelude to tackling other topics in finance. These other topics include: (1) valuation of securities and other assets; (2) capital budgeting; (3) cost of capital; (4) working capital; and (5) lease analysis.

I.   In borrowing or lending money, the amount due can be calculated using simple interest or compound interest.

    A.   The principal is the amount of money borrowed or invested, the term of a loan is the length of time or number of periods the loan is outstanding, and the rate of interest is the percent of the principal the borrower pays the lender per time period.

    B.   Simple interest is the interest paid on the principal sum only:

$$I = PV_0 \times i \times n$$

where I = simple interest in dollars, PV_0 = principal amount at time 0, i = interest rate per time period, and n = number of time periods.

    C.   For simple interest, the present value of the loan is:

$$PV_0 = \frac{I}{ixn}$$

    D.   The future value (amount due at time n) using simple interest is:

$$FV_n = PV_0 + I$$

$$FV_n = PV_0 + (PV_0 \times i \times n) = PV_0 [1 + (i \times n)]$$

II.   Compound interest refers to process where interest earned on principal is converted into interest-earning principal. That is, the interest that was earned in previous compounding periods is part of the principal on which interest is earned. The amount of interest due each period is the interest rate times the principal amount at the beginning of the period.

  A.   For one period, the future (compound) value is:

  $$FV_1 = PV_0 (1 + i)$$

  and for two periods, the future value is:

  $$FV_2 = FV_1 (1 + i)$$

  $$FV_2 = PV_0 (1 + i)(1 + i) = PV_0 (1 + i)^2$$

  B.   In general, the future value at the end of year n for a sum compounded at interest rate i is:

  $$FV_n = PV_0 (1 + i)^n$$

  C.   The term $(1 + i)^n$ is referred to as the Future Value Interest Factor ($FVIF_{i,n}$). Table 4-1 in the text shows the future value of $1 invested for n years at interest rate i:

  $$FVIF_{i,n} = (1 + i)^n$$

  D.   The future value of a lump sum can also be written as

  $$FV_n = PV_0 (FVIF_{i,n})$$

  E.   In future value problems, the present value (PV_0), the future value (FV_n), and the number of periods (n) are given and the objective is to solve for the interest rate (i).

III.   Present value calculations compute present value (PV_0), or the amount at time zero, that is equivalent to some future amount FV_n.

  A.   The present value of a future amount received in n years discounted at interest rate i is:

  $$PV_0 = FV_n \frac{1}{(1+i)^n} = FV_n (PVIF_{i,n})$$

  B.   Table 4-2 includes present value interest factors ($PVIF_{i,n}$) that show the present value of $1 discounted at interest rate i for n periods:

  $$PVIF_{i,n} = \frac{1}{(1+i)^n} \text{ or } 1/FVIF_{i,n}$$

  C.   The present value interest factor is the reciprocal of the future value interest factor.

D.   If i appears in the numerator, the interest rate is referred to as the compound interest rate or the growth rate. On the other hand, if i appears in the denominator, the interest rate is called the discount rate.

E.   The present value formula can also be used to calculate the interest rate (i) when the present value (PV_0), the future value (FV_n) and the number of periods (n) are given.

IV.   An annuity is a series of periodic payments of equal size. An *ordinary annuity* is one where the payments or receipts occur at the end of each period. An *annuity due* is one where payments or receipts occur at the beginning of each period.

A.   For an ordinary annuity, the future value at the end of year n ($FVAN_n$) can be found by multiplying the annuity payment (PMT) times the compound value of an annuity interest factor ($FVIFA_{i,n}$):

$$FVAN_n = PMT(FVIFA_{i,n})$$

where $$FVIFA_{i,n} = \frac{(1+i)^n - 1}{i}$$

B.   A number of values for FVIFA are shown in Table 4-3 in the text. Other values for the interest factor can be found with a financial calculator or by using the formula.

C. $FVIFA_{i,n}$ is the value at time n of $1 invested at the end of each of the next n periods earning interest rate i. For positive interest rates, the value of $FVIFA_{i,n}$ will exceed the value of n (i.e., $FVIFA_{i,n} > n$).

D.   One common use of the FVIFA is to find the annuity amount that must be invested each year to produce a future value:

R = $FVAN_n$/($FVIFA_{i,n}$)

This is called the sinking fund problem.

E.   The future value of an annuity due is simply equal to the future value of an ordinary annuity times one plus the interest rate:

$FVAND_n$ = PMT($FVIFA_{i,n}$)(1 + i)

F.   For an ordinary annuity, the present value of the annuity ($PVAN_0$) can be found by multiplying the annuity payment (PMT times the present value of an annuity interest factor ($PVIFA_{i,n}$) from Table 4-4.

$$PVAN_0 = PMT(PVIFA_{i,n})$$

where $$PVIFA_{i,n} = \frac{1 - \frac{1}{(1+i)^n}}{i}$$

G. $PVIFA_{i,n}$ is the value at time 0 of $1 received or paid at the end of each of the next n periods discounted at interest rate i. For positive interest rates, the value of $PVIFA_{i,n}$ will be less than the value of n (i.e., $PVIFA_{i,n} < n$).

H.   PVIFAs can be found in interest factor tables, computed from the formula, or computed on a financial calculator.

I.   Frequently, the PVIFA is used to find the annuity amount that is necessary to recover a capital investment:

$$PMT = PVAN_0/(PVIFA_{i,n})$$

This is called the capital recovery problem and an example of this problem would be to find the payments necessary to pay off a loan.

J.   The present value of an annuity due is equal to the present value of an ordinary annuity times one plus the interest rate:

$$PVAND_0 = PMT(PVIFA_{i,n})(1 + i)$$

V.   Some additional cash flow patterns encountered in finance are perpetuities, uneven cash flows, and deferred annuities.

A.   The present value of a perpetuity (which is an annuity with an infinite life) is:

$$PVPER_0 = \frac{PMT}{(1+i)^1} + \frac{PMT}{(1+i)^2} + \frac{PMT}{(1+i)^3} + \ldots$$

$$PVPER_0 = \sum_{t=1}^{\infty} \frac{PMT}{(1+i)^t} = \frac{PMT}{i}$$

where PMT is the equal periodic payment and $PVPER_0$ is the sum of the present values of these payments from time 1 to infinity.

B.   An uneven payment stream is a cash flow where the payments in each period are unequal. The present value of an uneven payment stream over n periods is given by:

$$PV_0 = \frac{PMT_1}{(1+i)^1} + \frac{PMT_2}{(1+i)^2} + \ldots + \frac{PMT_n}{(1+i)^n}$$

C.   A deferred annuity is an annuity that begins more than one period in the future. The present value of a deferred annuity may be calculated by first calculating the present value of the annuity as of the end of the period before the start of the annuity and then discounting this sum back to the present time (PV_0).

VI.   Interest may be compounded more frequently than once per year.

    A.   When interest is compounded frequently than annually, the basic compound interest formula must be modified. The modification occurs with the nominal interest rate i_{nom} and the formula exponent. Divide the nominal interest rate by the number of compounding periods per year to compute the per period interest rate.

    B.   The modified compound value formula is shown as:

$$FV_n = PV_0(1 + \frac{i_{nom}}{m})^{mn}$$

    where m is the number of compounding periods per year.

    C.   To discount cash flows under the assumption of intra-year compounding, the present value of a future amount discounted at an annual nominal interest rate i_{nom} compounded m times per year is:

$$PV_0 = FV_n \frac{1}{(1 + \frac{i_{nom}}{m})^{mn}}$$

    D.   The more frequently an annual *nominal* rate of interest (i_{nom}) is compounded, the greater the *effective* rate of interest (i_{eff}) is. The rate of interest per period (where there is more than one compounding period per year), i_m, which results from an effective annual rate of interest, i, is

$$i_m = (1 + i_{eff})^{1/m} - 1$$

    E.   Conversely, the effective annual rate of interest (i_{eff}) resulting from a rate of interest per period, i_m, compounded m times per year is

$$i_{eff} = (1 + \frac{i_{nom}}{m})^m - 1$$

VII.   (Chapter 4 Appendix) Continuous compounding is the case if interest is compounded a large number of times per year (i.e., if m approaches infinity).

    A.   The future value (FV_n) of some initial amount (PV_0) compounded at a continuous interest rate i for n periods is

$$FV_n = PV_0\, e^{in}$$

    B.   The present value of a future lump sum discounted at continuous rate i is

$$PV_0 = FV_n/e^{in} = FV_n\, e^{-in}$$

    C.   If the nominal interest (or growth) rate is i compounded continuously, the effective annual rate equivalent to this is

$$\text{Effective (annual) rate} = i_{\text{eff}} = e^i - 1$$

D.   If i is an annually compounded rate, the continuous rate equivalent to this is:

$$\text{Continuous Effective Rate} = \ln(1 + i_{\text{eff}}).$$

where ln is the natural logarithm operator.

TRUE AND FALSE QUESTIONS

Agree with each of the statements or **reject** it and modify it so that it is acceptable.

1.   For a given i and n, the present value interest factor (PVIF) is the reciprocal of the future value interest factor (FVIF).

2.   The present value of an annuity interest factor (PVIFA) is the reciprocal of the future value of an annuity interest factor (FVIFA).

3.   If an annuity of $1.00 per year is extended by one year (i.e, from n to n+1 years), the present value of the annuity increases by $1.00.

4.   If the discount rate decreases, the present value of a given future payment decreases.

5.   If the interest rate increases, the compound sum of an annuity and the present value of an annuity both increase.

6.   If one bank pays eight percent compounded annually on its savings deposits and a second bank pays eight percent compounded semiannually, the second bank is paying approximately twice as much interest.

7.   The present value of an annuity interest factor ($PVIFA_{i,n}$) is equal to the present value of an annuity interest factor ($FVIFA_{i,n}$) times the present value interest factor ($PVIF_{i,n}$).

8.   A four-year ordinary annuity has equal payments occurring at times 1, 2, 3, and 4 (time 1 = one year from today, etc.) and a four-year annuity due has equal payments occurring at times 0, 1, 2, and 3.

9.   If n increases and i decreases, the present value of a single future cash flow decreases.

10.   The future value of an annuity due is greater than the future value of an ordinary annuity ($FVAND_n > FVAN_n$) and the present value of an annuity due is greater than the present value of an ordinary annuity ($PVAND_0 > PVAN$).

Answers to True and False Questions

1.   True.
2.   False. It is true that the PVIFA<n and the FVIFA>n for i>0.
3.   The present value of the annuity increases by the present value of $1, the extra dollar received,

which is equal to:

$$\frac{1}{(1+i)^{n+1}} < 1.00$$

4.   If the discount rate <u>increases</u>, the present value of a given future payment <u>decreases</u>.

5. $FVIFA_{i,n}$ increases and $PVIFA_{i,n}$ decreases.

6.   A bank paying eight percent compounded semiannually is actually paying four percent every six months, which is only slightly more than eight percent compounded annually. (Eight percent compounded semiannually is actually equivalent to 8.16% compounded annually).

7.   True.

8.   True.

9.   In this case, the present value might increase or decrease.

10.   True.

MULTIPLE CHOICE QUESTIONS

1.   You invested $\$W$ in a savings account t periods ago earning a simple interest rate of r; how much money should you have in your account?
   - A. $\$Wrt$
   - B. $\$W + \$Wrt$
   - C. $\$W \times \$Wrt$
   - D. $\$W(1+r)^t$
   - E. $\$W + \$W(1+r)^t$

2.   You invested an amount of money is an account earning r percent compounded annually y years ago. If the value of that account today is $\$V$, what was the initial amount?
   - A. $\$V(1+r)^y$
   - B. $\$Vry$
   - C. $\$V/(1+r)^y$
   - D. $\$V/ry$
   - E. $\$Vr/y$

3.   Five years ago, you invested $\$V$ in a savings account. In the first two years, balances in your account earned k percent; in year three, the account earned s percent; and in years four and five, your account earned z percent. How much should be in your account today?
   - A. $\$V(1+k)^2(1+s)(1+z)^2$
   - B. $\$V(1+k)(1+s)(1+z)$
   - C. $\$V + \$Vk + \$Vs + \$Vz$
   - D. $\$V + \$Vk + \$Vk + \$Vs + \$Vz + \$Vz$
   - E. $\$V(1+k)(1+s)^2(1+z)^2$

4.   You are negotiating the purchase of a new automobile. What would be the monthly payments on the loan if you financed the purchase price of $\$P$ for 36 months at an annual interest rate of k?
   - A. $FVAN_0/(FVIFA_{k/12,36})$
   - B. $FVAN_0/(FVIFA_{k,36})$
   - C. $PVAN_0/(PVIFA_{k,36})$
   - D. $PVAN_0*(PVIFA_{k/12,36})$
   - E. $PVAN_0/(PVIFA_{k/12,36})$

5.   Given the following cash flows:

```
0        1        2        3        4        5        6        7
+--------+---------+--------+--------+---------+--------+---------+
               Pmt      Pmt      Pmt      Pmt
```

What is the value of this annuity at time = 7?
A. $Pmt(FVIFA_{i,4})(1+i)$
B. $Pmt(FVIFA_{i,5})(1+i)$
C. $Pmt(FVIFA_{i,7})$
D. $Pmt(FVIFA_{i,4})(1+i)^2$
E. $Pmt(FVIFA_{i,5})(1+i)$

6.   What is the value of the annuity (in question 4) at time = 0?
A. $Pmt(PVIFA_{i,4})(1+i)^{-2}$
B. $Pmt(PVIFA_{i,5})(1+i)^{-1}$
C. $Pmt(PVIFA_{i,5})$
D. $Pmt(PVIFA_{i,4})(1+i)^{1}$
E. $Pmt(PVIFA_{i,4})(1+i)^{-1}$

7.   You and your spouse are saving for a new home. You want to save enough over the next five years to accumulate \$W for a down payment. You will make five, equal annual payments into an account earning i percent with the first payment occurring in one year. How much will your payments need to be to have \$W at the end
A. $FVAN_0/(FVIFA_{i,5})(1+i)$
B. $PVAN_0/(PVIFA_{i,5})(1+i)$
C. $PVAN_0/(PVIFA_{i,5})$
D. $FVAN_0/(FVIFA_{i,5})$
E. $FVAN_0(1+i)/(FVIFA_{i,5})$

8.   A financial services company is offering a new annuity product. If you pay the firm a lump-sum payment of **\$P**, you will receive **\$V** forever. What rate of interest would you earn on this investment?
A.   \$P/\$V
B.   \$V/\$P
C.   \$V * \$P
D.   \$P - \$V
E.   \$P + \$V

9.   The effective rate of interest is equal to the annual nominal rate of interest only if:
A.   the nominal rate is continuously compounded.
B.   the nominal rate is compounded more than once a year.
C.   the nominal rate is compounded only once a year.
D.   the nominal rate is negative.
E.   the nominal rate is compounded monthly.

10.   Five years ago, you invest $V in a savings account earning r percent compounded continuously. How much money is in your account today?
    A. $V(1+r)^5$
    B. Ve^{r5}
    C. $V/(1+r)^5$
    D. V/r
    E. V/e^{r5}

Answers to Multiple Choice Questions

1.	B	5.	D	9.	C
2.	C	6.	E	10.	B
3.	A	7.	D		
4.	E	8.	A		

PROBLEMS

1.   If you deposit $5,000 in a savings account paying compound annual interest of 10%, what will the value of your account be in 1, 2, 3, 5, 10, and 20 years?

    Solution:

$$FV_n = 5,000(1.10)^n = 5,000(FVIF_{0.10,n})$$
$$FV_1 = 5,000(1.10)^1 = 5,000(1.10) = \$5,500.00$$
$$FV_2 = 5,000(1.10)^2 = 5,000(1.21) = \$6,050.00$$
$$FV_3 = 5,000(1.10)^3 = 5,000(1.331) = \$6,655.00$$
$$FV_5 = 5,000(1.10)^5 = 5,000(1.611) = \$8,052.55$$
$$FV_{10} = 5,000(1.10)^{10} = 5,000(2.594) = \$12,968.71$$
$$FV_{20} = 5,000(1.10)^{20} = 5,000(6.728) = \$33,637.50$$

2.   Fill in the missing information:

	PV	FV	i	n
a.	1000	--	10%	5
b.	--	50	1%	20
c.	144.25	250	4%	--
d.	600	3678	--	16

Solution:

a. $FV = PV(1 + i)^n = PV(FVIF_{i,n})$
       $FV = 1000(1.611) = \$1,611$ [\$1,610.51]

b. $PV = FV [1/(1+i)^n] = FV(PVIF_{i,n})$
       $PV = 50(.820) = \$41$ [\$40.98]

c. $PV = FV [1/(1+i)^n] = FV(PVIF_{i,n})$
       $144.25 = 250(PVIF_{.04,n})$
       $PVIF_{.04,n} = 144.25/250 = .577$
       From Table II, n = 14 [n = 14.021]

OR
       $FV = PV(1 = i)^n = PV(FVIF_{i,n})$
       $250 = 144.25(FVIF_{.04,n})$
       $FVIF_{.04,n} = 250/144.25 = 1.733$
       From Table I, n = 14 [n = 14.021]

d. $PV = FV [1/(1+i)^n] = FV(PVIF_{i,n})$
       $600 = 3678(PVIF_{i,16})$
       $PVIF_{i,16} = 600/3678 = .163$
       From Table II, i = 12% [12.00%]

3.   How long will it take to double your money if it grows at 12% annually?

Solution:

       $FV_n = PV_0(FVIF_{i,n})$
       $\$2 = \$1(FVIF_{.12,n})$
       $(1.12)^n = 2.000$
       From Table I, $FVIF_{.12,6} = 1.974$ and $FVIF_{.12,7} = 2.211$
       So it will take between six and seven years. (Actually, 6.12 years).

The "Rule of 72" gives a quick answer to the question. According to the rule, divide 72 by the interest rate percentage and this is the approximate number of years it takes the money to double (i.e., 72/12 = 6.0 years). Also, divide 72 by the number of periods to find the approximate interest rate per period required to double your money.

4.   David Riley bought a stock 10 years ago for \$10.00 a share. If it is now selling for \$50.00 a share, what is the stock price's compound annual growth rate?

Solution:

       $FV_n = PV_0(FVIF_{i,n})$
       $50.0 = 10.00(1+i)^{10}$
       $(1+i)^{10} = 50.0/10.0 = 5.0$
       $(1+i) = 1.1746$
       $i = 17.46\%$

5. You may purchase a 3-year certificate at the local savings and loan association for $500. The note pays no interest but will be redeemed for $1000 at maturity. What is the interest rate on the note?

Solution:

$$500 \, (FVIF_{i,3}) = 1000$$
$$FVIF_{i,3} = 2.0$$
$$i = 25.99\%$$

6. Ann Barry sold a farm for $10,000 per acre. She says she owned the land for 20 years and that the value of the property appreciated at an 11% annual rate. What did Ann originally pay for the land?

Solution:

$$FV_n = PV_0(1+i)^n$$
$$10,000 = PV_0(1.11)^{20}$$
$$10,000 = PV_0 \, (8.0623)$$
$$PV_0 = 1240.34$$

7. The Good Fairy has offered to give you $1,000,000 in 20 years. Because of your incredulity, the GF has volunteered to deposit the present value of the $1,000,000 in a trust managed by a bank or insurance company of your choice. How much must the BF deposit if the investment earns 5%? 10%? 20%?

Solution:

$$at \; 5\%, \; PV_0 \; = \; 1,000,000(.377) \; = \; \$377,000 \; [\$376,889.48]$$
$$at \; 10\%, \; PV_0 \; = \; 1,000,000(.149) \; = \; \$149,000 \; [\$148,643.63]$$
$$at \; 20\%, \; PV_0 \; = \; 1,000,000(.026) \; = \; \$26,000 \; [\$26,084.05]$$

$$PV_0 \; = \; 1,000,000 \, \frac{1}{(1+i)^{20}} \; = \; 1,000,000(\, PVIF_{i,20})$$

8. Suppose that the average house costs $100,000 in 1990. What annual inflation rate would cause the average house to cost $1,000,000 in the year 2010?

Solution:

$$FV_n = PV_0(FVIF_{i,n})$$
$$1,000,000 = 100,000(1+i)^{20}$$
$$(1+i)^{20} = 1,000,000/100,000 = 10$$
$$1+i = 1.122$$
$$I = 12.22\%$$

9.   Cabot Company's current $0.50 dividend is expected to grow at 20% annually for two years and then at 15% annually. What is the expected dividend in five years?

Solution:

$$FV = 0.50(1.20)^2(1.15)^3 = 0.50(1.44)(1.5209) = \$1.095$$

10.   Helen Steele is eligible for a student loan that will let him borrow $10,000 at the bargain rate of 4%. The loan will be repaid in a single payment at the end of four years. Helen plans to invest the funds in a certificate of deposit that earns 10% compounded annually and matures in four years. What will be Helen's net profit on the date the certificate of deposit matures and she repays the loan?

Solution:

The future value of the loan is:
$$FV = 10,000(1+0.04)^4 = 10,000(1.1699) = \$11,699$$

The future value of the certificate of deposit is:
$$FV = 10,000(1+0.1)^4 = 10,000(1.4641) = \$14,641$$

Stan's profit in four years is the difference between these two values:
$$\text{Profit} = \$14,461 - \$11,699 = \$2,762$$

11.   Brenda Jaeger is saving money for her daughter Sara's college education. Sara will begin college in eight years.

a.   If Brenda invests $500 at the end of each of the next eight years, how much will she have when Sara starts college? The interest rate is six percent.

b.   What will she have if she makes the eight installments at the beginning of the year instead of the end?

Solution:

a. $FVAN_n = 500(FVIFA_{.06,8}) = 500(9.897) = \$4,948.50$

b. $FVAND_n = 500(FVIFA_{.06,8})(1.06)$
      $FVAND_n = 500(9.897)(1.06) = \$5,245.41$

12.   Find the present value of the following stream of cash flows discounted at 15%.

End of Year	Cash Flow
0	-$200
1	+$100
2	+$200
3	+$ 50

Solution:

$$PV_0 = -200(PVIF_{.15,0}) + 100(PVIF_{.15,1}) + 200(PVIF_{.15,2}) + 50(PVIF_{.15,3})$$
$$PV_0 = -200(1.000) + 100(.870) + 200(.756) + 50(.658)$$
$$PV_0 = -200 + 87.0 + 151.2 + 32.9 = \$71.10$$

13.   One of your weird relatives deposited $10,000 in each of three banks that pay 12% interest. Bank A compounds annually, Bank B compounds semiannually, and Bank C compounds quarterly. If no other deposits or withdrawals occur and the interest rates do not change, how much will your weird relative have on deposit at each bank after five years?

Solution:

$$FV_n = PV_0(FVIF_{i,n})$$

In Bank A, use i = 12%, n = 5
$$FV = 10,000(FVIF_{.12,5})$$
$$FV = 10,000(1.762) = \$17,620$$

In Bank B, use i = 6%, n = 10
$$FV = 10,000(FVIF_{.06,10})$$
$$FV = 10,000(1.791) = \$17,910$$

In Bank C, use i = 3%, n = 20
$$FV = 10,000(FVIF_{.03,20})$$
$$FV = 10,000(1.806) = \$18,060$$

14.   Dolt Briscoe hates his job. However, he feels he can retire when he has $1,000,000. Dolt has invested $200,000 in a savings account earning 10% compounded annually which will eventually reach the required amount. Dolt figures he has a life expectancy of 25 more years. Will he be able to retire within his expected lifetime?

Solution::

$$FV_n = PV_0(1 + i)^n = PV_0(FVIF_{i,n})$$

$$1,000,000 = 200,000(FVIF_{.10,n})$$
$$FVIF_{.10,n} = 1,000,000/200,000 = 5.000$$
For i = .10, $FVIF_{.10,16} = 4.595$ and $FVIF_{.10,17} = 5.054$, so
Dolt can retire between 16 and 17 years from today. [The exact answer is 16.89 years.]

15.   Assume ordinary annuities with the following information given. Find the missing data.

a.	PMT =	100	i =	10%	n = 3	FV	=	331.00	
b.	PMT =	100	i =	10%	n = 3	PV	=	248.69	
c.	PV =	60,000	i =	13%	n = 25	PMT =		8185.55	
d.	i =	8%	n =	5	FV =	20,000	PMT =	3409.13	
e.	PMT=	198.71	i =	10%	PV =	1221	n	=	36
f.	PMT =	800	n =	12	PV =	4528	I	=	24

Solution:

a. $FVAN_n = PMT(FVIFA_{i,n}) = 100(3.310) = \$331.00$

b. $PVAN = PMT(PVIFA_{i,n}) = 100(2.487) = \$248.70$

c. $PVAN = PMT(PVIFA_{i,n})$
       $60,000 = PMT(7.330)$
       $PMT = 60,000/7.330 = \$8,185.54$

d. $FVAN_n = PMT(FVIFA_{i,n})$
       $20,000 = PMT(5.867)$
       $PMT = 20,000/5.867 = \$3,408.90$

e. $PVAN = PMT(PVIFA_{i,n})$
       $1221 = 198.71(PVIFA_{.10,n})$
       $PVIFA_{.10,n} = 1221/198.71 = 6.145$
       From Table IV, $n = 10$

f. $PVAN = PMT(PVIFA_{i,n})$
       $4528 = 800(PVIFA_{i,12})$
       $PVIFA_{i,12} = 4528/800 = 5.660$
       From Table IV, $i = 14\%$

16.   You are comparing two alternative investments to augment your pension. Do this exercise for your own edification.

   A.   Tax-sheltered medium: Take $2,000 of taxable income, invest the full amount at 5% interest at the end of each year for thirty years. At the end of thirty years, pay 40% taxes and see how much is left.

   B.   Taxable medium: Pay 40% taxes on the $2,000 of taxable and invest the remaining $1,200 at the end of each year for 30 years. Because income is taxable, the investment will grow by 3% per year. At the end of the 30 years, however, no taxes are due.

Solution:

   A.   Tax-sheltered investment:
          $FVAN_n = 2,000(FVIFA_{.05,30}) = 2,000(66.439) = 132,878$
          Taxes $= .40(132,878) = 53,151.20$
          Net proceeds $= 132,878 - 53,151.20 = \$79,726.80$

   B.   Taxable investment:
          $FVAN_n = 1,200(FVIFA_{.03,30}) = 1,200(47.575) = \$57,090$

The tax-sheltered investment results in a nest egg that is almost 40% larger than the taxable investment.

17.   Jim Rodriguez is borrowing $50,000 to buy a home. If he pays equal annual installments for 30 years and 8% interest on the outstanding balance, what is the size of his annual payment? What would his payment be if the interest rate were 12%?

Solution:

$$PV = PMT(PVIFA_{i,n})$$
At 8%, $50,000 = PMT(PVIFA_{.08,30}) = PMT(11.258)$
$PMT = 50,000/11.258 = \$4,441.29$
At 12%, $50,000 = PMT(PVIFA_{.12,30}) = PMT(8.055)$
$PMT = 50,000/8.055 = \$6,207.32$

18.   What is the equal annual installment on a four-year note if the amount borrowed is $10,000 and the interest rate is 20%? Prepare a table showing the interest paid and the remaining balance at the end of each year.

Solution:

$$PVAN = PMT(PVIFA_{i,n})$$
$10,000 = PMT(PVIFA_{0.20,4}) = R(2.589)$
$PMT = 10,000/2.589 = \$3,862.50$

Time	Payment	Interest	Principal Reduction	Remaining Principal
0	---	---	---	10,000.00
1	3862.50	2000.00	1862.50	8,137.50
2	3862.50	1627.50	2235.00	5,902.50
3	3862.50	1180.50	2682.00	3,220.50
4	3862.50	644.10	3218.40	2.10

The remaining balance should equal zero. If the PVIFA is not rounded off to three places, the installment is $3,862.89 and the remaining balance in the four years is almost exactly zero.

19.   Ann Hamilton is repaying a loan that currently has a remaining balance of $20,000. Her next payment of $4,000 is due in one year, and it will reduce the loan balance to $18,200. What interest rate is Ann paying?

Solution:

payment = interest + principal reduction
$4,000 =$ interest $+ (20,000 - 18,200)$
interest $= 4,000 - 1,800 = 2,200$
interest rate = interest/previous balance
$= 2,200/20,000 = .11 = 11\%$

20.   Congratulations! You have just won $250,000 in a contest. You have your choice of (1) $25,000 every year for 10 years (at the end of the year), or (2) $125,000 in cash today. The appropriate discount rate is 8%.

Solution:

The present value of the annuity is:
$PVAN = PMT(PVIFA_{i,n})$
$PVAN = 25,000(6.710) = \$167,750$
The annuity is worth more than $125,000.

21.   The dean of the college considers Professor X to be totally incompetent and would like to fire him/her. Unfortunately (from the dean's perspective) under the terms of Professor X's contract, the professor cannot be fired for five years. If Professor X's salary will be $30,000 each year (paid at the end of each year), how much will it cost the dean to buy up the contract if the dean thinks Professor X will quit in exchange for 30% of the present value of his/her salary? The discount rate is 8%.

Solution:

$PVAN = PMT(PVIFA_{i,n})$
$PVAN = 30,000(FVIFA_{.08,5}) = 30,000(3.993) = \$119,790$
The offer should be 30% of $119,790, or .30(119,790) = $35,937.

22.   James Smith is an indentured servant. Under his contract, he can buy his freedom for $1,000. If Smith can save $75 at the end of each year and he has nothing invested now, how long will it take for James Smith to become a free man? His investments earn 15%.

Solution:

$FVAN_n = PMT(FVIFA_{i,n})$
$1000 = 75(FVIFA_{.15,n})$
$FVIFA_{.15,n} = 1000/75 = 13.333$
From Table III, it will take about eight years.

23.   What is the present value of $10,000 received in 4 years discounted at 20% compounded annually? compounded semiannually? compounded quarterly?

Solution:

For annual compounding, use i = 20% and n = 4
$PV = \$10,000 \ (PVIF_{.20,4}) = \$10,000(.482)$
$PV = \$4,820$
For semiannual compounding, use i = 10% and n = 8
$PV = 10,000(PVIF_{.10,8}) = 10,000(.467)$
$PV = \$4,670$
For quarterly compounding, use i = 5% and n = 16
$PV = 10,000(PVIF_{.05,16}) = 10,000(.458)$
$PV = \$4,580 \quad [\$4,581.12]$

24.   You have $2,000 of income to invest. You have two alternatives:

   A.   Pay taxes at 30% on the income and invest the proceeds at 7% after taxes.

   B.   Invest in an IRA, which earns 10% and is taxed at 30% on the amount withdrawn after retirement. If you withdraw prior to retirement, you are subject to a 10% penalty (or a 40% total tax).

   If you reach retirement age in 25 years, how much do you net after taxes for each alternative if you withdraw your funds in one year? Five years? Twenty five years?

Solution:

   A.   tax = .30(2000) = 600, leaving 2000 - 600 = 1400
          one year: $FV = 1400(1.07)^1 = 1400 \ FVIF_{.07,1}$
                           $FV = 1400(1.07) = \$1,498.00$
          five years: $FV = 1400(1.07)^5 = 1400 \ FVIF_{.07,5}$
                           $FV = 1400(1.403) = \$1,964.20$
          25 years: $FV = 1400(1.07)^{25} = 1400 \ FVIF_{.07,25}$
                           $FV = 1400(5.427) = \$7,597.80$

   B.   Because of the penalty, if you withdraw prior to retirement, you net 60% of the withdrawal. After retirement, you net 70%.

          one year: $FV = .60(2000)(1.10)^1 = 1200 \ FVIF_{.10,1}$
                           $FV = 1200(1.10) = \$1,320.00$
          five years: $FV = .60(2000)(1.10)^5 = 1200 \ FVIF_{.10,5}$
                           $FV = 1200(1.611) = \$1,933.20$
          25 years: $FV = .70(2000)(1.10)^{25} = 1400 \ FVIF_{.10,25}$
                           $FV = 1400(10.835) = \$15,169.00$

25.   Willie Wilson plans to borrow $1,500 at the beginning of each of his four years of college. He will repay the loan in ten equal annual installments at the end of each year starting one year after he graduates. If the interest rate is 8%, how large will the installments be?

Solution:

   This can be solved in different ways. One way is to find the future value of the four-year $1,500 annuity due at t = 4 (his graduation date) and set this equal to the present value of a ten-year ordinary annuity of R dollars per year (at t = 4).

          $\$1,500(FVIFA_{.08,4})(1.08) = PMT(PVIFA_{.08,10})$
          $\$1,500(4.506)(1.08) = PMT(6.710)$
          $6.710PMT = \$7299.72$
          $PMT = \$1,087.89$

26.   Sarah N. Dippity believes the world will end in exactly five years. She has $200,000 in a Savings and Loan Association earning 6% interest. Sarah wants to withdraw an equal amount at the beginning of each of the next five years and to have exactly $50,000 left in five years to blow on one huge party just as the world is ending. What should be the size of her withdrawals?

Solution:

The $200,000 is the total present value of the five withdrawals (which are an annuity due) and the $50,000 future lump sum received at the end of five years.

$$200,000 = PMT(PVIFA_{.06,5})(1.06) + 50,000(PVIF_{.06,5})$$
$$200,000 = PMT(4.212)(1.06) + 50,000(.747)$$
$$200,000 = 4.465PMT + 37,350$$
$$4.465PMT = 200,000 - 37,350 = 162,650$$
$$PMT = 162,650/4.465 = \$36,427.77$$

27.   What is the present value of a perpetuity of $100 per year if the discount rate is 8%?

Solution:

$$PVPER = R/i = 100/.08 = \$1,250$$

28.   What is the effective annual rate of a loan that charges 1.5% interest per month?

Solution:

Interest is compounded m = 12 times per year and the interest rate per month is 1.5%. The effective annual rate is

$$i_{eff} = (1 + i_m)^m - 1 = (1 + .015)^{12} - 1 = (1.015)^{12} - 1$$

$$i_{eff} = 1.1956 - 1 = .1956 \text{ or } 19.56\%$$

29.   What is the future value in one year of $1,000,000 invested at:

a.   12% compounded annually?
b.   12% compounded semiannually?
c.   12% compounded quarterly?
d.   12% compounded monthly?
e.   12% compounded continuously?

Solution:

a. $FV = 1,000(FVIF_{.12,1}) = 1,000,000(1.120) = \$1,120,000$
b. $FV = 1,000,000(FVIF_{.06,2}) = 1,000,000(1.124) = \$1,124,000$
c. $FV = 1,000,000(FVIF_{.03,4}) = 1,000,000(1.126) = \$1,126,000$
d. $FV = 1,000,000(FVIF_{.01,12}) = 1,000,000(1.127) = \$1,127,000$
e. $FV = 1,000,000e^{.12(1)} = 1,000,000(1.127) = \$1,127,000$

30.   What is the present value of $20,000 received in five years discounted at

    a.   10% compounded annually?
    b.   10% compounded semiannually?
    c.   10% compounded continuously?

Solution:

    a. $PV = 20,000(PVIF_{.10,5}) = 20,000(.621) = \$12,420$
    b. $PV = 20,000(PVIF_{.05,10}) = 20,000(.614) = \$12,280$
    c. $PV = 20,000\ e^{-.10(5)} = 20,000\ e^{-.5} = 20,000(.6065) = \$12,130$

31.   First National Bank pays 12% compounded continuously and First Bank and Trust pays 12.5% compounded annually. Which bank is paying the higher effective rate?

Solution:

In order to make a fair comparison, convert FNB's continuous rate to an effective annual rate.
    effective annual rate $= e^{i} - 1 = e^{.12} - 1 = 1.1275 - 1 = .1275$ or 12.75%

The FNB effective annual rate of 12.75% is slightly higher than FB&T's 12.50%.

32.   Rework problem 18 using the excel template for loan amortization (Loanamort). The result should look as follows:

Loan Amortization Analysis

Loan Principal Amount	$10,000.00
Annual Percentage Rate	20.00%
Principal Payment Per Period	$0.00
Number of Payments per Year	1
Total Number of Payments	4
Timing of Payment:	0
End of Period - Enter 0	
Beginning of Period - Enter 1	

Period	Payment	Interest	Principal Reduction	Remaining Balance
0				$10,000.00
1	$3,862.89	$2,000.00	$1,862.89	$8,137.11
2	$3,862.89	$1,627.42	$2,235.47	$5,901.64
3	$3,862.89	$1,180.33	$2,682.56	$3,219.08
4	$3,862.89	$643.82	$3,219.08	($0.00)

33.   As you can see from problem 32, the excel templates make quick work of tedious problems such as those involving loan amortization schedules. Try the following problem using the loan amortization template (Loanamort).

Calculate the loan payment and provide a loan amortization table for a $12,000, 36 month auto loan. The interest rate is 8.5% per year.

Loan Amortization Analysis

Loan Principal Amount	$12,000.00
Annual Percentage Rate	8.50%
Principal Payment Per Period	$0.00
Number of Payments per Year	12
Total Number of Payments	36
Timing of Payment:	0
End of Period - Enter 0	
Beginning of Period - Enter 1	

Period	Payment	Interest	Principal Reduction	Remaining Balance
0				$12,000.00
1	$378.81	$85.00	$293.81	$11,706.19
2	$378.81	$82.92	$295.89	$11,410.30
3	$378.81	$80.82	$297.99	$11,112.31
4	$378.81	$78.71	$300.10	$10,812.21
5	$378.81	$76.59	$302.22	$10,509.99
6	$378.81	$74.45	$304.36	$10,205.62
7	$378.81	$72.29	$306.52	$9,899.10
8	$378.81	$70.12	$308.69	$9,590.41
9	$378.81	$67.93	$310.88	$9,279.53
10	$378.81	$65.73	$313.08	$8,966.45
11	$378.81	$63.51	$315.30	$8,651.15
12	$378.81	$61.28	$317.53	$8,333.62
13	$378.81	$59.03	$319.78	$8,013.84
14	$378.81	$56.76	$322.05	$7,691.80
15	$378.81	$54.48	$324.33	$7,367.47
16	$378.81	$52.19	$326.62	$7,040.85
17	$378.81	$49.87	$328.94	$6,711.91
18	$378.81	$47.54	$331.27	$6,380.64
19	$378.81	$45.20	$333.61	$6,047.03
20	$378.81	$42.83	$335.98	$5,711.05
21	$378.81	$40.45	$338.36	$5,372.69
22	$378.81	$38.06	$340.75	$5,031.94
23	$378.81	$35.64	$343.17	$4,688.77

24	$378.81	$33.21	$345.60	$4,343.17
25	$378.81	$30.76	$348.05	$3,995.12
26	$378.81	$28.30	$350.51	$3,644.61
27	$378.81	$25.82	$352.99	$3,291.62
28	$378.81	$23.32	$355.49	$2,936.12
29	$378.81	$20.80	$358.01	$2,578.11
30	$378.81	$18.26	$360.55	$2,217.56
31	$378.81	$15.71	$363.10	$1,854.46
32	$378.81	$13.14	$365.67	$1,488.78
33	$378.81	$10.55	$368.26	$1,120.52
34	$378.81	$7.94	$370.87	$749.65
35	$378.81	$5.31	$373.50	$376.15
36	$378.81	$2.66	$376.15	$0.00

Chapter
5
Analysis of Risk and Return

This chapter develops the relationship between risk and return and presents methods for measuring risk. The chapter also develops the concept of investment diversification and portfolio risk analysis.

I.   Many important concepts are utilized when risky securities or investments are evaluated.

    A.   *Risk* refers to the possibility that actual cash flows (returns) will be different than forecasted cash flows (returns). An investment is said to be risk-free if the dollar returns from the initial investment are known, in advance, with certainty.

    B.   Risk may be more precisely defined by using some probability concepts. The probability that a particular outcome will occur is defined as the percentage chance of its occurrence. A probability distribution consists of the probabilities of every possible outcome. Probability distributions may be objectively or subjectively determined.

    C.   The expected return is a weighted average of the individual possible returns:

$$\hat{r} = \sum_{j=1}^{n} r_j p_j$$

where

        $\hat{r}$ = expected return
        r_j = return for the jth case, where there are n possible outcomes
        p_j = probability of occurrence of the jth outcome

    D.   The standard deviation is an absolute measure of risk. This statistical measure is defined as the square root of the weighted average of the squared deviations of individual observations from the expected value.

$$\sigma = \sqrt{\sum_{j=1}^{n}(r_j - \hat{r})^2 p_j}, \ \ where \ \sigma = standard \ deviation$$

67

If the outcomes are normally distributed, the actual outcome should be between ± 1 standard deviation of the expected value 68.26 percent of the time, and between ± 2 standard deviations of the expected value 95.44 percent of the time.

E.   The number of standard deviations, z, that a particular value of r is from the expected value of $\hat{r}$ is computed with the relationship

$$z = \frac{r - \hat{r}}{\sigma}$$

F.   The coefficient of variation is a *relative* measure of risk. It is defined as the ratio of the standard deviation to the expected return

$$\textit{Coefficient of variation} = v = \frac{\sigma}{\hat{r}}$$

G.   Risk often is an increasing function of time with early returns being less risky than distant returns.

II.   The relationship between risk and return is a key element of effective financial decision making.

A.   The relationship between risk and required rate of return is defined as:

Required rate of return = Risk-free rate of return + Risk premium.

The rate of return required by investors is determined in the marketplace and depends on the supply of funds available and the demand for these funds.

B.   The risk-free rate of return, r_f, is equal to the real rate of return plus an expected inflation premium:

r_f = Real rate of return + Expected inflation premium.

The real rate of return is the return that investors would require from a security having no risk during a period of no expected inflation. The second component of the risk-free return compensates investors for the loss of purchasing power due to inflation.

C.   The risk premium is the "reward" a risk-averse investor expects for assuming risk. The risk premium for a given security is made of several different risk elements.

1.   The maturity risk premium depends on the maturity of a security. There is a *term structure of interest rates* such that yields (required returns) for securities differ for securities that differ in time to maturity.

a.   Yield curves are usually upward sloping, the longer the time to maturity, the higher is the required rate of return. Flat and downward sloping yield curves can often occur.

b.   One theory explaining the slope of the yield curve is the *expectations theory*. According to this theory, long-term rates are a function of expected future short-term rates. If expected future rates are expected to rise (perhaps due to inflation), the yield curve will have a positive slope. Conversely, if expected future rates are expected to fall, the yield curve has a negative slope.

c.   The *liquidity (or maturity) premium theory* holds that there is a larger liquidity premium on longer-term securities because they are riskier (their prices fluctuate more than short-term securities). This theory gives a positive tilt to the yield curve.

d.   The final theory is the *market segmentation theory*. In this theory, securities markets are segmented by maturity and interest rates for different maturities depend on the interaction of supply and demand for each maturity range.

2.   The default risk premium exists to compensate investors for investing in securities subject to default. U.S. government securities are considered default-free, while corporate securities have varying degrees of default risk.

3.   Seniority risk exists whenever corporations have more than one security outstanding. Securities have different claims on the income and assets of the corporation. A partial listing of securities from low to high seniority would be; common stock, preferred stock, income bonds, subordinated debentures, debentures, second mortgage bonds, and first mortgage bonds.

4.   Marketability risk refers to the ability of an investor to buy and sell a security quickly and without significant loss of value. Some securities of large firms are readily marketable and other securities of small firms are very costly to buy or sell.

5.   Individual securities also have significant differences in their business and financial risk.

   - *Business risk* is the variability of the firm's operating earnings over time.

   - *Financial risk* is the additional variability in a company's earnings per share caused by the use of fixed-cost sources of funds, such as debt and preferred stock.

6.   Risk can also be decomposed into *systematic* (undiversifiable) and *unsystematic* (diversifiable) risk. The systematic risk of a security is the portion of return variability caused by factors affecting the security market as a whole, such as the general business outlook. Unsystematic risk refers to the portion of return variability that is caused by factors unique to that security. Unsystematic risk can be reduced and even eliminated by investors who hold a broadly diversified portfolio of securities. Systematic risk cannot be diversified away.

7.   Securities have risk premiums that depend on their risk. Low risk securities (like U.S. treasury securities) have low expected returns, and higher risk securities (like common stocks) have higher expected returns.

III.   An understanding of the behavior of risk and return in a portfolio context is important because most individuals and institutions (including firms) invest in a portfolio of assets. The evaluation of risk becomes more difficult when multiple assets are held in contrast to when the holding is confined to a single asset.

    A.   A *portfolio* is simply a collection of assets. When investing in a portfolio of assets, it may not be appropriate to consider independently the risk of an individual asset. From a portfolio perspective, an individual asset should be evaluated on the basis of its own returns and also in the light of the relationship between its returns and the returns of other assets in the portfolio.

    B.   The *portfolio effect* is the risk reduction accompanying diversification. The size of the portfolio effect is inversely related to the correlation between a given asset's returns and those of the rest of portfolio. Thus, a firm that invests in a project having cash flows or returns with a low (or perhaps even negative) correlation to the rest of the firm's returns or cash flows will reduce the overall risk of the firm more than a project with a higher correlation.

IV.   The expected return and risk of a portfolio is a function of the characteristics of the securities (or assets) comprising the portfolio and the relative weight of each security in the portfolio.

    A.   The expected return of a portfolio (r_p) is a weighted average of the expected returns of the individual securities. If w is the proportion invested in each asset, for two assets, the portfolio return is:

$$\hat{r}_p = w_A \hat{r}_A + w_B \hat{r}_B, \text{ where } w_A + w_A = 1$$

For n assets, the portfolio return is

$$\hat{r}_p = \sum_{j=1}^{n} w_j \hat{r}_j, \text{ where } \sum_{j=1}^{n} w_j = 1, \ 0 \le w_j \le 1.$$

    B.   The standard deviation of the portfolio return (σ_p) is used as a measure of portfolio risk. For a two-security portfolio, the standard deviation is:

$$\sigma_p = \sqrt{w_A^2 \sigma_A^2 + w_B^2 \sigma_B^2 + 2 w_A w_B \rho_{AB} \sigma_A \sigma_B}$$

where σ_A^2 and σ_B^2 are the variances of returns for securities A and B, σ_A and σ_B are their standard deviations, and ρ_{AB} is the correlation coefficient of the returns between securities A and B.

    C.   The lower the correlation coefficient (ρ_{AB}), the greater will be the risk reduction accompanying diversification between A and B. If A and B are perfectly positively correlated ($\rho_{AB} = 1$), then there is no benefit from diversification--the risk of the portfolio is equal to the weighted average of the risk of the individual securities making up the portfolio. However, if A and B are perfectly negatively correlated, the optimal combination of these securities will result in the complete elimination of portfolio risk.

      D.   An efficient portfolio has the highest possible return for a given standard deviation or has the lowest possible standard deviation for a given expected return.

            1.   The efficient frontier is the set of risk-return choices associated with efficient portfolios. The efficient frontier is locus of points along a curve graphed in expected return and risk space.

            2.   The capital market line is a straight line running though the risk-free rate and tangent to the efficient frontier. The capital market line shows the risk and return caused by lending at the risk-free rate and investing in the risky portfolio associated with the tangency on the efficiency frontier or borrowing at the risk-free rate and investing in that risky portfolio.

V.   A well-known method for analyzing the relationship between risk and return for risky assets is the Capital Asset Pricing Model (CAPM).

      A.   Two types of risk are inherent in all securities: systematic risk and unsystematic risk. The sum of the two types of risk equal the total risk of the security.

            1.   Systematic risk is the portion of the variability of a security's returns caused by factors affecting the market as a whole.

                  a.   Some of these general factors include interest rate changes, changes in purchasing power, or changes in investor expectations about the economy.

                  b.   Systematic risk is nondiversifiable; diversifying across more securities does not affect systematic risk.

            2.   Unsystematic risk is caused by factors unique to the firm.

                  a.   Firm-specific factors such as management's decisions and capabilities, strikes, the availability of raw materials, some government actions and regulations, and foreign competition, can affect unsystematic risk.

                  b.   To the extent these factors are unique to the firm and do not affect the market as a whole, the unsystematic risk inherent in individual securities can be eliminated through diversification.

      B.   In a well-diversified portfolio, the relevant risk is each security's systematic risk (because the unsystematic risk is assumed to be diversified away).

      C.   The security market line (SML) shows the relationship between the required rate of return for a security and its systematic risk. The SML may be expressed as

$$k_j \;=\; r_f \;+\; \theta_j$$

where k_j is security j's required rate of return, r_f is the risk-free rate, and θ_j is the risk premium required by investors.

D.   The risk-free rate (r_f) is composed of two parts, a real return and a premium for expected inflation. Changes in inflationary expectations would change the risk-free rate in the SML for all securities and change their required rates of return.

E.   Beta is the most commonly used measure of the systematic risk of a security.

1.   A security's beta is determined by the standard deviation of the security's returns (σ_j), the standard deviation of the returns from the market portfolio (σ_m), and the correlation between the security and market returns (ρ_{jm}).

2.   Security j's beta is equal to the covariance of the returns on security j and the market portfolio divided by the variance of the returns on the market portfolio. This can be represented as:

$$B_j = \frac{Covariance_{j,m}}{Variance_m} \qquad \text{or} \qquad B_j = \frac{\rho_{jm}\sigma_j\sigma_m}{\sigma_m^2} .$$

3.   In practice, beta may be computed as the slope of a regression line where the return on security j is the dependent variable and the return on the market portfolio (measured by a market index such as the Standard and Poor's 500 index) is the independent variable. This relationship is shown as:

$$k_j = a_j + B_j r_m + e_j$$

where k_j is the return for security j, r_m is the return of the market index, a_j is the constant term in the regression, B_j is the regression coefficient (slope term) which is the beta for security j, and e_j is a random error term. This equation is estimated from a number of observations over a historical period. A regression equation of the form above is called security j's *characteristic line*.

4.   By definition the beta for the market portfolio is equal to 1.0.

5.   A security with a beta equal to 1.0 indicates that it has average systematic risk. A security with beta greater (less) than 1.0 has systematic risk that is above (below) average.

6.   The beta of a portfolio of n securities is a weighted-average of the individual security betas. This is shown as:

$$B_p = \sum_{j=1}^{n} w_j B_j$$

7.   Using beta as a systematic risk measure, the risk premium for a security is proportional to its beta:

$$\theta_j = B_j(\hat{r}_m - r_f)$$

The security market line gives the required rate of return for security j (k_j) and is written as:

$$k_j = r_f + B_j(\hat{r}_m - r_f)$$

where $\hat{r}_m$ is the required rate of return for the market, r_f is the risk-free rate and, of course, B_j is the beta for security j.

8. The risk-free rate of return consists of a real rate of return plus a premium due to the effects of inflation. Changes in inflationary expectations will change the security market line. An increase (decrease) in the inflation premium will cause the required rate of return for all securities to increase (decrease).

9. The average risk premium (which is the slope of the security market line), $(\hat{r}_m - r_f)$ will increase or decrease with uncertainties about the future economic outlook and the degree of risk aversion of investors as a group.

F. The capital asset pricing model may be used to estimate the cost of equity capital for the firm or to estimate the required rates of return for capital budgeting projects. Given estimates of r_f, r_m, and B_j, the security market line (SML) equation immediately above is used to find r_j--the required rate of return on security j.

G. The capital asset pricing model (CAPM) is based on a number of crucial assumptions.

1. The CAPM assumptions are:

   a. Investors hold well-diversified portfolios and are influenced by the systematic risk (rather than total risk) of each security.

   b. Securities are actively traded in a competitive market, where information is freely available.

   c. Investors can borrow and lend at the risk-free rate that is constant over time.

   d. There are no brokerage charges for buying and selling securities.

   e. There are no taxes.

   f. Investors are risk averse.

   g. All investors have homogeneous expectations regarding the expected returns, variances, and correlations of returns among all assets.

2. While these assumptions are restrictive, the CAPM has been used somewhat successfully in the face of violations of assumptions.

3.   In practical applications of the CAPM, some of the major problems encountered are:

    a.   Estimating expected future market returns.

    b.   Determining an appropriate risk-free rate.

    c.   Determining the best estimate of an asset's future beta.

    d.   Assuming that systematic risk is the relevant risk measure in some instances where unsystematic risk should not be ignored.

    e.   Betas are frequently unstable over time.

    f.   There is some evidence that required returns are determined by factors in addition to the risk-free rate of interest and the systematic risk of a security. These factors can be macroeconomic factors such as interest rates and inflation.

VI.   International investing appears to offer diversification benefits.

    A.   The returns from domestic companies (DMC's) tend to have high, positive correlations to the overall level of economic activity in a given country. The returns from multinational companies (MNC's) tend to have a lower correlation to the overall level of economic activity, and thus have lower systematic risk and promise more benefits from diversification.

    B.   In order to obtain the benefits of international diversification, an investor could invest in MNC's or invest in DMC's operating in other countries.

VII.   Risk of failure is not necessarily captured by risk measures that focus on return variability (total variability measured by a standard deviation or coefficient of variation or systematic variability measured by a beta).

    A.   For undiversified investors, risk of failure is especially relevant.

    B.   If a failing firm goes into bankruptcy, it suffers costs including:

        1.   The loss of funds that occurs when assets are sold at distressed prices during liquidation,

        2.   The legal fees and selling costs incurred when a firm enters bankruptcy proceedings, and

        3.   The opportunity costs of funds unavailable to investors during extended bankruptcy proceedings.

TRUE AND FALSE QUESTIONS

Agree with each of the statements or **reject** it and modify it so that it is acceptable.

1.   A riskless security should have an expected rate of return of zero.

2.   The standard deviation is defined as

$$\sigma = \sum_{j=1}^{n}(r_j - \hat{r})^2 p_j$$

3.   The expected portfolio return and standard deviation of the portfolio return are weighted averages of the individual security expected returns and standard deviations.

4.   The portfolio standard deviation is directly related to the correlation coefficients between securities.

5.   Systematic risk can be eliminated through diversification.

6.   Changes in the level of interest rates are one source of unsystematic risk.

7.   The characteristic line shows the relationship between the required rate of return for a security and its systematic risk.

8.   Beta, a commonly used systematic risk measure, is the covariance between a security's return and the market return.

9.   A portfolio beta is a weighted average of its individual security betas.

10.   According to the security market line, the required rate of return for a security is equal to the risk-free rate plus a risk premium that is proportional to the security's beta.

Answers to True and False Questions

1.   The risk premium for a riskless security should be zero and its expected return should be equal to the risk-free rate of return.

2.   The standard deviation formula is:

$$\sigma = \sqrt{\sum_{j=1}^{n}(r_j - \hat{r})^2 p_j}$$

3.   The expected portfolio return is a weighted average of the individual security expected returns. However, the portfolio standard deviation is a weighted average of the individual security standard deviations only if the securities are perfectly correlated ($\rho = +1.0$). When the correlations are less than 1.0, the portfolio standard deviation is less than the weighted-average of individual security standard deviations.

4.   True.

5.   Unsystematic risk can be eliminated through diversification.

6.   Changing interest rates would affect all securities and therefore would be part of nondiversifiable or

systematic risk.

7.   The security market line shows the relationship between the required rate of return and systematic risk. The characteristic line is a regression with the security returns as the dependent variable and the market returns as the independent variable.

8.   Beta, a commonly used systematic risk measure, is the covariance between a security's return and the market return divided by the variance of the market return.

9.   True.

10.   True.

MULTIPLE CHOICE QUESTIONS

1.   _____ is a measure of the absolute risk of an investment, where _____ is a measure of the relative risk of an investment..
   A.   Beta;   coefficient of variation
   B.   Standard deviation;   beta
   C.   Coefficient of variation; standard deviation
   D.   Standard deviation;   coefficient of variation
   E.   Beta;   standard deviation

2.   The _____ theory of the term structure of interest rates suggests that investors require higher rates of return for holding securities with longer maturities.
   A.   Expectations
   B.   Market segmentation
   C.   Liquidity premium
   D.   Seniority
   E.   Marketability

3.   _____ risk refers to the ability of an investor to buy and sell a security quickly and without significant loss of value.
   A.   Systematic
   B.   Financial
   C.   Business
   D.   Seniority
   E.   Marketability

4.   To achieve diversification through the combination of two assets, the correlation between those assets must be:
   A.   less than +1.0.
   B.   equal to zero.
   C.   equal to -1.0.
   D.   less than zero.
   E.   greater than +1.0.

5.   Diversifying across securities reduces _____ risk.
   A.   Systematic
   B.   Unsystematic
   C.   Business
   D.   Financial
   E.   Market

6.   The _____ shows the relationship between the required rate of return for a security and its systematic risk.
   A.   Capital market line
   B.   Efficient frontier
   C.   Security market line
   D.   Characteristic line
   E.   Portfolio effect

7.   The size of the portfolio effect is inversely related to the:
   A.   Correlation between the assets held in the portfolio.
   B.   Relative marketability of the assets held in the portfolio.
   C.   Number of assets held in the portfolio.
   D.   Size of the variance of returns of the assets held in the portfolio.
   E.   Beta of the assets held in the portfolio.

8.   A securities that has a beta of 1.5 will have expected returns that are _____ than the market and _____ systematic risk than the market on average.
   A.   lower; greater
   B.   lower; lower
   C.   greater; lower
   D.   greater; greater

9.   What should happen to the security market line if an investor predicts that the following changes will occur in financial markets:
          A reduction in inflationary expectations; and,
          A reduction in the collective degree of risk aversion of investors.
   A.   The SML should shift up and have a greater slope.
   B.   The SML should shift down and have less slope.
   C.   The SML should shift down and have a greater slope.
   D.   The SML should shift up and have less slope.

10.   The slope of the Security Market Line (SML) is:
   A.   The beta of the security.
   B.   The coefficient of variation of the security.
   C.   The standard deviation of the returns of the security.
   D.   The risk-free rate of return on the market.
   E.   The average market risk premium.

Solutions to the Multiple Choice Questions

1.	D	6..	C
2.	C	7.	A
3.	E	8.	D
4.	A	9.	B
5.	B	10.	E

PROBLEMS

1. Jan Caparis owns a piece of property that has the following distribution of returns:

Probability	Return r_j
0.15	10.00%
0.35	15.00%
0.40	20.00%
0.10	30.00%

    a. What is the expected return on Joe's property?

    b. Compute the standard deviation.

    c. Compute the coefficient of variation.

    Solution:

    a. Find the expected return:

r_j	p_j	$r_j p_j$	(r_j-r)	$(r_j-r)^2$	$(r_j-r)^2 p_j$
10.00	0.10	1.50	-7.75	0.600	0.0901
15.00	0.15	5.25	-2.75	0.076	0.0265
20.00	0.40	8.00	2.25	0.051	0.0203
30.00	0.10	3.00	12.25	1.501	0.0150
	100.0	17.75			0.2870

    $$\hat{r} = \sum_{j=1}^{4} r_j p_j = 17.75\%$$

    b. Find the standard deviation.

    $$\sigma = \sqrt{\sum_{j=1}^{4}(r_j - \hat{r})^2 p_j} = \sqrt{0.287} = 5.356\%$$

    c. Find the coefficient of variation

    $$Coefficient\ of\ variation = v = \frac{\sigma}{\hat{r}} = \frac{5.356}{17.75} = 0.302$$

2. An investment has an expected return of 30% and a standard deviation of 20%. If the returns are normally distributed,

    a. what is the probability of a negative return?

b.   what is the probability of a return below 30%?

c.   what is the probability of a return above 50%?

Solution:

a.   Probability of a return less than zero = $P(r < 0)$

$$z = \frac{r - \hat{r}}{\sigma} = \frac{0 - 30}{20} = -1.5$$

$$P(r < 0) = P(z < -1.50) = .067$$

b.   Probability of a return below 30%

$$z = \frac{r - \hat{r}}{\sigma} = \frac{30 - 30}{20} = 0$$

$$P(r < 30) = P(z < 0) = .50$$

c.   Probability of a return above 50%

$$z = \frac{r - \hat{r}}{\sigma} = \frac{50 - 30}{20} = 1.0$$

$$P(r > 50) = P(z > 1.0) = .159$$

3.   Frank Robins is investing in four securities with the following expected returns:

Security	Expected Return (%)
W	10
X	35
Y	20
Z	18

a.   If Frank invests 20% of his money in Security W, 30% in X, 40% in Y, and 10% in Z, what is the expected portfolio return?

b.   If Frank invests 25% in W, 25% in X, 25% in Y, and 25% in Z, what is the portfolio return?

c.   How could Frank earn the highest possible and lowest possible returns?

Solution:

a. $\hat{r}_p = \sum_{i=1}^{4} w_i \hat{r}_i = 0.20(10) + 0.30(35) + 0.40(20) + 0.10(18) = 22.3\%$

b. $\hat{r}_p = \sum_{i=1}^{4} w_i \hat{r}_i = 0.25(10) + 0.25(35) + 0.25(20) + 0.25(18) = 20.75\%$

c.   If Frank invested 100% of her funds in X, the expected return would be 35%.   100% invested in W results in a 10% expected return.

4.   Two securities have the following expected returns and standard deviations:

	Security 1	Security 2
Expected return	.12	.20
Standard deviation	.08	.30

If you invest 40% of your money in Security 1 and 60% of your money in Security 2:

a.   What is your expected portfolio return?

b.   What is your portfolio standard deviation if the correlation coefficient is +1.0, +0.5, 0.0, -0.5, and -1.0?

Solution:

a. $\hat{r}_p = w_1\hat{r}_1 + w_2\hat{r}_2 = .4(12) + .6(.20) = .168$

b.   Use the portfolio standard deviation formula:

$$\sigma_p = \sqrt{w_1^2\sigma_1^2 + w_2^2\sigma_2^2 + 2w_1w_2\rho_{12}\sigma_1\sigma_2}$$

For $\rho_{12} = 1.0$, $\sigma = \sqrt{(.4)^2(.08)^2 + (.6)^2(.30)^2 + 2(.4)(.6)(1.0)(.08)(.30)}$

$\sigma = \sqrt{.001024 + .0324 + .01152} = \sqrt{0.044944} = .2120$

For $\rho_{12} = 0.5$, $\sigma = \sqrt{(.4)^2(.08)^2 + (.6)^2(.30)^2 + 2(.4)(.6)(0.5)(.08)(.30)}$

$\sigma = \sqrt{0.039184} = .1979$

For $\rho_{12} = 0.0$, $\sigma = \sqrt{(.4)^2(.08)^2 + (.6)^2(.30)^2 + 2(.4)(.6)(0.0)(.08)(.30)}$

$\sigma = \sqrt{0.033424} = .1828$

For $\rho_{12} = -0.5$, $\sigma = \sqrt{(.4)^2(.08)^2 + (.6)^2(.30)^2 + 2(.4)(.6)(-0.5)(.08)(.30)}$

$\sigma = \sqrt{0.027664} = .1663$

For $\rho_{12} = -1.0$, $\sigma = \sqrt{(.4)^2(.08)^2 + (.6)^2(.30)^2 + 2(.4)(.6)(-1.0)(.08)(.30)}$

$\sigma = \sqrt{0.021904} = .1480$

5.   Arizona Mining Company has a standard deviation on its common stock of 60% and a correlation with market returns of 0.65. The market's standard deviation and expected return are 15% and 14%, respectively, and the risk-free rate of return is 8%.

   a.   What is Arizona Mining's beta?

   b.   Calculate Arizona Mining's expected rate of return.

   Solution:

   a. $B_j = r_{jm}\, \sigma_j\, \sigma_m / \sigma_m^2$

           $B_j = .65(60\%)(15\%) / (15\%)^2 = 2.60$

   b. $k_j = r_f + B_j\,(r_m - r_f)$

           $k_j = 8\% + 2.60\,(14\% - 8\%)$

           $k_j = 8\% + 15.6\% = 23.6\%$

6.   Susan Conners has invested 50% of her portfolio in Atlantic Richfield, 20% in Coca Cola, and 30% in Union Pacific. Assume that the betas for Atlantic Richfield, Coca Cola, and Union Pacific are 1.20, 0.85, and 1.30, respectively. What is her portfolio beta?

   Solution:

$$B_p = \sum_{j=1}^{n} w_j B_j$$

   $B_p = (.50)(1.20) + (.20)(0.85) + (.30)(1.30) = 1.16$

7.   Abqaiq Baking expects to pay $2.40 dividend next year ($D_1 = 2.40$) and the dividend is expected to grow at 4% annually. Abqaiq has an estimated standard deviation of .24, the market portfolio has a standard deviation of .12, the market expected return is .13 and the risk-free rate is .05. The correlation between Abqaiq and market returns is 0.8.

   a.   What is Abqaiq's beta?

   b.   What is the required rate of return?

   c.   What is the value of a share of stock?

   Solution:

   a. $B = r_{jm}\, \sigma_j\, \sigma_m / \sigma_m^2 = .8(.24)(.12)/(.12)^2 = 1.6$

   b. $k_j = r_f + B_j(r_m - r_f) = .05 + 1.6(.13 - .05) = .05 + .128 = .178$

   c. $P = D_1/(k - g) = 2.40/(.178 - .04) = 2.40/.138 = \$17.39$ per share.

8.   Consider the following information about two securities.

Security	Exp Ret	Std Dev	Beta	% Invested (W)
OHV	10%	20%	.85	.30
Turbo	12%	28%	1.15	.70

a.   Compute the expected portfolio return.

b.   If the returns of the two securities have a correlation of 0.50, compute its portfolio standard deviation.

c.   Compute the beta of the portfolio.

Solution:

a. $\hat{r}_p = w_1\hat{r}_1 + w_2\hat{r}_2 = .30(.10) + .70(.12) = .114$

b.

$$\sigma_p = \sqrt{w_1^2\sigma_1^2 + w_2^2\sigma_2^2 + 2w_1w_2\rho_{12}\sigma_1\sigma_2}$$

$$\sigma_p = \sqrt{(.3)^2(.20)^2 + (.7)^2(.28)^2 + 2(.3)(.7)(0.5)(.20)(.28)}$$

$$\sigma_p = \sqrt{.0036 + .038416 + .01176} = \sqrt{0.053776} = .232$$

c.

$$B_p = w_1B_1 + w_2B_2$$

$$B_p = .3(.85) + .7(1.15) = 1.06$$

9.   David Brown has $12,000 invested in American Cyanamid, $15,000 in Gannett Company, and $3,000 in Texas International. If American Cyanamid has a beta of 1.05, Gannett a beta of .85, and Texas International a beta of 1.30, what is David's portfolio beta?

Solution:

The total portfolio is $12,000 + $15,000 + $3,000 = $30,000. The portfolio weights are:

American Cyanamid: w_1 =   12,000/30,000 =   0.40
Gannett Company: w_2 =   15,000/30,000 =   0.50
Texas International: w_3 =   3,000/30,000 =   0.10

The portfolio beta is

$B_p = w_1B_1 + w_2B_2 + w_3B_3$

$B_p = .40(1.05) + .50(.85) + .10(1.30) = 0.975$

Chapter
6
Fixed-Income Securities: Characteristics and Valuation

Long-term debt, preferred stock, and common stock are the major sources of capital for a firm. Chapter 6 focuses on the characteristics and valuation of fixed income securities, namely long-term debt (bonds) and preferred stock.

I.   If a company borrows money in the capital markets, it issues long-term debt securities (bonds) to investors. Bonds are issued in denominations of $1,000 (principal amount) which constitutes a promise by the firm to repay the principal by a particular date (the maturity date) and to pay a specified amount of interest at fixed intervals (usually twice a year).

     A.   Long-term debt can be classified in a number of ways according to the security, repayment provisions and other features.

          1.   Secured debt issues are called *mortgage* bonds; unsecured bonds are called *debentures*.

          2.   Senior debt issues have a higher priority claim to the earnings or assets of the firm than junior issues.

          3.   Debt may be *subordinated* or *unsubordinated*. In the event of liquidation or reorganization, claims of subordinated debenture holders are considered only after the claims of unsubordinated debt holders. The debt to which a debenture is subordinated varies from firm to firm.

     B.   Special types of long-term debt can be created.

          1.   *Equipment trust certificates* are securities used largely by railroads and trucking companies to purchase specific assets such as rolling stock. Technically, the certificate holders own the equipment and lease it to the firm. Oversight and payments are through a trustee.

2.   *Collateral trust bonds* are backed by securities of other corporations. These are used primarily by holding companies that borrow against their interest in their subsidiaries and then re-lend the funds to the subsidiaries.

3.   *Income bonds* promise to pay interest only if the firm has sufficient income. These are not commonly used today.

4.   *Pollution control bonds* and *industrial revenue bonds* are tax-exempt securities issued by local governments for the benefit of a firm that guarantees the bonds.

C.   Long-term debt contains a number of standard features and common optional features.

1.   An *indenture* is a legal contract between the issuing firm and the lenders which specifies payment procedures and contains any restrictive *covenants* intended to enhance the security of the debt issue. Typical restrictions apply to minimum levels of working capital, limitations on dividends, limitations on additional debt, and poison puts. (A poison put allows bondholders to sell their debt back to the company at par value in the event of a leveraged buyout transaction and a downgrade in the credit rating of the debt issue to below investment grade.) Debt covenants are used to resolve agency problems among debtholders, stockholders, and managers.

2.   The Trust Indenture Act of 1939 requires that a *trustee* represent the debtholders in dealings with the firm. This role is usually performed by a commercial bank or trust company that is responsible for ensuring that all terms of the agreement are upheld.

3.   A *call feature* is an option that allows the firm to redeem or call a debt issue prior to maturity. The call price is higher than the par value by an amount called the *call premium*. Bonds are most likely to be called when interest rates have declined since the time of issuance. A *bond refunding* occurs when a company redeems a callable issue and sells a lower-cost issue to take its place.

4.   A sinking fund provision requires the gradual retirement of a debt issue during its life either through repurchase in the open market, use of the call provision, or by contributions to a sinking fund account. The alternative chosen depends on the relative costs involved.

5.   Some debt issues (and some preferred stock issues) are linked to the equity of the firm through a conversion feature that allows the holder to exchange the security for shares of common stock at the option of the debtholder. *Convertible debt* is convertible at the option of the holder into common stock of the issuing company. Another form of equity-linked debt is the issuance of warrants with debt securities. A *warrant* is an option to purchase shares of a firm's common stock at a specified price during a given time period.

6.   Debt issues sold to the public usually range in size from $25 to $200 million although large companies occasionally issue larger amounts. Private placements are usually in the $5 to $10 million range.

7. The coupon rates on new bonds are normally fixed and chosen so that the bond will sell at or near par value when issued. A few bonds have been issued with floating coupon rates that are pegged to another interest rate such as on 91-day Treasury bills.

8. Original issue discount (OID) bonds are bonds issued with a coupon below prevailing rates and, therefore, are issued at a discount to par. Zero coupon bonds are OID bonds that pay no interest at all.

9. Long-term debt typically matures in 20 to 30 years although longer and shorter maturities do occur. Debt with maturities over 1 year is classified as long-term for accounting purposes.

D. Most debt issues are traded in the over-the-counter (OTC) market. The financial press contains information for the secondary market

1. A typical quote as it might appear in the financial press (such as the *Wall Street Journal*) is as follows:

Bonds	Cur Yld	Vol	Close	Net Chg
XYZ7s05	6.8	20	1025/8	-1/8

Bond prices are quoted as a percentage of the bond's par value (usually $1,000). The closing price for this company's bond is $1,026.25). The "7s05" next to the name of the issuer indicates that the bond pays a coupon rate of 7% per year and matures in the year 2005. The current yield is the annual interest rate divided by the closing price. Net change is the change in closing price from the previous trading day's closing price. The closing price for this bond was 1/8 less than the previous trading day.

2. The U.S. government raises funds by selling debt securities. These securities take the form of Treasury bills (with a maturity of less than one year), Treasury notes (typical maturity of 1 to 10 years), and long term Treasury bonds (typical maturity of 10 to 30 years).

E. Debt issues are rated according to credit risk. Moody's rates bonds from high to low as Aaa, Aa, A, Baa, Ba, B, Caa, Ca, C. Standard and Poor's uses the designations AAA, AA, A, BBB, BB, B, and lower.

1. Moody's applies numerical modifiers to many of its letter bond rating classes, where 1 indicates that the bond is in the higher end, 2 the middle range, and 3 the lower end of a ranking (e.g., A1 or Baa3). Standard and Poor's adds a plus (+) or minus (-) sign to show relative standing within its major categories (e.g., A+ or BBB-). Standard and Poor's also attaches an 'r' to highlight derivative, hybrid, and certain obligations likely to experience high volatility.

2. Higher rated bonds generally carry lower market yields.

3. Firms with the most profitability and lowest leverage ratios tend to have the highest bond ratings.

4.   Some companies in weak financial positions have issued high yield debt called junk bonds. These junk bonds are rated Ba or lower by Moody's (BB or lower by Standard and Poor's) and typically yield at least 3 percentage points more than high quality corporate bonds.

F.   Using long-term debt has a number of advantages and disadvantages.

    1.   Tax deductibility of interest provides relatively low cost.

    2.   Financial leverage can increase potential EPS.

    3.   Ownership is not diluted through additional equity issues.

    4.   Financial risk is increased.

    5.   Bond indenture provisions may restrict the firm's flexibility.

G.   International bonds are bonds that are initially sold to investors outside the home country of the borrower. When U.S. firms go to other countries to raise capital, the two major types of long-term instruments they use are Eurobonds and foreign bonds.

    1.   *Eurobonds* are bonds issued by U.S. corporations, for example, denominated in U.S. dollars, but sold to investors outside of the U.S. such as in Europe and Japan. There are advantages to Eurobond financing that can lead to costs below that of domestic financing.

        a.   There may be less regulatory interference in the issuing country.

        b.   There may be less stringent disclosure requirements.

        c.   Eurobonds are bearer bonds (the name and country of the bond owner are not on the bond, which provides the bondholder with tax anonymity and an opportunity to avoid the payment of taxes).

    2.   *Foreign bonds* are underwritten by an investment banking syndicate and sold in a single country. Foreign bonds are denominated in the currency of the country of sale, which means that interest and principal are paid in that foreign currency.

II.   The value of an asset is based on the expected future benefits its owner will receive over the life of an asset.

A.   The value of a financial asset is based on the expected cash flows it will generate over the holding period.

B.   The capitalization-of-cash flow method of valuation determines the value of an asset as the present value of the stream of future cash flows discounted at an appropriate required rate of return.

1.   Algebraically, this approach is equal to:

$$V_0 = \sum_{t=1}^{n} \frac{CF_t}{(1+i)^t}$$

where CF_t is the expected cash return at time t, i is the required rate of return or discount rate, n is the length of the holding period, and V_0 is the value of the asset.

2.   The required rate of return (i) on an asset is a function of the asset's risk as well as the risk-free interest rate. If the asset's returns are known with certainty (there is no risk), the investor's required rate of return is the risk-free rate.

C.   The market value of an asset is determined by the demand for and the supply of that assets.

1.   The transaction price at which an asset is sold is the market price.

2.   In market equilibrium there is no tendency for the price of an asset to change. However, as investors' required rates of return or expected returns from an asset change, the price changes.

3.   When large numbers of buyers and sellers operate in a market, the market price represents a consensus judgment about an asset or security's worth. The market value of securities that are not publicly traded can be estimated from the prices of publicly traded firms with similar operating and financial characteristics.

D.   The book value of an asset is its accounting value -- historical acquisition cost minus accumulated depreciation. An asset's book value and its market value are not necessarily related.

III.   Bonds may be valued using the capitalization of cash flows method. The future cash flows consist of the interest payments and the principal value repaid at the end of maturity. The discount rate (required rate of return) depends upon the risk-free rate and the default risk of the particular bond.

A.   Using the capitalization-of-cash flow method, the value of a bond is:

$$P_0 = \frac{I_1}{(1+k_d)^1} + \frac{I_2}{(1+k_d)^2} + ... + \frac{I_{n-1}}{(1+k_d)^{n-1}} + \frac{I_n + M}{(1+k_d)^n}$$

where P_0 is the present value of the bond, I_t is the interest payment at time t, n the time to maturity, M the principal payment, and k_d the investor's required rate of return for the bond.

1.   Since the interest payments are equal, the value can be expressed using summation notation as:

$$P_0 = \sum_{t=1}^{n} \frac{I}{(1+k_d)^t} + \frac{M}{(1+k_d)^n}$$

2.   Using present value factors, the value of the bond is

$$P_0 = I(\text{PVIFA}_{k,n}) + M(\text{PVIF}_{k,n})$$

3.   There is an inverse relationship between a bond's value (P_0) and its required rate of return (k_d).

4.   An equal change in the required rate of return changes the value of a long-term bond more than the value of a short-term bond.

5.   Bonds are subject to interest rate risk and reinvestment rate risk. Interest rate risk refers to the potential loss that an investor would experience from a reduction in a bond's market price due to a change in market interest rates. Reinvestment rate risk occurs when a bond issue matures (or is called) and because of a decline in interest rates, the investor has to reinvest the principal at a lower coupon rate.

B.   Most bonds pay interest semi-annually. With semi-annual interest payment and compounding, the bond valuation formula becomes:

$$P_0 = \sum_{t=1}^{2n} \frac{I/2}{(1 + k_d/2)^t} + \frac{M}{(1 + k_d/2)^{2n}}$$

C.   A perpetual bond, or perpetuity, promises to pay interest indefinitely and has no maturity date. The general valuation formula for a perpetual bond that pays interest (I) per period forever and has a required rate of return k_d is

$$P_0 = \sum_{t=1}^{\infty} \frac{I}{(1 + k_d)^t} = \frac{I}{k_d}$$

D.   The *yield to maturity* of a bond is the expected rate of return earned on a bond purchased at a given price and held to maturity.

1.   The yield to maturity is found by solving the following formula for k_d given values for P_0, I, M, and n.

$$P_0 = \sum_{t=1}^{n} \frac{I}{(1 + k_d)^t} + \frac{M}{(1 + k_d)^n}$$

In practice, k_d may be found by using bond tables, by using special financial calculators, or by trial and error.

2.   For *zero coupon bonds* that pay no interest over their lives, the only payment to holders is the principal payment at maturity. The yield to maturity on a zero coupon bond can be found directly from the relationship:

$$P_0 = \frac{M}{(1+k_d)^n} = M(PVIF_{k_d,n})$$

3.   The yield to maturity for a perpetual bond is $k_d = I/P_0$.

4.   If sold prior to maturity, the realized rate of return for a bond will generally differ from its yield to maturity. Variation in the market value of a fixed income security (and in realized rates of return) due to fluctuations in interest rate levels is called interest rate risk.

E.   In many restructurings during the 1980s and 1990s, firms were acquired through LBOs (leveraged buyouts). In many LBOs, the buyer of the firm financed the purchase with a large amount of debt. Often, stockholders made a large gain while bond prices plummeted because of the higher leverage the firm had assumed. This is an example of an ethical issue and of the agency conflict between stockholders and creditors.

IV.   Preferred stock has characteristics similar to both common stock and long-term debt. It is a part of stockholders' equity like common stock; but it is considered a fixed income security like debt and increases the financial leverage of the firm.

A.   Dividends on preferred stock are not tax deductible like interest on debt. This makes the effective cost considerably higher than debt and limits the popularity of preferred stock.

B.   Preferred stock is so called because it usually has preference over common stock with regard to claims against the firm's earnings, assets, or both.

1.   Dividends may not be paid on common stock unless the preferred dividend for the period has been paid.

2.   Preferred stock usually has a higher claim (than common stock) against the assets of the company in the event of bankruptcy or liquidation.

C.   Preferred stock is characterized by a number of features.

1.   The selling price is the price at which preferred shares are sold to the public.

2.   The par value is the value assigned to the stock by the firm for accounting purposes.

3.   Preferred stock is usually designated by the annual dollar dividend per share.

4.   Recently, some adjustable rate preferred stock has been issued. The dividends on adjustable rate preferred stock are reset periodically and are tied to some interest rates specified in their indentures.

5.   Most preferred stock is cumulative. No common dividend may then be paid unless all unpaid back preferred dividends have been paid.

6.   Most preferred stock is non-participating. Participating preferred shares in increased earnings of the firm.

7. Although some preferred stock is perpetual with no maturity, many preferred issues have sinking fund provisions that guarantee retirement over a specified period.

8. Preferred stock may have options of callability and convertibility like long-term debt.

9. Preferred stock is usually nonvoting although special provisions may give preferred stockholders some voting rights if dividends are in arrears.

10. Preferred shares are traded both on the major exchanges and over-the-counter.

11. Utility companies are the most frequent issuers of preferred stock. However, firms that require additional capital but are restricted in their borrowing abilities or suffering from depressed prices of their common stock may resort to issues of preferred stock.

D. Preferred stock has a number of advantages and disadvantages.

1. Preferred stock increases financial leverage with less serious consequences in the event of missed dividends than defaulted interest payments.

2. Preferred stock is expensive when compared to long-term debt because preferred dividends are not a tax-deductible expense.

3. From an investor's perspective, preferred stock confers a tax advantage to companies that purchase preferred stock of other companies.

V. Most preferred stock issues are perpetuities, promising fixed dividends forever. The value of preferred stock, then, is

$$P_0 = \sum_{t=1}^{\infty} \frac{D_p}{(1+k_p)^t} = \frac{D_p}{k_p}$$

where D_p is the fixed dividend per period and k_p is the required rate of return.

VI. (Appendix 6A) Bond refunding occurs when a company redeems a callable issue and replaces it with a lower cost issue.
A. Bond refunding decisions are based on the present value of the cash flows associated with maintaining the old issue versus those of refunding.

B. Because the cash flows associated with refunding decisions are known with certainty, the after-tax cost of the new debt is used for discounting rather than the firm's cost of capital.

C. Factors included in the refunding decision are: the savings in periodic interest payments; the call premium on the old bonds; the flotation cost on the new bonds; the unamortized flotation costs on the old bonds; and, the double interest payments between the time the new debt is issued and the old recalled.

1. The value of the interest savings is computed as:

    Annual interest, old issue = (issue size)(coupon)(1-tax rate)
    —   Annual interest, new issue = (issue size)(coupon)(1-tax rate)
    Annual after-tax interest savings

    The present value of the annual after-tax savings is computed using the after-tax interest rate on the new debt.

    PV interest saving = (annual after-tax savings)(PVIFA$_{r,n}$)

2. The call premium is tax deductible. The call premium after taxes is computed as (call premium) $(1 - T)$, where T is the tax rate.

3. Flotation costs on the new bonds are an immediate cash outflow. These costs are amortized over the life of the issue. Each year, the amortization is deducted from taxable income. The present value effect is given by:

    Present value of flotation costs of new issue
        = new cost - (new cost/years)(T)(PVIFA$_{r,n}$)

4. The unamortized portion of the flotation costs for the old issue will be taken as an expense immediately rather than being amortized over the remaining life of the issue. The present value effect of this is given by

    Present value of flotation costs of old issue
        = (old cost/years left)(T)PVIFA$_{r,n}$) - (old cost)(T)

5. In order to prevent a gap in financing, the new bonds are usually issued before the old bonds are retired. The interest expense on the old issue during this overlap is called the overlapping interest.

    Overlapping Interest
        = (issue size)(coupon rate)(1-T)(overlap as fraction of year)

6. The present value of the net investment in refunding is

    Call Premium
    +   PV of flotation costs on new issue
    -   PV of flotation costs on old issue
    +   Overlapping interest
    Net Investment (cash outflow)

7. The interest savings and the net investment are combined to obtain the net present value of refunding.

    NPV of refunding = PV of interest savings - PV Net Investment

8.   Refunding is undertaken if the NPV is greater than zero. Consideration should also be given to the possibility that more advantageous refunding opportunities may occur in the relatively near future.

TRUE AND FALSE QUESTIONS

Agree with each of the statements or **reject** it and modify it so that it is acceptable.

1.   Secured debt issues are called mortgage bonds; unsecured bonds are called indentures.

2.   Income bonds are bonds that guarantee regular interest income to investors.

3.   Sinking fund provisions may be met by purchasing bonds in the open market.

4.   If a preferred stock is cumulative, common dividend may be paid even if preferred dividends in arrears have not been paid.

5.   Preferred stock is frequently more expensive than debt.

6.   The value of an asset is the present value of its expected future net income stream discounted at an appropriate discount rate.

7.   While the market value of an asset may be above or below book value in the short run, on average book value equals market value.

8.   There is a direct relationship between the value of a bond and its required rate of return.

9.   If two bonds with different maturities have the same price and yield to maturity, the short-term bond's price will change less in response to a change in interest rates than the long-term bond's price will change in response to an equal interest rate change.

10.   For a perpetual bond, the yield to maturity and coupon yield will be equal.

11.   A warrant is an order to arrest the officers of a corporation.

12.   The yield to maturity is the discount rate that equates the present value of all expected interest payments and the repayment of principal from a bond with the present bond price.

13.   Bond refunding frequently occurs in order to replace a high interest debt issue with an issue of lower cost.

14.   If interest rates decline, a bond issue should be refunded.

15.   Overlapping interest must be paid because the new issue is usually sold before the old issue is retired.

Answers to True and False Questions

1. Unsecured bonds are called debentures. The legal agreement of a bond issue is called the indenture.
2. Income bonds pay interest only if earnings are sufficient to pay it. Otherwise no obligation exists.
3. True.
4. If a preferred stock is cumulative, no common dividend may be paid until all preferred dividends in arrears have been paid.
5. True.
6. The value of an asset is the present value of its expected future cash flows.
7. There is no necessary relationship between book and market values.
8. There is an <u>inverse</u> relationship between the value of a bond and its required rate of return.
9. True.
10. True.
11. A warrant is a security issued by a company that is a long-term option to purchase a specified number of shares of the firm's stock at a specified price during a specified time period.
12. True.
13. True.
14. This is oversimplified. The present value of interest savings must be compared to the present value of the net investment in the refunding process including call premium, changes in flotation cost amortization, and overlapping interest.
15. True.

MULTIPLE CHOICE QUESTIONS

1. Unsecured long-term debt is referred to as _____.
    A.   mortgage bonds.
    B.   debentures.
    C.   subordinated debt.
    D.   junior debt.
    E.   treasury notes.

2. _____ are debt issues backed by securities issued by other corporations or government agencies.
    A.   Equipment trust certificates
    B.   Industrial revenue bonds
    C.   Pollution control bonds
    D.   Collateral trust bonds
    E.   Senior mortgage bonds

3. Which of the following standard provisions in a bond issues indenture requires the firm to gradually retire the security issue throughout its life?
    A.   Call provision
    B.   Sinking fund provision
    C.   Convertible provision
    D.   Subordinate provision
    E.   Original issue discount

4.   Given the following bond quotes, which statement best describes the previous day's changes in the bond's price and yield?

ABC7s10   7.2   20   98³/₈   +1/8

   A.   The bond's price rose and its yield fell during the previous day's trading.
   B.   The bond's price fell and its yield fell during the previous day's trading.
   C.   The bond's price rose and its yield rose during the previous day's trading.
   D.   The bond's price fell and its yield fell during the previous day's trading.

5.   Which of the following bonds should have the <u>highest</u> yield in normal market conditions?
   A.   30-year Treasury bonds
   B.   30-year BBB-rated Corporate Bonds
   C.   30 year B-rated Corporate Bonds
   D.   30-year AAA-rated Corporate Bonds

6.   The Eurobond market is a popular source of long-term capital because Eurobonds:
   A.   Are subject to less regulatory oversight than are domestic bond issues.
   B.   Are more liquid than domestic bond issues.
   C.   Provide greater financial leverage than do domestic bond issues.
   D.   Generate higher average returns on average to the bond issuer.
   E.   Are easily traded in US capital markets.

7.   A large number of buyers and sellers operate in US financial markets; thus, the market price of a financial asset represents:
   A.   the book value of the asset.
   B.   the historical cost of the asset.
   C.   the replacement value of the asset.
   D.   the expected future value of the asset.
   E.   the consensus judgment of the asset's worth.

8.   _____ refers to the potential losses that investors experience from changes in the market price of bonds due to changes in the prevailing interest rate.
   A.   Credit risk
   B.   Reinvestment rate risk
   C.   Interest rate risk
   D.   Principal uncertainty
   E.   Basis risk

9.   Which of the following statements concerning preferred stock is <u>not</u> true?
   A.   Utility companies are the most frequent issuers of preferred stock.
   B.   Using preferred stock by a firm increases the firm's financial leverage.
   C.   Preferred stock has a preference over common stock with regards to claims against the firm's assets or earnings.
   D.   Dividends paid on preferred stock are tax-deductible like interest payments on debt.
   E.   Preferred stock is valued like a perpetuity.

10.   Bond refunding occurs when:
   A.   current market interest rates are higher than the existing bond's coupon rate.
   B.   current market interest rates are lower than the existing bond's coupon rate.
   C.   current market interest rates are lower than the existing bond's call premium.
   D.   current market interest rates are higher than the existing bond's call premium.
   E.   current market interest rates are equal to the existing bond's coupon rate.

Answers to Multiple Choice Questions:

1.	B	5.	C	9.	D
2.	D	6.	A	10.	B
3.	B	7.	E		
4.	A	8.	C		

PROBLEMS

1.   If a perpetual bond pays fixed interest of $100 at the end of each year, what is the value of the bond if the investor's required rate of return is 10%? 12%? 15%?

Solution:

$P_0 = I/k_d$

At 10%, $P_0 = 100/0.10 = \$1,000$
At 12%, $P_0 = 100/0.12 = \$833.33$
At 15%, $P_0 = 100/0.15 = \$666.67$

2.   Suppose that General Electric (GE) has two issues of preferred stock outstanding, one paying a dividend of $12.75 per year and the other paying $15.00 annually.

   a.   If the $12.75 GE preferred is selling for $95.50 and the $15.00 GE preferred is selling for $107.50, what are the required rates of return for each issue?

   b.   Five years later the $12.75 preferred is selling for $91.75 and the $15.00 preferred is selling for $96.50. What are the new rates of return?

Solution:

   $k_p = D_p/P_0$

   a.   For the $12.75 preferred, $k_p = 12.75/95.50 = 0.1335$ or 13.35%.
          For the $15.00 preferred, $k_p = 15.00/107.50 = 0.1395$ or 13.95%.

   b.   For the $12.75 preferred, $k_p = 12.75/91.75 = 0.1389$ or 13.89%.
          For the $15.00 preferred, $k_p = 15.00/96.50 = 0.1554$ or 15.54%.

3.   If the Edins Company has a 7 3/4% bond that matures in twenty years, what will be its value if the yield to maturity is 6%? 8%?

Solution:

$$P_0 = \sum_{t=1}^{n} \frac{I}{(1+k_d)^t} + \frac{M}{(1+k_d)^n}$$

$$P_0 = I(PVIFA_{k_d,n}) + M(PVIF_{k_d,n})$$

At 6%, $P_0 = 77.50(PVIFA_{.06,20}) + 1000(PVIF_{.06,20})$

$P_0 = 77.50(11.4699) + 1000(.3118) = 888.91 + 311.80 = \$1,200.71$

At 8%, $P_0 = 77.50(PVIFA_{.8,20}) + 1000(PVIF_{.8,20})$

$P_0 = 77.50(9.8181) + 1000(.2145) = 760.90 + 214.50 = \$975.40$

4.   Suppose Pacific Gas and Electric (PGE) has a 9 3/8% bond outstanding that matures in 30 years. The bond has an annual coupon and is selling for 72 7/8 (72 7/8% of $1,000 or $728.75). What is the exact yield to maturity?

Solution:

a. $P_0 = I(PVIFA_{i,n}) + M(PVIF_{i,n})$

The yield to maturity may be found using trial and error. Since the bond is selling for a discount, its yield to maturity is above the coupon rate.

Trial 1: i = 14% $P_0 = 93.75(7.003) + 1000(.020) = \$676.53$
Trial 2: i = 12% $P_0 = 93.75(8.055) + 1000(.033) = \$788.16$
Trial 3: i = 13% $P_0 = 93.75(7.496) + 1000(.026) = \$728.75$

The yield to maturity is 13%.

5.   a.   What would Walt Eckardt have to pay for a 10-year, $1000 face value
           bond with a 6.5% annual coupon if its yield to maturity is 8.0%?

      b.   If the yield increases to 9.0% one year after Walt purchases the bond, what is the new bond
           value and Walt's realized rate of return if he sells it?

      c.   If the yield drops to 7.0% one year after Walt buys the bond, what is the bond value and
           realized rate of return?

Solution:

a. $P_0 = I(PVIFA_{k,n}) + M(PVIF_{k,n})$

$P_0 = \$65.00(PVIFA_{.08,10}) + \$1,000(PVIF_{.08,10})$
$P_0 = \$65.00(6.710) + \$1,000(.463)$
$P_0 = \$436.15 + \$463.00 = \$899.15$

b. $P_1 = \$65.00(PVIF_{.09,9}) + \$1,000(PVIF_{.09,9})$

$P_1 = \$65.00(5.995) + \$1000(.460)$
$P_1 = \$389.68 + \$460.00 = \$849.68$

$$Realized\ Return = \frac{P_1 - P_0 + I}{P_0}$$

$$Realized\ Return = \frac{849.68 - 899.15 + 65.00}{899.15} = \frac{15.53}{899.15} = .0173\ (1.73\%)$$

c. $P_1 = \$65.00(PVIFA_{.07,9}) + \$1,000(PVIF_{.07,9})$

$P_1 = \$65.00(6.515) + \$1,000(.544)$
$P_1 = \$423.48 + \$544.00 = \$967.48$

$$Realized\ Return = \frac{P_1 - P_0 + I}{P_0}$$

$$Realized\ Return = \frac{967.48 - 899.15 + 65.00}{899.15} = \frac{133.33}{899.15} = .1483\ (14.83\%)$$

6.   What is the value of a share of Wisconsin Gas $2.55 preferred stock if the investor's required rate of return is

a.   8%?
b.   11%?
c.   14%?

Solution:

$P_0 = D_p/k_p$

a. $P_0 = 2.55/.08 = \$31.875.$
b. $P_0 = 2.55/.11 = \$23.18.$
c. $P_0 = 2.55/.14 = \$18.21.$

7.   A zero coupon bond with a current market price of $480.30 promises to pay $1000 at maturity in six years. What is the yield-to-maturity?

Solution:

$P_0 = M(PVIF_{k,n})$

$480.30 = 1000\ (PVIF_{k,n})$

$$PVIF_{k,n} = .4803$$

for $n = 6$, $k_d = 13\%$

8. International Velvet Company has $20 million of 12% debentures outstanding. After tax net income is $3 million. The bond indenture requires that the debt coverage ratio as measured by times-interest-earned be maintained at 2.5 or better. Their tax rate is 40%.

   a.   What is their times-interest-earned ratio?

   b.   How much additional debt at 10% could they have without violating the restrictive covenant?

   Solution:

   a.   Net income = (Earnings before taxes)(1 - t)
        $3 million = (Earnings before taxes)(.6)
        Earnings before taxes = $5 million
        EBIT = EBT + Interest = $5 million + .12($20 million) = $7,400,000
        TIE = EBIT/Interest = 7,400,000/2,400,000 = 3.08

   b.   Maximum allowable interest occurs when 2.5 x interest = EBIT so maximum allowable interest = 7,400,000/2.5 = 2,960,000.
        Maximum allowable interest - current interest = allowable increase
        2,960,000 - 2,400,000 = 560,000
        $5,600,000 of additional debt at 10% can be incurred without exceeding the restrictive covenant.

9. Lesscan B. More, Inc. is considering whether to purchase bonds yielding 14% or preferred stock yielding 10%. Their tax rate is 40%.

   a.   What after-tax yield can they expect from the bonds?

   b.   What after-tax yield can they expect from the preferred?

   Solution:

   a.   After-tax yield = (Before-tax yield) (1-t) = 14% x .6 = 8.4%

   b.   Dividends received by a corporation are 70% exempt from taxation.

        After-tax yield = before-tax yield - taxes

        After-tax yield = before-tax yield - (before-tax yield x .30 x tax rate)

        After-tax yield = 10% - (10% x .30 x .40) = 8.8%

10.   Spiess Corporation bonds mature in 10 years and have a maturity value of $1,000. The coupon rate on the bond is 12%. The Spiess Corporation can call the bonds in 5 years at a call premium of 12% above the maturity value. If you expect the bonds to be called in 5 years, what is a bond's value discounted at 9%?

Solution:

The trick is to recognize the maturity value as $1,000 plus the call premium of $120, or M = $1,120.

$$P_0 = \sum_{t=1}^{5} \frac{120}{(1.09)^t} + \frac{1120}{(1.09)^5}$$

$P_0 = 120(PVIFA_{.09,5}) + 1,120(PVIF_{.09,5})$
$P_0 = 120(3.890) + 1,120(.650) = 466.80 + 728.00 = \$1,194.80$
[more exactly, $P_0 = 466.76 + 727.92 = \$1,194.68$]

11.   The Sure-Bond Glue Company has outstanding $100 million of 12% bonds with 20 years to maturity. These bonds are callable at 105. $600,000 of flotation costs have not yet been amortized. Sure-Bond is considering replacing the outstanding bonds with an issue of the same maturity bearing interest at 10%. Flotation costs will amount to 1% of the amount issued. If the refunding is undertaken, there will be a 4 week overlap between the time the new bonds are issued and the old retired. The company's tax rate is 40%. Find the net present value of refunding. For simplicity, assume that the tax benefits of writing off the flotation costs of the old issue are available immediately. Assume interest is paid annually.

Solution:

We begin by finding the present value of the interest savings.

After tax interest on old issue=100 million x 12% x.6	=$7,200,000
- After tax interest on new issue=100 million x 10% x.6	=$6,000,000
After tax interest savings	$1,200,000
x PVIFA$_{0.06,20}$ (use after tax-rate on new bonds)	11.470
Present value of after tax interest savings	$13,764,000

The next step is to determine the present value of the net investment in refunding. The components of this include the call premium, the unamortized flotation costs on the old issue, the flotation costs on the new issue, and the overlapping interest.

The after tax cash flow associated with the call premium on the old issue is:

        (size of issue)(call premium)(1 - T)
        ($100,000,000)(.05)(.6) = $3,000,000

If the old issue is refunded, the unamortized flotation costs will be written off immediately rather than amortized over the remaining 20 years. This results in a current tax deduction of the unamortized costs but a reduction in future tax benefits. The result is given by:

Present value of flotation costs of old issue
        = (Unamortized costs/years left)(T)(PVIFA$_{0.06,20}$)-(Unamortized costs)(T)

$$= (600,000/20)(.4)(11.470)-(600,000)(.4) = -102,360$$

The negative sign indicates that this is a net cash inflow since the immediate write-off is more valuable than the amortized write-off.

The flotation costs on the new issue represent an immediate cash outflow which will be partially offset by the tax benefits arising from the annual amortization. Thus we have

Present value of flotation costs of new issue
$$= costs - (costs/years)(T)(PVIFA_{.06,20})$$
$$= 1,000,000 - (1,000,000/20)(.4)(11.470) = 770,600$$

Overlapping interest is given by

Overlapping interest
$$= (size\ of\ issue)(rate\ on\ old\ issue)(fraction\ of\ year)(1-T)$$
$$= (100,000,000)(.12)(4/52)(.6) = 553,846$$

The net investment in refunding is summarized as:

Call premium	3,000,000
Flotation costs on old issue	-102,360
Flotation costs on new issue	770,600
Overlapping interest	553,846
Net investment in refunding	4,222,086

The net present value of refunding is:

Present value of interest savings - present value of net investment
$$= 13,764,000 - 4,222,086 = \$9,541,914$$

12.   Using the excel template for bond valuation (Bondval) solve problem 3 assuming semi-annual compounding and a required rate of return of 11% per year.

Bond Valuation - Computing The Price Of A Bond

Coupon Bonds

Par Value	$1,000.00
Call or Sale Value	$1,000.00
Annual Coupon Rate	9.25%
Coupon Periods Per Year	2
Years To Maturity or Holding Period	20
Required Rate Of Return	11.00%
Current Price	$859.60

13.   Solve this problem using the bond valuation excel template (bondval). Assume you purchased a Spiess Corporation bond described in problem 10 for $1,050. What is the expected yield to maturity if this bond is called in 5 years?

Bond Valuation - Computing The Yield To Maturity Of A Bond

Coupon Bonds

Par Value	$1,000.00
Call or Sale Value	$1,120.00
Coupon Rate	12.00%
Coupon Periods Per Year	1
Years To Maturity or Holding Period	5
Current Price	$1,050.00
Yield To Maturity	12.47%

14.   Solve the bond refunding problem (problem 12) using the excel template (Bondref).

Analysis Of Bond Refunding

Information Concerning Original Issue

Issue Size	$100,000,000
Coupon Interest Rate	12.00%
Coupon Periods Per Year	1
Remaining Years To Maturity	20
Call Price ($ Per Bond)	$1,050
Unamortized Flotation Costs	$600,000

Information Concerning New Issue

Issue Size	$100,000,000
Coupon Interest Rate	10.00%
Coupon Periods Per Year	1
Original Years To Maturity	20
Flotation Cost	$1,000,000

Overlap Period (# Of Weeks)	4
Overlap Rate (1=Old, 2=New)	1
Annual Rate Of Return (Overlap Period)	0.00%

Marginal Tax Rate   40.00%

Benefits Of
Refunding
Annual Interest $1,200,000
Savings
Present Value Of Interest Savings $13,763,905

Less: Costs Of
Refunding
After-Tax Call $3,000,000
Premium
Present Value Flotation Costs (New $770,602
Issue)
Present Value Floatation Costs (Old   ($102,361)
Issue)
Overlapping $553,846
Interest
                                                          _____

Total Cost Of $4,222,087
Refunding

Net Present Value Of Refunding $9,541,819
Decision
                                                          ========================

Chapter
7
Common Stock: Characteristics, Valuation, and Issuance

Chapter 7 describes the various characteristics of common stock and develops various models that can be used to value this security. The process by which common stock is offered for sale and the role of the investment banker in this process are also covered in this chapter.

I.   Understanding stock quotations is an important element of how stocks are valued.
        A typical quotation as it might appear in the popular press is shown below:

52 WEEKS					YLD		VOL				NET
HI	LO	STOCK	SYM	DIV	%	PE	100s	HI	LO	CLOSE	CHG
881/8	641/2	MYCorp	MY	2.25	5.0	22	1100	473/4	433/8	45	+21/2

A.   The first two columns show the high and the low price at which the stock traded in the preceding 52 weeks.

B.   The third column shows the name of the stock (MY Corp.).

C.   This is followed by the unique ticker symbol for the stock (MY).

D.   The fifth column shows the annualized dividend per share ($2.25) based on the most recent quarterly dividend.

E.   YLD % is the dividend yield calculated as the dividend per share divided by the closing price of the stock ($2.25/$45 = 5.0%).

F.   The P/E ratio is a relative valuation measure (market price/earnings per share) calculated as closing price of the stock divided by the sum of the latest four quarters of earnings per share.

G.   The next figure is the volume of shares traded expressed in hundreds.

H.   The next three columns show the high, low, and closing price of the stock.

I.   The final column shows the net change in the closing price from the previous trading day's closing price.

II.   Common stock is the permanent long-term financing of the firm and represents the true residual ownership of the firm.

    A.   Three balance sheet accounts are associated with the common stock of the company.

        1.   The common stock account contains the par value of common stock issued.

        2.   Contributed capital in excess of par, also known as additional paid in capital or sometimes capital surplus, represents the difference between the proceeds of issuing the common stock and the par value of the stock.

        3.   The retained earnings account represents the accumulation of net income that has been reinvested in the business.

        4.   The book value per share is found by dividing total common stockholders' equity by the number of shares outstanding.

    B.   Common stockholders have a number of general rights.

        1.   *Dividend rights.* All common stockholders have a right to share equally on a per share basis in any dividends paid.

        2.   *Asset rights.* In the event of liquidation, stockholders have the right to share assets remaining after senior claims are satisfied.

        3.   *Preemptive rights.* Some common stock carries a preemptive right that gives stockholders the right to share proportionately in any new stock sold.

        4.   *Voting rights.* Unless the stock is specifically nonvoting, common stockholders have the right to vote on stockholder matters.

    C.   One of the rights of stockholders is the right to elect the board of directors. Two rules for electing the Board of Directors are commonly used.

        1.   *Majority voting* requires that a group have more than 50% of the votes to elect a director.

        2.   *Cumulative voting* makes it easier for minorities to elect a favorable board member.

        3.   Under cumulative voting, the number of shares required to obtain representation on the Board is given by:

$$\text{No. of shares} = \frac{\begin{array}{c}\text{No. of directors} \\ \text{desired}\end{array} \times \begin{array}{c}\text{No. of shares} \\ \text{outstanding}\end{array}}{\text{No. of directors being elected} + 1} + 1$$

    D.   There can be other features and management actions that affect common stockholders.

        1.   Corporations may issue more than one class of common stock. Firms may sell voting and nonvoting stock allowing the voting owners to maintain control of the firm. Some classes of stock may represent ownership of a part of the firm rather than the whole firm.

        2.   The stock may be split to create a larger number of lower valued shares and, thus, attracting a wider range of investors.

            a.   A stock split of itself has no value.

           b.   A stock split may increase the wealth of existing shareholders if the lower price increases market activity so that the overall market value of the common stock increases.

           c.   A stock split does not change the dollar value of any accounts. The par value and the number of shares outstanding are the only changes.

    3.   A reverse stock split may be used to reduce the number of shares and increase the market price of the stock if it is felt that the stock is so low priced as to discourage investors because of commission costs or a low-price stigma.

    4.   A stock dividend is a dividend to shareholders that consists of additional shares of stock instead of cash.

           a.   Stock dividends involve a transfer from retained earnings to common stock and additional paid in capital.

           b.   Unless market activity is increased due to the reduced price, stock dividends have no real value.

    5.   Firms sometimes repurchase their own stock, which is known as treasury stock. Management may repurchase stock if they feel it is a good investment if the stock is undervalued. Repurchased stock may also be available for use in mergers or executive stock option plans. By issuing debt and repurchasing stock, the firm can increase its leverage and accomplish a financial restructuring. Share repurchases can dispose of excess cash and can also be a tactic to help reduce takeover risk.

    F.   There is a number of advantages and disadvantages to common stock financing.

        1.   Common stock financing is flexible since no fixed obligation exists.

        2.   Common stock financing can reduce the financial leverage and lower the cost of capital if leverage is excessive.

        3.   Issuing common stock dilutes earnings per share until the new investments pay off.

        4.   Flotation costs make issuing common stock relatively expensive.

III.   Investment bankers are experts in capital market issues including long-range financial planning, issuance of securities, the arrangement of long-term loans and leases, and the negotiation of mergers.

    A.   Securities are sold in the primary market to the public in public cash offers, to a few large investors in private or direct placements, or to existing stockholders of the firm through a *rights offering*.

    B.   Public cash offerings are usually purchased by an investment banker or an investment banking syndicate and then resold to the general public. This process is called *underwriting*. The terms of the underwriting agreement are agreed upon through negotiation or by competitive bid. The underwriters are compensated by the difference between their purchase price and the price to the public. This difference is called the *underwriting discount* or *underwriting spread*:

        Underwriting spread = Selling price to public - Proceeds to company

        In some cases, the investment bankers only market the securities on a "best effort" basis without actually underwriting them.

C.   Direct or private placement of securities with one or more institutional investors is often arranged by an investment banker in exchange for a "finder's fee." Direct placement avoids underwriting costs and registration requirements and offers greater flexibility in terms although interest rates are often slightly higher.

D.   Common stock may be sold through the issuance of "rights" to existing stockholders that entitle them to purchase the new stock at a subscription price below the current market price. For these issues, investment bankers encourage rights holders to purchase the issue. In a standby underwriting, they also agree to purchase any unsold shares at the subscription price.

E.   Direct issuance costs consist of the underwriting spread and all other issue expenses of the company. These other expenses include legal and accounting fees, taxes, the cost of registration with the Securities and Exchange Commission, and printing costs. Direct issuance costs are usually directly related to the riskiness of the security.

F.   In addition to direct costs, other costs include:
- management time in preparing the offerings,
- underpricing a new equity offering below its correct market value,
- stock price declines for stock offerings by firms whose stock is already outstanding, and
- other incentives provided to the investment banker, such as the "Green Shoe" option in which the investment bankers have a short term option to buy additional new shares at the initial offering price.

G.   Any company planning to sell an interstate security totaling over $1.5 million and having a maturity greater than 270 days is required to register the issue with the SEC. The registration statement contains a vast amount of information about the company's legal, operational and financial position. The prospectus summarizes the information contained in the registration statement and is intended for the use of potential investors. The SEC makes no judgment about the quality of security issues, it simply requires extensive disclosure. All buyers of the new securities must be provided with a final copy of the prospectus.

H.   Shelf registration is an option for larger firms (such as those with outstanding equity of at least $150 million) with an investment-grade rating. Under this procedure, the firm files a master registration statement with the SEC. The company is then free to sell small increments of the offering over an extended time period of up to 2 years by simply filing a short-form statement with the SEC only hours before the actual offering.

I.   Many firms have their stocks trading in several stock exchanges around the world. As the capital markets becomes globally integrated, more firms will raise capital in the markets that will yield the lowest cost to the firm.

IV.   The valuation of common stock is based on the same principles underlying the valuation of bonds or preferred stock. The value of common stock is the discounted value of the stock's expected stream of returns.

A.   The valuation of common stock is more difficult than other securities.

      1.   The returns from owning common stock are a mixture of dividends and capital gains (or losses).

      2.   Dividends are not constant and typically are expected to grow over time.

      3.   The future returns from common stock are much more uncertain than the returns from bonds and preferred stock.

B.   The present value of a share of common stock is based on the expected dividends received during the investor's holding period and the expected selling price at the end of the holding period.

      1.   The one-period dividend valuation model is:

$$P_0 = \frac{D_1}{1+k_e} + \frac{P_1}{1+k_e}$$

where k_e is the required rate of return, D_1 is the expected dividend at time 1, and P_1 is the expected selling price at time 1.

      2.   The two-period dividend valuation model is

$$P_0 = \frac{D_1}{(1+k_e)^1} + \frac{D_2}{(1+k_e)^2} + \frac{P_2}{(1+k_e)^2}$$

where the investor receives dividends for two periods and the stock is sold at the end of the second period.

      3.   The multiple-period dividend valuation model is

$$P_0 = \frac{D_1}{(1+k_e)^1} + \frac{D_2}{(1+k_e)^2} + \ldots + \frac{D_n}{(1+k_e)^n} + \frac{P_n}{(1+k_e)^n}$$

or

$$P_0 = \sum_{t=1}^{n} \frac{D_t}{(1+k_e)^t} + \frac{P_n}{(1+k_e)^n}$$

where the investor receives dividends for n periods and P_n is the selling price after n periods.

C.   The value of the stock at the end of the holding period (P_n) depends on the value of future dividends after time n. The value of common stock at time zero (P_0) depends directly on dividends received during the holding period and indirectly on dividends after the holding period (through their effect on P_n). The general dividend model simply establishes the value of a firm's common stock to the investor to be equal to the present value of the expected future dividend stream.

$$P_0 = \sum_{t=1}^{\infty} \frac{D_t}{(1+k_e)^t}$$

V.   The general dividend valuation model can be simplified if the dividends follow a regular pattern. Three patterns considered here are zero growth, constant growth, and nonconstant growth.

A.   The zero growth dividend model is the simplest dividend valuation model.

    1.   If the dividends are expected to be constant forever, the general valuation model is

$$P_0 = \sum_{t=1}^{\infty} \frac{D}{(1+k_e)^t} = \frac{D}{k_e}$$

    2.   The value is the present value of a perpetuity. This can also be visualized as a special case of the constant growth model (presented next) where g=0.

B.   The constant growth dividend valuation model assumes that dividends grow at a constant rate g per period forever.

    1.   The future dividend at time t is $D_t = D_0(1 + g)^t$.

    2.   The general dividend model becomes

$$P_0 = \sum_{t=1}^{\infty} \frac{D_0(1+g)^t}{(1+k_e)^t}$$

    3.   Assuming $k_e > g$, this model reduces to

$$P_0 = \frac{D_1}{k_e - g}$$

where D_1 is the next period's dividend, $D_1 = D_0(1+g)$.

    4.   This constant growth dividend model is usually referred to as the Gordon model.

    5.   If P_0, g, and D_1 are given, the Gordon model can be used to find the investor's required rate of return on equity

$$k_e = \frac{D_1}{P_0} + g$$

The investor's required rate of return is equal to the expected dividend yield (D_1/P_0) plus the capital gains yield (g).

    6.   Growth rate forecasts are available from the Value Line Investment Survey, the Institutional Brokers Estimate System (IBES), and Zack's Earnings Estimates.

C.   The nonconstant growth model allows for varying dividend patterns over various future time periods.

    1.   One example of this model is where the firm's dividends fluctuate over the next few years and then grow at a constant rate after that. The value of this stock is:

$$P_0 = \begin{array}{c} \textit{Present value of} \\ \textit{expected dividends} \\ \textit{during period of} \\ \textit{nonconstant growth} \end{array} \quad \begin{array}{c} \textit{Present value of the} \\ \textit{expected stock price} \\ \textit{at the end of the} \\ \textit{nonconstant growth period} \end{array}$$

If the dividends fluctuate until time m and then grow at a constant rate g_2 during period M+1 and after, the value of the stock at time m is P_m, which is:

$$P_m = \frac{D_{m+1}}{k_e - g_2}$$

If P_m is discounted back for m periods, this is the second half of the equation for P_0 above.

2. A special case of the nonconstant growth model occurs if there is rapid above-normal growth of dividends for a period of time after which the growth rate of dividends is lower. Assume that dividends grow at a rate g_1 over the first m years and that dividends grow at a rate g_2 after that. The value of the stock can be expressed as:

$$P_0 = \sum_{t=1}^{m} \frac{D_0(1+g_1)^t}{(1+k_e)^t} + \frac{P_m}{(1+k_e)^m}$$

This gives the present value of the first m dividends plus the present value of the value of the stock at end of year m (P_m).

3. Because dividends will grow at a constant rate g_2 beginning in year m + 1, the Gordon model may be used to find the stock value in year m: $P_m = D_{m+1}/(k_e-g_2)$. By substituting this into the equation for P_m above, the above-normal growth dividend valuation model becomes

$$P_0 = \sum_{t=1}^{m} \frac{D_0(1+g_1)^t}{(1+k_e)^t} + \frac{1}{(1+k_e)^m}\left(\frac{D_{m+1}}{k_e-g_2}\right)$$

VI. Many small firms are closely held and no active market for their shares exists. Small business owners occasionally need appraisals for such reasons as mergers and acquisitions, divestitures or liquidations, initial public offerings, estate and gift tax returns, leveraged buyouts, recapitalizations, employee stock ownership plans, divorce settlements, estate valuation, and other litigation matters.

A. Many factors are considered when valuing a small business. These factors include the nature and history of the business, the general economic outlook and the condition of the firm's industry. Also include are the earnings capacity of the firm, its dividend paying capacity, the book value of the company, the company's financial condition, whether the shares represent a majority or minority interest, and whether the stock is voting or nonvoting.

B. A basic approach to valuing a closely held company is the "capitalization of earnings" approach. In this approach, the value of the firm is the normal earnings level multiplied by an appropriate price-earnings multiple. When warranted, a minority interest discount is applied to this value.

TRUE AND FALSE QUESTIONS

Agree with each of the statements or **reject** it and modify it so that it is acceptable.

1.   A 2 for 1 stock split does not affect shareholders' wealth.

2.   The future returns from common stock are generally more uncertain than the future returns from bonds and preferred stock.

3.   Cumulative voting provisions make it easier for groups of stockholders with minority views to obtain representation.

4.   In the constant growth dividend model, the dividend growth rate can be zero.

5.   In the constant growth dividend model, the value of the stock is inversely related to the dividend growth rate.

6.   In the general dividend valuation model, the value of a firm's common stock is equal to the present value of the expected earnings stream.

7.   In the basic constant growth dividend model, the dividend is assumed to grow at a rate g, and because the stock value increases as dividends increase, the stock price should also grow at a rate g.

8.   The Securities and Exchange Commission insures that all securities sell for a price within a reasonable range of their actual value.

9.   An underwriting investment banker in a public cash offering assists the issuing firm on a best efforts basis.

10.   Flotation costs are usually higher for high quality securities.

11.   An underwriting discount is a special price break for firms which often issue new securities.

12.   Privately placed debt usually carries a higher interest cost than debt issued through underwriters.

Answers to True and False Questions

1.   True.
2.   True.
3.   The growth rate is assumed to be constant.
4.   True.
5.   All other things held constant, the value of common stock and the dividend growth rate are positively related.
6.   In the general dividend valuation model, the value of a firm's common stock is equal to the present value of the expected <u>dividend</u> stream.
7.   True.
8.   The SEC regulates trading but makes no judgment as to the value of a security.

9. An underwriting investment banker purchases the issue from the firm and then resells it. Assistance provided on a best effort basis is not underwriting.
10. Flotation costs are usually higher for more risky securities.
11. An underwriting discount is the difference between the price the underwriter pays the firm for the security and sells the security to the public.
12. True.

MULTIPLE CHOICE QUESTIONS

1. The book value per share of a company is determined by dividing the firm's _____ by the number of share outstanding.
    A. Total assets
    B. Total liabilities
    C. Asset book value
    D. Total common equity
    E. Retained earnings

2. Among the general rights of commons shareholders are _____ rights that gives shareholders the right to share proportionately in any new stock sold.
    A. Dividend
    B. Asset
    C. Preemptive
    D. Voting
    E. Ownership

3. Which of the following statements best represents the management's motive for a stock split?
    A. To reduce the value of the firm's stock.
    B. To bring market attention to the firm.
    C. To generate new shares for employee stock options.
    D. To prevent a unfriendly takeover.
    E. To create a larger number of lower-valued shares.

4. A major advantage of using common stock to finance the capital needs of a firm is that the use of common equity:
    A. creates no fixed obligation of repayment.
    B. increases the firm's financial leverage.
    C. reduces the overall cost of funding.
    D. dilutes the firm's earnings per share.
    E. rewards shareholders for continued investment.

5. Your firm is in the process of issuing new long-term debt. The firm's underwriter has found one or more institutional investors that are willing to purchase the entire issue. This is an example of a
    _____
    A. Rights offering
    B. Private placement
    C. Best efforts basis
    D. Restructure
    E. Direct issuance

6.   Any company planning to sell an interstate security totaling over _____ and having a maturity greater than _____ is required to register the issue with the Securities and Exchange Commission.
- A. $1 million;   1 year
- B. $1 million;   180 days
- C. $1.5 million;   270 days
- D. $2 million;   1 year
- E. $2 million;   270 days

7.   Which of the following is not an appropriate rationale for a firm to repurchase shares of its stock on the open market?
- A.   If management feels it is a good investment.
- B.   For use in mergers and executive stock option plans.
- C.   To increase its leverage and accomplish financial restructuring.
- D.   To dispose of excess cash and reduce the risk of a hostile takeover.
- E.   All of the above are good reasons to repurchase shares on the open market.

8.   The valuation of common stock is more difficult than the valuation of fixed income securities because:
- A.   The appropriate discount rate is more difficult to determine for common stock than it is for fixed income securities.
- B.   The future cash flows from common stock are more uncertain than the cash flows from fixed income securities.
- C.   The market for common stock is more volatile than the market for fixed income securities.
- D.   Common stock represents a residual claim on the firm's assets where debt and preferred stock have senior claims on the assets.

9.   Which of the following is <u>not</u> a general assumption of the dividend discount model?

$$P_0 = \frac{D_1}{k_e - g}$$

- A.   The required rate of return must exceed the expected rate of growth.
- B.   The expected rate of growth must be constant.
- C. $D_1 = D_0(1+g)$
- D.   The expected rate of growth must be positive.
- E.   All of the above are assumptions of the model.

10.   The investors required rate of return on an equity investment is equal to the expected dividend yield:
- A.   plus the capital gains yield.
- B.   minus the expected growth rate.
- C.   plus the appropriate discount rate.
- D.   minus the present value of the expected stock price.
- E.   plus the present value of the expected stock price.

Solutions to Multiple Choice Questions

1.	D	5.	B	9.	D
2.	C	6.	C	10.	A
3.	E	7.	E		
4.	A	8.	B		

PROBLEMS

1.   You bought a stock at $27 per share and sold it at $34. While you owned it you received a $2 per share dividend. What was your percentage return?

Solution:

Return = (Selling price - Cost + Dividend) / Cost
Return = (34 - 27 + 2)/ 27 = 9 / 27 = .333 = 33.3%

2.   Aardvark Exterminators Inc. has the following financial statements and other information.

Balance Sheet (millions)

Current assets	$ 80	Current liabilities	$30
Other assets	100	Long-term debt	40
		Preferred stock	20
		Common stock ($2 par)	10
		Additional paid in capital	35
		Retained earnings	45
Total assets	$180	Total liabilities and capital	$180

Income Statement (millions)

		Miscellaneous	
Sales	$82	Preferred dividends	$2 million
Cost of goods sold	51	Common dividends	$5 million
EBIT	31	Market price	
Interest expense	4	common	$33/share
EBT	27		
Taxes @ 37%	10		
Net Income	$17		

Find the following:

a.   Earnings per share common
b.   Price-earnings ratio on common
c.   Book value of common
d.   Interest coverage
e.   Dividend yield on common
f.   Dividend payout ratio

Solution:

a.   EPS = Earnings available to common / No. of shares
     EPS = (Net income - Pref div) / (Common stock account / Par value)
     EPS = (17,000,000 - 2,000,000) / (10,000,000 / 2) = $3

b.   Price/Earnings = 33/3 = 11x

c.   Common Stock $10 million
      + Additional paid in capital   35 million
      + <u>Retained Earnings</u>   <u>45 million</u>
      Total Common Equity $90 million
      ÷ <u>No. of shares</u>   <u>5 million</u>
      Book Value per share $18

d.   Interest coverage = EBIT/Interest = 31/4 = 7.75x

e.   Dividend yield = dividends per share/price = 1/33 = 3.03%

f.   Payout ratio = dividends per share/earnings per share = 1/3 = 33.33%

3.   Suppose Aardvark (Problem 2) declares a 10% stock dividend. Show the changes in the stockholders' equity portion of their balance sheet.

Solution:

Preferred Stock   20
Common Stock   11   = 10 + (.5 million new shares)($2 par)
Additional Paid
     in Capital   50.5   = 35 + (new shares)(market price-par)
Retained Earnings   <u>28.5</u>   = 45 - (new shares)(market price)
     Total   110.0

4.   The ABC Company has 12 members on their board of directors. Four positions are up for election at the annual meeting. The company has 40 million shares of common stock outstanding. You are a member of a group that wishes to be assured of electing at least one of your group members to the board of directors.

a.   How many shares of stock must your group control if a simple majority voting rule is followed?

b.   How many shares of stock must your group control if the company uses cumulative voting?

Solution:

a.   Under simple majority voting, you must have 50% of the stock outstanding plus one share or 20,000,001 shares.

b.   Under cumulative voting, the number of shares required is given by

$$\text{No. of shares} = \frac{\text{No. of directors desired} \times \text{No. of shares outstanding}}{\text{No. of directors being elected} + 1} + 1$$

$$No. \, of \, shares = \frac{1x \, 40,000,000}{4+1} + 1 = 8,000,001$$

5.   George Franks can buy shares of Ace Rocket Launcher for $45.00. George expects dividends to be $3.00 in one year and $5.00 in two years, and he expects to sell the stock for $58.00 in two years. Should George buy any ARL? George feels that 18% is the appropriate discount rate.

Solution:

$$P_0 = \frac{3.00}{(1.18)^1} + \frac{5.00}{(1.18)^2} + \frac{58.00}{(1.18)^2}$$

$P_0 = 3.00(PVIF_{.18,1}) + 5.00(PVIF_{.18,2}) + 58.00(PVIF_{.18,2})$
$P_0 = 3.00(.8475) + 5.00(.7182) + 58.00(.7182)$
$P_0 = 2.542 + 3.591 + 41.65 = \$47.78$

George should invest in ARL because its estimated value of $47.78 per share exceeds the $45.00 that he would have to pay for it.

6.   Blather Broadcasting's current dividend per share of $3.20 is expected to grow at 5% per year indefinitely. What is the value of a Blather share if the required rate of return is

    a.   10%?
    b.   12%?
    c.   14%?

Solution:

Next year's dividend should be 5% greater than the current dividend.

$D_1 = D_0(1 + g) = 3.20(1.05) = 3.36$

a. $P_0 = \dfrac{D_1}{k_e - g} = \dfrac{3.36}{.10 - .05} = \dfrac{3.36}{.05} = \$67.20$

b. $P_0 = \dfrac{D_1}{k_e - g} = \dfrac{3.36}{.12 - .05} = \dfrac{3.36}{.07} = \$48.00$

c. $P_0 = \dfrac{D_1}{k_e - g} = \dfrac{3.36}{.14 - .05} = \dfrac{3.36}{.09} = \$37.33$

7.   Union Aquatech Company has a current share price of $11.00 and an expected dividend of $0.66 in one year.

    a.   If the dividend growth rate is 7%, what is the required rate of return for Union Aquatech shares?

    b.   If the required rate of return is 11.5%, what dividend growth is expected if the Gordon model fits this stock?

Solution:

a. $k_e = (D_1/P_0) + g = (.66/11.00) + .07 = .06 + .07 = .13$ or 13%

b. $k_e = (D_1/P_0) + g$
$.115 = (.66/11.00) + g$
$g = .115 - .06 = .055$ or 5.5%

8.   Because of a lucky breakthrough, Philadelphia Pharmaceutical's current dividend per share of $2.00 is expected to grow at a very high 32% per year for the next three years and then to grow at a more normal 6% per year. What is the value of a Philadelphia share if the investors' required rate of return is 20%?

Solution:

The above-normal growth dividend valuation model may be used. The current value of the common stock would be the present value of the first three dividends plus the present value of the stock in three years (which is found with the Gordon model).

Present value of the first three years dividends:

Year	Dividend	PVIF$_{.20,n}$	Present value of D$_t$
1	$2.00(1 + .32)^1 = 2.64$	.833	2.20
2	$2.00(1 + .32)^2 = 3.48$	.694	2.42
3	$2.00(1 + .32)^3 = 4.60$	.579	2.66
			7.28

Present Value of stock at end of year three, $P_3 = D_4/(k_e - g_2)$

    $D_4 = D_3(1 + g_2) = 4.60(1 + .06) = 4.88$

    $P_3 = 4.88/(.20 - .06) = 4.88/.14 = 34.86$

Present value of $P_3 = P_3/(1 + k_e)^3$

    $PV(P_3) = 34.86/(1 + .20)^3 = 34.86(PVIF_{.20,3}) = 34.86(.579) = 20.18$

Value of common stock $= P_0 = PV(\text{first three dividends}) + PV(P_3)$

    $P_0 = 7.28 + 20.18 = \$27.46$

9.   Rework Problem 8 using the Excel template (Cstockvl) accompanying the text. The result is:

Stock Valuation - Nonconstant Dividend Growth

Current Dividend (Do)		$2.00
Required Rate of Return		20.00%
Constant Growth Rate		6.00%

Super-Normal Growth

Year	Growth Rate	Dividend	Present Value of Dividend	
1	32.00%	$2.64	$2.20	
2	32.00%	$3.48	$2.42	
3	32.00%	$4.60	$2.66	
4	6.00%	$4.88	$2.35	
5	6.00%	$5.17	$2.08	
6	6.00%	$5.48	$1.83	
7	6.00%	$5.81	$1.62	
8	6.00%	$6.16	$1.43	
9	6.00%	$6.53	$1.26	
10	6.00%	$6.92	$1.12	
Present Value of Dividends			$18.98	
Year 10 Stock Price		$2.00	$52.37	
Present Value of Year 10 Stock Price			$8.46	
Current Stock Price				$27.44

8

Capital Budgeting and Cash Flow Analysis

Chapter 8 provides an overview of the capital budgeting process and shows how to estimate the relevant cash flows associated with an investment project.

I.   Capital expenditures are important to a firm both because they require sizable outlays and because they have a significant impact on the firm's long-term performance.

     A.   *Capital budgeting* is the process of planning for purchases of assets whose returns are expected to continue beyond one year.

     B.   A *capital expenditure* is a cash outlay which is expected to generate a flow of future cash benefits. Normally, a capital project is one with a life of more than one year.

     C.   Capital budgeting models are used to evaluate a wide variety of capital expenditure decisions, including:

          1.   investments in assets to expand an existing product line or to enter a new line of business.

          2.   replacement of an existing capital asset.

          3.   expenditures for an advertising campaign.

          4.   expenditures for research and development.

          5.   investments in permanent increases in inventory or receivables levels.

          6.   investments in education and training.

          7.   refunding an old bond issue with new bonds paying a lower interest rate.

8.   leasing decisions.

9.   merger and acquisition decisions.

D.   The firm's *cost of capital* is the combined cost of funds from all sources. The cost of capital is also called the investors' required rate of return, because it is the minimum rate of return that must be earned on the capital invested in the firm. The required rate of return helps provide a basis for evaluating capital investment projects.

E.   Projects under consideration may be independent of each other or have some types of interdependencies.

1.   An *independent project* is one whose acceptance or rejection has no effect on other projects under consideration.

2.   Two projects are *mutually exclusive* if one or the other can be accepted, but not both.

3.   A *contingent project* is one whose acceptance is contingent upon the adoption of one or more other projects.

4.   One additional complication is *capital rationing*, which occurs when the firm has a limited total amount of dollars available for investment and the outlay for profitable investments exceeds this limit. On the other hand, when the firm has sufficient funds available to invest in all profitable projects, we say the firm is operating without a funding constraint.

II.   A widely employed framework exists for capital budgeting.

A.   Economic theory demonstrates that the firm should expand its output until marginal revenue equals marginal cost.

B.   In capital budgeting, the firm should invest in its most profitable projects first and should continue accepting projects as long as the last project's rate of return exceeds the marginal cost of funds to the firm.

C.   Practical problems are encountered when this capital budgeting model is used.

1.   The firm's management may be unaware of all potential capital projects at a single point in time. Changing markets, technology, and corporate strategies make some current proposals obsolete and make new ones profitable.

2.   The behavior of the marginal cost of capital may be difficult to determine. This topic is discussed extensively later in the text.

3.   Estimates of future costs and revenues can be made subject to varying degrees of uncertainty.

D.   Capital budgeting can be broken into four steps. (The first two are discussed in this chapter and the last two are in the following chapter). These steps include:

   1.   Generating capital investment project proposals.

   2.   Estimating cash flows.

   3.   Evaluating alternatives and selecting projects to be implemented.

   4.   Reviewing or post-auditing prior investment decisions.

III.   The initial step in the capital budgeting process is generating capital investment project proposals.

   A.   The process of soliciting and evaluating investment proposals varies greatly among firms.

   B.   Investment projects can be classified as:

      1.   projects generated by growth opportunities in existing product lines or new lines.

      2.   projects generated by cost reduction opportunities.

      3.   projects required to meet legal requirements and health and safety standards.

   C.   The size of an investment proposal frequently determines who has authority to approve the project. A very large outlay might require approval of the corporation president or board of directors, where smaller outlays can be authorized by lower and lower levels of management.

   D.   If an investment decision is critical and must be made fast, a lower level manager can approve it or it can by-pass the normal time-consuming review process to reach the appropriate responsible manager as fast as possible.

IV.   Estimating the cash flows associated with investment projects is crucial to the capital budgeting process. The cash flows associated with a project are the basis for evaluation rather than the project's accounting profits. Typically, capital expenditures are associated with a net investment (at time 0) and a series of net (operating) cash flows expected to be received over a number of future periods. Several principles should be kept in mind when determining project cash flows. These principles include:

   A.   Cash flows should be measured on an incremental basis. The cash flow stream for a project is the difference between the cash flows to the firm with the project compared to the cash flows to the firm without adopting the project.

   B.   Cash flows should be measured on an after-tax basis.

   C.   All the indirect effects of a project should be included in the cash flow estimates. For example, increases in cash balances, receivables, and inventory necessitated by a capital project should be included in the project's net investment.

D.   Sunk costs should not be considered since sunk costs result from previous decisions, they are not truly incremental costs.

E.   Resources should be measured in terms of their opportunity costs. The opportunity costs of resources are the cash flows they would generate if not used in the project under consideration.

V.   The *net investment* (NINV) is the initial cash outlay for a project (usually at time zero).

A.   A project's net investment is estimated as:

	The new project cost plus any installation and shipping costs associated with acquiring the asset and putting it into service;
PLUS	Any increases in net working capital initially required as a result of the new investment
PLUS	The net proceeds from the sale of existing assets when the investment is a replacement decision;
PLUS or MINUS	The taxes associated with the sale of the existing asset and/or the purchase of a new one;
EQUALS	Net investment (NINV).

B.   Most projects involve outlays over more than one year. The NINV for a multiple-period investment is the present value of the series of outlays discounted at the firm's cost of capital.

VI.   The future net operating cash flows (NCF) are computed using the proposed project's accounting information:

A.   After-tax net operating cash flow is:

$NCF = \Delta OEAT + \Delta Dep - \Delta NWC$
where,
NCF = net operating cash flow,
$\Delta OEAT$ = change in operating earnings after tax,
ΔDep = change in depreciation, and
ΔNWC = increase in the net working capital investment.

B.   The change in operating earnings after tax is:

$\Delta OEAT = \Delta OEBT(1 - T)$
where,

$\Delta OEBT$ = change in operating earnings before tax, and T is the tax rate.

C.   The change in operating earnings before tax is $\Delta OEBT = \Delta R - \Delta 0 - \Delta Dep$

where

$\Delta R = R_w - R_{wo}$ = change in revenues

R_w = revenues with project
R_{wo} = revenues without project
$\Delta 0 = 0_w - 0_{wo}$ = change in operating costs
0_w = operating costs with project exclusive of depreciation
0_{wo} = operating costs without project exclusive of depreciation
$\Delta Dep = Dep_w - Dep_{wo}$ = change in depreciation
Dep_w = depreciation with project
Dep_{wo} = depreciation without project

D.   Based on these definitions, two useful expanded versions of the basic NCF equation are

$$NCF = (\Delta R - \Delta 0 - \Delta Dep)(1 - T) + \Delta Dep - \Delta NWC$$

$$NCF = [(R_w - R_{wo}) - (0_w - 0_{wo}) - (Dep_w - Dep_{wo})](1-T) + (Dep_w - Dep_{wo}) - \Delta NWC$$

VII.   There are two potential cash flows at the end of a project's life.

A.   Cash inflow due to the incremental salvage must be included at the end of the project. The incremental salvage is the difference between the salvage with the project and without the project. There will be taxes due or saved when an asset is sold for more or less than book value. Book value is the installed cost of the asset less accumulated depreciation. There are four possible tax situations:

Case 1: Sale of an asset for book value. There are no tax consequences.

Case 2: Sale of an asset for less than book value. The loss is treated as an operating loss to offset operating income. The tax saving is the marginal tax rate times the amount of the loss.

Case 3: Sale of an asset for more than book value but less than original cost. The IRS considers the gain a recapture of depreciation. The gain is taxed as operating income, with taxes due equal to the marginal tax rate times the amount of the gain.

Case 4: Sale of an asset for more than original cost. The part of the gain that represents a recapture of depreciation is treated as an operating gain and the gain in excess of original cost is treated as a capital gain. Under the Revenue Reconciliation Act of 1993, both ordinary income and capital gains are taxed at the same corporate rate (35%).

Don't forget that the recovery of book value is tax-free, only gains and losses from book value result in tax savings or obligations.

B.   Recovery of net working capital can be a cash inflow. There are no tax consequences of liquidating working capital.

VIII.   It is important to note that interest charges were not considered in estimating a project's net cash flows. This was done so that measures of the value of a project (in the next chapter) can be constructed independent of how a project is financed. Furthermore, if interest charges are deducted from cash flows and then the remaining cash flows are discounted to adjust for the time value of money, this would constitute a double counting of the time value of money when evaluating the value of an asset.

IX.   Depreciation policy can have a significant impact on the determination of cash flows because of its impact on taxes.

    A.   Depreciation is the allocation of the cost of an asset over more than one year.

    B.   Depreciation charges affect the cash flows of the firm. With a 35% tax rate, an additional $1.00 depreciation charge will reduce earnings before taxes by $1.00, reduce taxes by $.35, reduce net income after taxes by $.65, and increase the period's cash flow by $.35.

    C.   Firms can depreciate using the straight-line method or one of several accelerated methods of depreciation.

        1.   In the straight-line depreciation method, the annual depreciation charge is:

$$\text{Annual depreciation amount} = \frac{\text{Cost - Estimated salvage value}}{\text{Estimated economic life (years)}}$$

        2.   In the accelerated depreciation methods (of which there are several), the asset is depreciated at a rate higher than straight-line depreciation in the early years. However, the depreciation rate declines rapidly over time. For tax purposes the use of accelerated depreciation methods is desirable since it reduces tax outlays in the initial years thereby increasing the present value of the cash flows. For tax purposes firms use the Modified Accelerated Cost Recovery Systems (MACRS) depreciation method. This is described in the appendix at the end of the book.

TRUE AND FALSE QUESTIONS

Agree with each of the statements or **reject** it and modify it so that it is acceptable.

1.   If Investment B can be made only after Investment A is made, then the two investments are mutually exclusive.

2.   A decision to keep the old machine or replace it with a new one can be a mutually exclusive decision.

3.   The president of the firm ordinarily accepts or rejects investment proposals regardless of their size.

4.   Changes in net working capital are not included in the calculation of net investment and net cash flows.

5.   If an old asset has been fully depreciated to zero and is sold for more than original cost, a tax liability on the gain is incurred.

6.   For capital budgeting purposes, interest paid is deducted when finding a project's future net cash flows.

7.   Because a business has no choice about paying taxes, taxes are generally ignored in evaluating capital projects.

8.   Given the same revenues and costs, a larger depreciation charge would result in a smaller net income and a larger net cash flow.

9.   Sunk costs are an important component of the net investment outlay in many capital budgeting decisions.

10.   If the tax rate is 40 percent, an additional one dollar depreciation charge results in a sixty cent net cash flow.

Answers to True and False Questions

1.   Investment B is contingent upon Investment A.
2.   True.
3.   Presidential (or board) approval might be required for very large investments, but authority to accept or reject smaller projects is normally delegated to lower management levels.
4.   Initial change in net working capital is included in net investment, while subsequent changes in net working capital are included in the determination of net cash flows over the life of the project.
5.   True.
6.   For capital budgeting purposes, interest paid is <u>not</u> deducted when finding a project's future net cash flows..
7.   Taxes must be deducted to find the net cash flow.
8.   True.
9.   Sunk costs should not be considered since they result from previous decisions and are not truly incremental costs.
10.   The net cash flow will be the tax rate times the additional depreciation charge, or only forty cents. In the basic equation
$$NCF = (\Delta R - \Delta 0 - \Delta Dep)(1 - T) + \Delta Dep,$$
let ΔR and $\Delta 0$ be zero:
$$NCF = -\Delta Dep(1 - T) + \Delta Dep = T\Delta Dep = .40(\$1) = \$.40$$

MULTIPLE CHOICE QUESTIONS

1.   The firm's _____ is the combined cost of funds from all sources.
    A.   capital budget
    B.   capital ration
    C.   capital expenditure
    D.   cost of capital
    E.   cost of funds

2.   _____ occurs when a firm has limited financial resources available for investment.
    A.   Capital budgeting
    B.   Capital rationing
    C.   Capital expenditure
    D.   Capital limitation
    E.   Funding limits

3.   Economic theory suggests that the profit-maximizing firm should expand its output until:
    A.   all available funds are invested.
    B.   all proposed projects are accepted.
    C.   all independent projects are accepted.
    D.   operating costs are minimized.
    E.   marginal cost equals marginal revenue.

4.   The initial step in the capital budgeting process is:
    A.   generating capital investment project proposals.
    B.   estimating cash flows.
    C.   evaluating alternatives and selecting projects.
    D.   selecting the appropriate evaluation techniques.
    E.   determining the proposed project's marginal cost of funding.

5.   Which of the following statements concerning project cash flows is incorrect?
    A.   Sunk costs should be disregarded.
    B.   Resources should be measured in terms of their opportunity costs.
    C.   Cash flows should be measured on a before-tax basis.
    D.   Cash flows should be measured on an incremental basis.
    E.   The indirect effects of the project should be included in the cash flow estimates.

6.   Which of the following should not be considered in the initial cash outlay or net investment (NINV) of a proposed investment?
    A.   The purchase price of the new machine.
    B.   An increase in the working capital necessary to support the new investment.
    C.   Net proceeds from the sale of the asset to be replaced.
    D.   Taxes associated with the sale of the new asset.
    E.   The installation and shipping costs of the new machine.

7.   Which of the following should not be considered in the future net operating cash flows (NCF) of a proposed project?
    A.   Changes in revenues associated with the project
    B.   Salvage value of the asset
    C.   Changes in operating costs associated with the project
    D.   Additional depreciation charges associated with the project
    E.   Additional net working capital associated with the project

8.   At the end of the asset's life, if the market value of the asset is less than its book value:
    A.   There is no tax consequence.
    B.   There is an additional tax equal to the marginal tax rate times the amount of the gain.
    C.   There is a tax savings equal to the marginal tax rate times the amount of the loss.
    D.   There is an operating gain and a capital gain both of which are taxed at the ordinary rate.

9.   Interest charges should not be considered in estimating the project's net cash flows because:
        A.   The value of the project should be measured independently of how the project is financed.
        B.   Interest charges are not tax-deductible for all project types.
        C.   The project may be financed with funds that do not require interest payments.
        D.   The project's expected cash flows should be discounted at the after-tax cost of debt.

10.   The use of accelerated depreciation instead of straight-line depreciation increases the value of the project to the firm because the use of:
        A.   Accelerated depreciation techniques increases the total net cash flows of the proposed investment.
        B.   Straight-line depreciation increases the total depreciation expense of a proposed project and thus reduces the project's net cash flows.
        C.   Accelerated depreciation techniques reduces the total tax liability of the proposed investment expected net cash flows.
        D.   Accelerated depreciation techniques eliminates the unfavorable treatment of salvage values.
        E.   Accelerated depreciation techniques reduces tax outlays in the project's early years and thereby increase the present value of the project's expected cash flows.

Answers to Multiple Choice Questions

1.	D	5.	C	9.	A
2.	B	6.	D	10.	E
3.	E	7.	B		
4.	A	8.	C		

PROBLEMS

1.   Lewis and Sons Company is considering a new machine that would increase annual revenues by $500,000, increase annual cash operating expenses by $140,000, and increase depreciation charges by $70,000 per year. If Lewis is in the 40 percent tax bracket, what annual net cash flows result from this investment?

Solution:

NCF = ΔOEAT + ΔDep - ΔNWC
NCF = (ΔR - Δ0 - ΔDep)(1 - T) + ΔDep - ΔNWC $(0 - (-4500) - 3000)(1-0.4) + 3000 - 0$
NCF = (500,000 - 140,000 - 70,000)(1 - 0.4) + 70,000 - 0
NCF = 290,000(.6) + 70,000
NCF = 174,000 + 70,000 = $244,000

2.   Acme Farms bought a tractor ten years ago for $200,000. The crane is being depreciated (straight-line) over a 15-year life to a salvage value of $20,000. Acme pays taxes equal to 48% of ordinary income and 30% of capital gains. What is the tax liability (or saving) if the crane is sold now for:

        a. $80,000?   c. $120,000?
        b. $60,000?   d. $240,000?

Solution:

This asset is being depreciated using a pre-ACRS straight-line method.

Annual depreciation = ($200,000 - $20,000)/15 = $12,000
Current book value = $200,000 - $12,000(10) = $80,000

a.   The selling price equals the current book value so there is no tax consequence.

b.   Tax saving equals the ordinary rate times the loss.
        Tax saving = .48(80,000 - 60,000) = .48(20,000) = $9,600.

c.   Tax liability equals the ordinary rate times the gain.
        Tax = .48(120,000 - 80,000) = .48(40,000) = $19,200.

d.   Tax liability equals the ordinary rate times (200,000 - 80,000) plus the capital gains rate
        times (240,000 - 200,000).
        Tax = .48(200,000 - 80,000) + .30(240,000 - 200,000)
        Tax = .48(120,000) + .30(40,000) = 57,600 + 12,000 = $69,600.

3.   What is the after-tax cash proceeds for Acme Farming for each selling price above in Problem 2?

Solution:

a. $80,000
b. $60,000 + $9,600 = $69,600
c. $120,000 - $19,200 = $100,800
d. $240,000 - $69,600 = $170,400

4.   Speedy Delivery Company bought a light duty truck in 1999 for $80,000. What will be Barry's
        future depreciation charges. Modified ACRS rules apply.

Solution:

Speedy's truck is classed as 5-year property and there is no investment tax credit. The depreciation
charges will be:

Year	MACRS rate	Rate x $80,000
1	20.00%	$16,000
2	32.00	25,600
3	19.20	15,360
4	11.52	9,216
5	11.52	9,216
6	5.76	4,608
7 and after	0.00	0

5.   NPR Enterprises is thinking of starting a new commercial lawn care business. This project will have a life of 5 years. The project will require the purchase of new equipment costing $150,000 (including shipping costs). Initial net working capital is anticipated to equal $15,000. The equipment will be depreciated using the straight-line method over the five-year period assuming an estimated salvage value of zero. Revenue for year 1 is expected to equal $150,000 and, thereafter, is expected to grow at the rate of 10% per year. Cash operating expenses are estimated to equal $60,000 in year 1 and, thereafter, growing at the rate of 8% per year. An additional investment of $5,000 in net working capital is projected at the end of year 1; no further changes in net working capital are anticipated for the remainder of the project life. At the end of year 5 assume that the equipment is sold for $30,000.

   a.   What is the net investment required for this project?
   b.   What are the net cash flows associated with the project in each of the five years?

Solution:

   a.   The net investment is determined as follows:
              Cost of equipment (including shipping) $150,000
              Initial net working capital $ 15,000
                        Net Investment $165,000

   b.   Determining the net cash flows requires that we first calculate the revenues, operating, expenses and depreciation for each of the 5 years.

          The projected revenues and operating expenses for each of the next five years are as follows:
          Year   Revenues   Operating expenses
          1         $150,000 $60,000
          2         $150,000(1.10)=$165,000 $60,000(1.08) = $64,800
          3         $165,000(1.10)=$181,500 $64,800(1.08) = $69,984
          4         $181,500(1.10)=$199,650 $69,984(1.08) = $75,583
          5         $199,650(1.10)=$219,615 $75,583(1.08) = $81,630

          The annual depreciation is: ($150,000-0)/5 years = $30,000
          The net cash flows are:
          Year $(\Delta R - \Delta O - \Delta Dep)(1 - T) + \Delta Dep - \Delta NWC = NCF$
          1   (150,000 - 60,000 - 30,000)(1-.4) + 30,000 - 5,000= $61,000
          2   (165,000 - 64,800 - 30,000)(1-.4) + 30,000 - 0 = $72,120
          3   (181,500 - 69,984 - 30,000)(1-.4) + 30,000 - 0 = $78,910
          4   (199,650 - 75,583 - 30,000)(1-.4) + 30,000 - 0 = $86,440
          5   (219,615 - 81,630 - 30,000)(1-.4) + 30,000 + 20,000 = $114,791

          Note above that in year 1 we subtracted $5,000 for additional net working capital and added $20,000 in year 5 for recovery of the total net working capital (initial net working capital and the additional net working capital amount in year 1). In addition to the above, we need to modify year 5 cash flow to include the proceeds (after-tax) from the sale of the equipment:

          $NCF_5 = 114,791 + 30,000 - (.4)(30,000) = \$ 132,791$

6.   Charlie's Cleaners is considering replacing its old equipment with more efficient equipment. The old equipment was purchased five years ago for $90,000. New equipment would cost $135,000 plus $5,000 for shipping and $10,000 for installation. Under Modified ACRS rules, the new equipment is classed as 7-year property. The new equipment has a 10-year economic life and a $10,000 estimated salvage. The new equipment would have no effect on sales, but it would reduce annual cash operating expenses by $10,000 (from $60,000 per year with the old equipment to $50,000 with the new). No change in receivables or inventories will be associated with the new equipment. Charlie's Cleaners is in the 34 percent tax bracket.

a.   If Charlie buys the new equipment, what is his net investment at time zero?

b.   If Charlie buys the new equipment, what is his net cash flow for each of the next ten years?

Solution:

a.   The net investment can be found in four steps.

Step 1	Asset cost	$135,000	
	Shipping cost	5,000	
	Installation cost	10,000	$150,000
Step 2	Increase in working capital	0 +	0
Step 3	Proceeds on sale of old assets (before tax)	30,000 -	30,000
Step 4	Tax saving on old asset sold at loss*	10,200 -	10,200
	Net Investment		$109,800

*The book value on the old equipment = 90,000 - 5(6,000) = $60,000.
The loss was 60,000 - 30,000 = $30,000.
The tax saving was .34(30,000) = $10,200.

b.   The annual depreciation on the old equipment for each year is 90,000/15 = $6,000. The depreciable basis of the new equipment is $150,000. The depreciation charges for the new equipment will be:

Year	MACRS Rate	Depreciation MACRS Rate x $150,000
1	14.29%	$21,435
2	24.49	36,735
3	17.49	26,235
4	12.49	18,735
5	8.93	13,395
6	8.92	13,380
7	8.93	13,395
8	4.46	6,690
9	0.00	0
10	0.00	0

The annual operating net cash flows are computed with the formula:

$$NCF = (\Delta R - \Delta O - \Delta Dep)(1 - T) + \Delta Dep$$
$$NCF = [(R_w - R_{wo}) - (O_w - O_{wo}) - (D_w - D_{wo})](1 - T) + (D_w - D_{wo})$$

For all 10 years, $\Delta R = 0$
For all 10 years, $\Delta O = 50,000 - 60,000 = -\$10,000$
The depreciation charge is:

Year	new depr	old depr	Δ Dep
1	$21,435	$6,000	$15,435
2	36,735	6,000	30,735
3	26,235	6,000	20,235
4	18,735	6,000	12,735
5	13,395	6,000	7,395
6	13,380	6,000	7,380
7	13,395	6,000	7,395
8	6,690	6,000	690
9	0	6,000	-6,000
10	0	6,000	-6,000

Year	$(\Delta R - \Delta O - \Delta Dep)(1 - T)$	+ ΔDep	=	$\Delta OEAT$	+ ΔDep	=	NCF
1	$(0 + 10,000 - 15,435)(1-.34)+$	15,435	=	-3,587	+ 15,435	=	11,848
2	$(0 + 10,000 - 30,735)(1-.34)+$	30,735	=	-13,685	+ 39,735	=	17,050
3	$(0 + 10,000 - 20,235)(1-.34)+$	20,235	=	-6,755	+ 20,235	=	13,480
4	$(0 + 10,000 - 12,735)(1-.34)+$	12,735	=	- 1,805	+ 12,735	=	10,930
5	$(0 + 10,000 - 7,395)(1-.34) +$	7,395	=	1,719	+ 7,395	=	9,114
6	$(0 + 10,000 - 7,380)(1-.34) +$	7,380	=	1,729	+ 7,380	=	9,109
7	$(0 + 10,000 - 7,395)(1-.34) +$	7,395	=	1,719	+ 7,395	=	9,114
8	$(0 + 10,000 - 690)(1-.34) +$	690	=	6,145	+ 690	=	6,835
9	$(0 + 10,000 + 6,000)(1-.34) -$	6,000	=	10,560	- 6,000	=	4,560
10	$(0 + 10,000 + 6,000)(1-.34) -$	6,000	=	10,560	- 6,000	=	4,560

In addition, in year 10, Charlie's Cleaners will sell the new equipment for salvage for $10,000, which will be taxed at 34%. So the year 10 net cash flow will be:

$$NCF_{10} = 4,560 + 10,000 - .34(10,000) = \$11,160.$$

Chapter

9

Capital Budgeting Decision Criteria and Real Option Considerations

This chapter explains four commonly used capital budgeting criteria, discusses project review and post audit procedures, and discusses how capital rationing and inflation are included in capital budgeting analysis. Real options and international capital budgeting are also covered.

I. Four capital budgeting criteria are widely known and used. These are the net present value (NPV), internal rate of return (IRR), profitability index (PI), and the payback period (PB).

  A. The *net present value* (NPV) of an investment project is defined as the present value of the stream of future net cash flows from a project minus the project's net investment.

    1. The net present value is:

$$NPV = PVNCF - NINV$$

$$NPV = \sum_{t=1}^{n} \frac{NCF_t}{(1+k)^t} - NINV$$

where:

NPV = net present value
NCF_t = expected net cash flow in period t
n = expected project life
k = cost of capital
NINV = net investment

k = cost of capital (interest rate

NPV ≥ 0 Accept.
mutually exclusive - if both ≥ 0, choose highest NPV.
NPV ≤ 0 = reject

Decision rule.

NPV, k is specified, NPV computed

IRR, r is unknown, cause NPV = 0   Rate of discount that makes NPV = 0

3.   Like the NPV, the IRR takes account of the magnitude and timing of a project's net cash flows over its entire life.

4.   One occasional difficulty with the IRR is that an unusual cash flow pattern (cash flows switching signs from positive to negative and vice versa) can result in multiple rates of return.

5.   When two or more mutually exclusive projects are acceptable using the IRR and NPV criteria, and if the two criteria disagree on which is best, the NPV criterion is generally preferred.

6.   Both the NPV and IRR criteria will always agree on accept/reject decisions (i.e., if NPV > 0, then IRR > k; and if NPV < 0, then IRR < k), even if the NPV and IRR do not rank the projects the same.

7.   Different rankings result from the implicit reinvestment rate assumptions of the two techniques: the NPV assumes that cash flows over the project's life may be reinvested at the cost of capital k while the IRR assumes that cash flows may be reinvested at the IRR. *The cost of capital is considered to be a more realistic reinvestment rate.*

C.   The *profitability index* (PI) or benefit-cost ratio is the ratio of the present value of future net cash flows over the life of the project to the net investment.

1.   Algebraically, the profitability index is

$$PI = \frac{\sum_{t=1}^{n} \frac{NCF_t}{(1+k)^t}}{NINV}$$

PI > 1 = Accept
PI < 1 = Reject
(Decision rule

2.   The *PI decision rule* is to accept a project whose PI is greater than or equal to one and to reject a project whose PI is less than one.

3.   The PI has the same advantages and disadvantages as the NPV criterion.

4.   The NPV is an *absolute* measure of the amount of wealth increase from a project, whereas the PI is a *relative* measure showing the wealth increase per dollar of investment.

D.   The *payback period* (PB) of an investment is the number of years required for the cumulative net cash inflows from a project to equal the initial cash outlay.

1.   If the future net cash inflows are equal in each year, the payback period is simply the ratio of the net investment to the annual cash inflows.

Whenever a project has multiple internal rates of return, the pattern of cash flows over the project's life contains more than one sign change —↑ + + ↑— 2 sign changes - from minus to plus & again from plus to minus.

mult rr - NPV

$$PB = \frac{Net\ investment}{Annual\ net\ cash\ flow}$$

When the future net cash flows are unequal, interpolation is frequently used in the final period to get an accurate payback period.

2.   The advantages of the payback method are that it is simple, it provides a measure of project liquidity, and, in a sense, it may also be a measure of risk.

3.   On the other hand, the payback period is not a true measure of profitability and, therefore, is not a good criterion for decision making. The payback period ignores cash flows after the payback is reached and it ignores the time value of money of the cash flows occurring within the payback period.

II.   Capital budgeting analysis can be complicated by *capital rationing*, that is, when the total outlay for projects exceeds available funds. One method for maximizing the wealth of the firm given a funds constraint is the profitability index approach, which involves the following steps:

[handwritten margin note: Constraints (upper limit) on amt allocated for investment. Self imposed by mgmt or externally imposed by capital markets.]

A.   Step 1: Calculate the profitability index (PI) for each of a series of investment projects.

B.   Step 2: Array the projects from the highest to the lowest PI.   *[handwritten: ↑ to ↓]*

C.   Step 3: Starting with the project with the highest ratio, proceed through the list and accept until the entire capital budget is utilized.

D.   In the event some capital investment funds cannot be fully utilized because the next acceptable project is too large, there are three alternatives:

1.   Alternative 1: Search for another combination of projects, perhaps including some smaller, less profitable projects, which will allow for a more complete utilization of available funds <u>and</u> increase the NPV of the combination of projects.

2.   Alternative 2: Attempt to relax the funds constraint so that sufficient resources are available to accept the last project.

[handwritten margin note: depressed stock mkt, ↑ int rates "Tight money" policy - Fed reserve. Sample pg 354 (9-5)]

3.   Alternative 3: Accept as many projects as possible and invest any excess funds in short-term securities until the next period, or pay out the excess funds to reduce outstanding debt or as common stock dividends.

III.   Reviewing or post-auditing is a final step to review the performance of investment projects after they have been implemented.

A.   While projected cash flows are uncertain and one should not expect actual values to agree with predicted values, the analysis should attempt to find systematic biases or errors by individuals, departments, or divisions and attempt to identify reasons for these errors.

B.   Another reason to audit project performance is to decide whether to abandon or continue projects that have done poorly.

↑ Inflation
↓ Capital expenditures

IV.   Inflation is easily incorporated into the basic capital budgeting criteria.

      A.   Make sure the cost of capital takes account of inflationary expectations.

      B.   Make sure that future cash flow estimates also include expected price and cost increases.

      C.   If these are done, the capital budgeting techniques outlined in these chapters serve the financial decision-maker reasonably well.

V.   *Real options* are not incorporated into the conventional discounted cash flow techniques (NPV, IRR, and PI). A real option gives the firm the right, but not the obligation, to buy, sell, or otherwise transform an asset at a set price during a specified time period.

      A.   The firm will exercise its real options in the future if it is advantageous to do so. These real options can be a major part of the value of capital projects. The bad news is that option valuation in capital budgeting is complicated. Managers must recognize their presence.

      B.   Five types of real options exist.

            1.   *Investment timing options.* Delaying investment in a project, i.e. for a year or so, may allow the firm to evaluate additional information about demand, costs, or technology. Then the firm can make a better decision. The "waiting-to-see" option is a very common real option.

            2.   *Abandonment option.* A project can be abandoned by shutting it down completely, selling the asset, or by switching it to some alternative use. The abandonment option can reduce the downside risk of a project.

            3.   *Shutdown options.* A firm may have the option of shutting down temporarily a project to avoid negative cash flows.

            4.   *Growth options:* Many projects can be expanded later. Examples of growth options are in research programs, building a small plant that can be expanded if the market grows, or making a strategic acquisition in a new line of business.

            5.   *Designed-in options.* Some options occur naturally, and others can be designed in. These designed-in options are input flexibility options, output flexibility options, or expansion options.

      C.   Using conventional discounted cash flow analysis in capital budgeting without considering the value of real options can result in a downward-bias in estimates of a project's true net present value.

VI.   International capital budgeting must account for cash flows in different currencies and for financial market conditions in different countries.

    A.   The net present value of a foreign investment can be found in simple steps. First, find the present value of the foreign cash flows denominated in the foreign currency and discounted by that foreign country's applicable cost of capital:

$$PVNCF_f = \sum_{t=1}^{n} \frac{NCF_t}{(1+k)^t}$$

    Then convert the present value of the cash flows to the home country's currency by multiplying by the spot exchange rate (expressed in units of home currency per unit of foreign currency):

$$PVNCF_h = PVNCF_f \times S_0$$

    Finally, subtract the parent company's net investment from the $PVNCF_h$ to get the NPV.

$$NPV = PVNCF_h - NINV$$

    B.   The amount and timing of the cash flows to a foreign subsidiary and to a parent may not be the same for several reasons.

        1.   Differential tax rates for foreign and domestic companies exist in many countries.

        2.   There may be legal and political constraints on cash remittances from the foreign country to the home country.

        3.   Many governments offer subsidized loans, which obviously are valuable only in the country that grants them.

VII.   The principles of capital budgeting apply to entrepreneurial, or small, firms as well as large firms. However, there are some differences in practice.

    A.   Large firms tend to use the conceptually correct NPV and IRR methods while small firms often use incorrect procedures such as the payback and accounting rate of return.

    B.   There are logical reasons for the discrepancy in how large and small firms apply capital budgeting techniques.

        1.   Small firms may lack the expertise to implement formal capital budgeting procedures, or they may have the expertise but it is simply stretched too thin to do a careful analysis.

2.   There are more costs associated with a formal, complete analysis. The smaller projects being considered by small firms may not justify this expensive analysis.

3.   Many small firms may have critical cash shortages, which causes them to focus on the payback period.

VIII.   (Appendix to Chapter 9) When two or more mutually exclusive projects have unequal lives, the net present value and internal rate of return criteria can be unreliable unless the projects are being evaluated for an equal period of time. The two basic approaches to evaluate unequal lives, mutually exclusive projects are the replacement chain approach and the equivalent annual annuity approach.

A.   In the *replacement chain* approach, follow these logical steps:

1.   Find the least common multiple of the projects' lives (i.e., find the smallest number that is an integer multiple of each project's life).

2.   For each project, lay out the replacement chain cash flows over the least common multiple of lives (you may have to reinvest in each project one or more times over a long time period).

3.   Find the net present value of the replacement chain cash flows for each project. Choose the alternative with the best NPV.

B.   In the *equivalent annual annuity* approach, follow these steps:

1.   Compute the net present value of each project over its expected economic life.

2.   Obtain an equivalent annual annuity for each project by dividing its net present value by the present value of an annuity factor (PVIFA) over its original life. Choose the project with the better equivalent annual annuity.

3.   If a net present value is desired, the net present value for each project may be found by assuming the equivalent annual annuity is a perpetuity. The net present value of a perpetuity is found by dividing the equivalent annual amount by the cost of capital. Choose the project with the greater NPV. (This will always agree with your decision in step 2.)

TRUE AND FALSE QUESTIONS

Agree with each of the statements or **reject** it and modify it so that it is acceptable.

1.   A project with a rapid payback will have a positive net present value (NPV).

2.   Assume a project has a positive NPV. If the net investment and expected future cash flows double with the cost of capital remaining constant, then the NPV doubles.

3.   If a project's required rate of return increases with the expected cash flows remaining constant, the investment's internal rate of return (IRR) decreases.

4.   The NPV and IRR criteria agree on accept/reject decisions for individual projects, but they may rank a set of projects differently.

5.   The profitability index (PI) decision rule is to accept a project whose PI exceeds zero and to reject a project with a negative PI.

6.   When the cost of capital increases, the NPV and IRR decrease and the payback increases.

7.   If Project A's NPV is $2,000 and its IRR is 15%, and Project B's NPV is $3,000, then Project B's IRR is greater than 15%.

8.   The NPV criterion is not a true measure of profitability and an objective criterion for decision making because it ignores the cash flows after the payback is reached.

9.   One reason to review or post-audit the performance of investment projects after they have been implemented is to decide to abandon or continue projects that have done poorly.

10.   One way that inflation may be incorporated into capital budgeting criteria is by making sure that inflationary expectations are reflected in both the cost of capital and future cash flow estimates.

11.   Financial managers must be aware that using conventional discounted cash flow techniques in capital budgeting without considering real options results in a downward-biased estimate of the project's true net present value.

12.   A real option to abandon a project at some future point should result in a lower net present value.

Answers to True and False Questions

1.   A project with a rapid payback can have a negative payback. For example, if you lend me $1,000 for one year and I pay you back, you have an investment with a one-year payback and a negative NPV.

2.   True.

3.   If the required rate of return increases, the investment's net present value decreases; the internal rate of return remains constant.

4.   True.
5.   Accept if PI≥ 1.0 and reject if PI < 1.0.
6.   The higher discount rate decreases the NPV but does not change the calculated IRR and payback.
7.   The NPV and IRR may rank projects differently.
8.   The NPV criterion evaluates all cash flows. The comment in the statement applies to the payback criterion, not to the NPV criterion.
9.   True.
10.   True.
11.   True.
12.   A real option to abandon a project should not lower a project's net present value since you would not exercise the option unless it were to your advantage to exercise it. The abandonment option actually reduces your downside risk.

MULTIPLE CHOICE QUESTIONS

1.   The _____ of an investment project is defined as the present value of the stream of future net cash flows from a project minus the project's net investment.
      A.   Profitability index
      B.   Payback period
      C.   Internal rate of return
      D.   Net present value
      E.   Replacement chain

2.   The NPV decision rule is to accept a proposed project when the NPV is:
      A.   greater than the cost of capital.
      B.   less than the present value of expected cash inflows.
      C.   greater than the internal rate of return.
      D.   less than zero.
      E.   greater than zero..

3.   Which of the following is not a stated benefit of using NPV as a decision-making technique?
      A.   It adheres to the principle of value additivity.
      B.   It is consistent with the goal of shareholder wealth maximization.
      C.   It is a relative measure showing the wealth increase per dollar of investment.
      D.   It accounts for the magnitude and timing of a project's cash flows over its entire life.

4.   The internal rate of return is the discount rate that makes the project's NPV:
      A.   equal to zero.
      B.   equal to the cost of capital.
      C.   positive.
      D.   negative.
      E.   acceptable.

2.   The *NPV decision rule* is to accept a project when the NPV is positive and to reject a project when its NPV is negative. If the present value of the project's net cash flows exceeds the project's net investment outlay, the project contributes to the total value of the firm.

3.   The benefits of using the NPV criterion include: (1) It accurately accounts for the magnitude and timing of a project's cash flows over its entire life. (2) It shows whether a proposed project yields the rate of return required by the firm's investors and, therefore, consistent with the goal of shareholder wealth maximization. (3) It adheres to the principle of value additivity.

4.   A disadvantage of the NPV criterion is that it is not as easily understood by untrained decision-makers as the payback or internal rate of return.

5.   What causes some projects to have positive or negative NPV's? When product and factor markets are not perfectly competitive, it is possible for a firm to earn above-normal profits and invest in positive NPV projects. Some examples of conditions that allow above-normal profits include:

   a.   buyer preferences for established brand names;
   b.   ownership or control of favored distribution systems;
   c.   patent control of superior product designs or production techniques;
   d.   exclusive ownership of superior natural resource deposits;
   e.   inability of new firms to acquire necessary factors of production (management, labor, equipment);
   f.   superior access to financial resources at lower costs (economies of scale in attracting capital);
   g.   economies of large-scale production and distribution arising from capital intensive production processes and high initial start-up costs; and
   h.   access to superior labor or managerial talents at cost which are not fully reflective of their value.

B.   The *internal rate of return* (IRR) is defined as the rate of discount that equates the present value of net cash flows of a project with the present value of the net investment. In other words, the IRR is the discount rate that makes a project's NPV equal zero.

AKA
(DCF)
Discounted
Cash Flow

1.   The algebraic definition of the IRR is:

$$\sum_{t=1}^{n} \frac{NCF_t}{(1+r)^t} = NINV$$

where r = IRR.

2.   The *IRR decision rule* is to accept a project when its IRR exceeds the cost of capital (k) and to reject a project when its IRR is less than k.

When 2 or more independent projects w/ normal cash flows are considered, PI, NPV, IRR approaches all w'll yield identical accept-reject signals.

No Constraints, no capital rationing = use NPV for largest total $ increase.

5.   If NPV > 0, then:
      A.   IRR = k.
      B.   IRR > k.
      C.   IRR > 0.
      D.   IRR < 0.
      E.   IRR < k.

6.   The reinvestment rate assumption is more realistic for the net present value approach to project evaluation than the internal rate of return because NPV assumes that intermediate cash flows will be invested at _____ where IRR assumes these cash flows will be reinvested at _____.
      A.   cost of capital;   internal rate of return.
      B.   project's payback;   internal rate of return.
      C.   internal rate of return;   cost of capital
      D.   internal rate of return;   project's payback
      E.   cost of capital;   project's payback

7.   Each of the following are advantages of using the Payback Period except:
      A.   It provides a measure of a project's liquidity.
      B.   It is simple to compute.
      C.   It is a crude measure of risk.
      D.   It is a measure of profitability.
      E.   It is a measure of time.

8.   Using conventional discounted cash flow analysis in capital budgeting without considering the value of real options can result in:
      A.   an overstatement of the project's true net present value.
      B.   the acceptance of unprofitable projects.
      C.   an understatement of the project's true net present value.
      D.   an overstatement of the project's expected future cash flows.

9.   Which of the following statements concerning capital budgeting for small firms is not true?
      A.   Small firms tend to use incorrect procedures such as payback and accounting rate of return.
      B.   Small firms tend to lack the expertise to implement formal capital budgeting procedures.
      C.   Small firms cannot afford the additional costs of formal capital budgeting procedures.
      D.   Small firms face cash shortages that leads to focus on capital budgeting techniques that measure liquidity.
      E.   Net present value is not an appropriate capital budgeting technique for small firms.

10.   Replacement Chains and Equivalent Annual Annuities are used to evaluate mutually exclusive projects with:
      A.   similar cash flows.
      B.   unequal lives.
      C.   cashflows arising in different currencies.
      D.   contain real options.
      E.   limited funding.

Answers to Multiple Choice Questions:

1.	D	5.	B	9.	E
2.	E	6.	A	10.	B
3.	C	7.	D		
4.	A	8.	C		

PROBLEMS

1. An outlay of $180,000 is expected to yield the following cash flows:

Year	Net Cash Flow
1	75,000
2	55,000
3	60,000
4	25,000
5	15,000
6	10,000

The depreciation tax benefits and salvage value are already included in the cash flows and the cost of capital is 12 percent.

a. What is the payback period?
b. What is the project's NPV?
c. Should the project be adopted?

Solution:

a. Payback = 2 5/6 years.

b.

Year	NCF$_t$	PVIF @ 15%	PV Cash Flows	
1	75,000 *22,000*	.8929 *. 8 0*	66,964	*19,644*
2	55,000 *22000*	.7972	43,846	*17,538*
3	60,000 *22000*	.7118	42,707	*15,659*
4	25,000 *22000*	.6355	15,888	*13,981*
5	15,000 *22000*	.5674	8,511	*12,483*
6	10,000 *22000*	.5066	5,066	*11,145*
7	*22000*		182,982	*90,449*
	Less: Net Investment		(180,000)	*<76,000>*
	NPV=		$2,982	

c.   The project should be accepted because of its positive NPV.

2.   What is the internal rate of return for the cash flows in Problem 1?

Solution:

We can find the IRR with trial and error and interpolation.

Year	NCF_t	PVIF @ 13%	PV of Cash Flows
1	75,000	.8850	66,372
2	55,000	.7831	43,073
3	60,000	.6931	41,583
4	25,000	.6133	15,333
5	15,000	.5428	8,141
6	10,000	.4803	4,803
			179,305
	Less:	NINV	(180,000)
		NPV =	$-695

This indicates that the internal rate of return is slightly less than 13%.
The calculated solution is 12.81%..

The IRR criterion rates the project as acceptable because the IRR (12.81) is greater than the cost of capital (12%).

3.   Two mutually exclusive projects have the following cash flows:

Year	NCF for A	NCF for B
0	-10,000	-10,000
1	4,000	0
2	4,000	0
3	4,000	0
4	4,000	19,000

a.   Find the net present value of each project discounted at 0%, 5%, 10%, 15%, and 24%. Plot the NPVs as a function of the discount rate.

b.   What is the IRR of each project?

c.   Assuming a cost of capital of 10%, which project should be chosen?

Solution:

a.

Discount Rate	NPV for A	NPV for B
0%	$-10,000 + 4,000(4.0) = 6,000$	$-10,000 + 19,000(1.0) = 9,000$
5%	$-10,000 + 4,000(3.546) = 4,184$	$-10,000 + 19,000(.823) = 5,637$
10%	$-10,000 + 4,000(3.170) = 2,680$	$-10,000 + 19,000(.683) = 2,977$
15%	$-10,000 + 4,000(2.855) = 1,420$	$-10,000 + 19,000(.572) = 868$
20%	$-10,000 + 4,000(2.589) = 356$	$-10,000 + 19,000(.482) = -842$
24%	$-10,000 + 4,000(2.404) = -384$	$-10,000 + 19,000(.423) = -1,963$

b.   Discounted at 21%, $NPV_A = -10,000 + 4,000(2.540) = 160$
Discounted at 22%, $NPV_A = -10,000 + 4,000(2.494) = -24$

$$r = 21\% + \frac{160}{160 + 24}(22\% - 21\%) = 21\% + .87(1\%) = 21.87\%$$

Interpolating for IRR:
[More precisely, IRR = 21.86%]
Discounted at 17%, $NPV_B = -10,000 + 19,000(.534) = 146$
Discounted at 18%, $NPV_B = -10,000 + 19,000(.516) = -196$
Interpolating for IRR:

$$r = 17\% + \frac{146}{146 + 196}(18\% - 17\%) = 17\% + .43(1\%) = 17.43\%$$

[More precisely, IRR = 17.41%]

c.   If the cost of capital is 10%, $NPV_A = 2,680$ and $NPV_B = 2,977$, which means that Project B is superior. However, $IRR_A = 21.87\%$ and $IRR_B = 17.43\%$, implying that Project A is superior. The choice of projects would depend on which reinvestment assumption was appropriate. For example, if the NPV reinvestment assumption of 10% (the cost of capital) is correct, then Project B would be chosen.

4.   The Worst Management Company is evaluating the following seven independent projects

Project	Outlay	NPV
A	$ 100	$ 20
B	500	125
C	400	90
D	200	20
E	250	40
F	300	18
G	50	9

a.   Calculate the profitability index (PI) for each project and rank the seven projects according to their PI's.

b.   If the total outlay cannot exceed $750, choose the set of projects that maximizes Worst's NPV.

Solution:

a.

Project	Outlay	NPV	PV*	PI**	Rank
A	100	20	120	1.200	3
B	500	125	625	1.250	1
C	400	90	490	1.225	2
D	200	20	220	1.100	6
E	250	40	290	1.160	5
F	300	18	318	1.060	7
G	50	9	59	1.180	4

*PV = present value of future NCF's = Outlay + NPV
**PI = PV/Outlay

b.   This can be solved by trial and error. Generally, projects with high PI's are chosen, but in this case, the best two projects (C and B) cannot both be bought because they exceed the $750 budget.

Projects	Total Outlay	Total NPV
B, E	$750	$165
A, C, E	750	150
B, A, G	650	154
B, D, G	750	154

Projects B and E are the set of projects that maximizes your NPV subject to the $750 capital outlay constraint.

5.   Calculate the NPV of the equipment replacement decision being considered by Fred's Deli. The cost of capital is 8%.

Solution:

Time	Cash flow	PVIF @ 8%	PV @ 8%
0	-$109,800	1.000	-$109,800.00
1	11,848	.926	10,971.25
2	17,050	.857	14,611.85
3	13,480	.794	10,703.12
4	10,930	.735	8,033.55
5	9,114	.681	6,206.63
6	9,114	.630	5,741.82
7	9,114	.583	5,313.46
8	6,830	.540	3,688.20
9	4,560	.500	2,280.00
10	4,560	.463	5,167.08
		Total	-$37,083.04

6.   Melissa Welsh is evaluating a capital budgeting project for his employer. Melissa has determined the relevant facts to be as follows:

installed cost = $100,000
project life = 10 years
incremental revenue = $45,000 annually
incremental cash operating expenses = $20,000
cost of capital = 10%
tax rate = 40%
depreciation: straight-line over ten years to a salvage value of $10,000.
liquidation value in 10 years = $10,000
investment in working capital = zero

Please use this information to find (a) the project's payback period, (b) net present value, (c) profitability index, and (d) internal rate of return.

Solution:

Annual depreciation = (100,000 - 10,000)/10 = $9,000
NCF = (ΔR - Δ0 - ΔD)(1 - T) + ΔD - ΔNWC
NCF = (45,000 - 20,000 - 9,000)(1 - .4) + 9000 - 0
NCF = 9,600 + 9,000 = 18,600

a.   Since the future cash flows are equal,
      PB = net investment/annual net cash flow
      PB = 100,000/18,600 = 5.38 years

b.
Year	NCF	Interest Factors @ 10%	PV of Cash Flows
1-10	18,600	6.145	114,297
10	10,000	.386	3,860
			118,157
	Less:	NINV	(100,000)
		NPV =	$ 18,157

c.   PI = PV of Cash Flows/NINV
      PI = 118,157/100,000 = 1.18

d.   We will use trial and error and interpolation to get the IRR.

Year	NCF	PVIF @ 13%	PV of Cash Flows	PVIF @ 14%	PV of Cash Flows
1-10	18,600	5.426	100,923.60	5.216	97,017.60
10	10,000	.295	2,950.00	.270	2,700.00
			103,873.60		99,717.60
Less:	NINV		(100,000.00)		(100,000.00)
	NPV =		$ 3,873.60	NPV =	$ -282.40

Interpolating for IRR:

$$r = 13\% + \frac{3,873.60}{3,873.60 + 282.40}(14\% - 13\%) = 13\% + .93(1\%) = 13.93\%$$

This is a profitable project. It has a positive net present value, a profitability index greater than 1.0, and an internal rate of return greater than the cost of capital.

7.   Reevaluate Problem 6 using the MACRS depreciation schedule. The relevant data are now:

installed cost = $100,000
no investment tax credit
project life = 10 years
incremental revenue = $45,000 per year
incremental cash operating expenses = $20,000 per year
cost of capital = 10%
tax rate = 40%
depreciation: Modified ACRS, 7-year class
liquidation value in 10 years = $10,000
investment in working capital = zero

Please use this information to find (a) the project's payback period, (b) net present value, (c) profitability index, and (d) internal rate of return.

Solution:

Year	ACRS rate	Depreciation (rate x $100,000)
1	14.29%	$14,290
2	24.49%	24,490
3	17.49%	17,490
4	12.49%	12,490
5	8.93%	8,930
6	8.92%	8,920
7	8.93%	8,930
8	4.46%	4,460
9	0.00%	0
10	0.00%	0

$$\underline{\text{Year}} \qquad (\Delta R - \Delta O - \Delta D)(1 - t) + \Delta D = \text{NCF}$$

1	(45,000 - 20,000 - 14,290)(1 - .4)	+	14,290	=	20,716.00
2	(45,000 - 20,000 - 24,490)(1 - .4)	+	24,490	=	24,796.00
3	(45,000 - 20,000 - 17,490)(1 - .4)	+	17,490	=	21,996.00
4	(45,000 - 20,000 - 12,490)(1 - .4)	+	12,490	=	19,996.00
5	(45,000 - 20,000 - 8,930)(1 - .4)	+	8,930	=	18,572.00
6	(45,000 - 20,000 - 8,920)(1 - .4)	+	8,920	=	18,568.00
7	(45,000 - 20,000 - 8,930)(1 - .4)	+	8,930	=	18,572.00
8	(45,000 - 20,000 - 4,460)(1 - .4)	+	4,460	=	16,784.00
9	(45,000 - 20,000 - 0)(1 - .4)	+	0	=	15,000.00
10	(45,000 - 20,000 - 0)(1 - .4)	+	0	=	15,000.00

In year 10, the cash flow also increases by the salvage value and declines by the tax on the gain on salvage.

$$\text{NCF}_{10} = 15,000 + 10,000 - .40(10,000) = 21,000$$

a.   To find the PB, we see how long it takes for the cumulative cash flow to equal the outlay.

Year	Cash Flow	Cumulative Cash Flow
1	20,716.00	20,716.00
2	24,796.00	45,512.00
3	21,996.00	67,508.00
4	19,996.00	87,504.00
5	18,572.00	106,076.00
6	18,568.00	124,644.00
7	18,572.00	143,216.00
8	16,784.00	160,000.00
9	15,000.00	175,000.00
10	21,000.00	196,000.00

$$\text{PB} = 4 \text{ years} + \frac{100,000.00 - 87,504.00}{106,076.00 - 87,504.00}(1\text{year}) = 4.67 \text{years}$$

It takes between 4 and 5 years to recover the $100,000 net investment. Interpolating for the payback gives:

b.

Year	NCF	PVIF @ 10%	PV of NCF
1	20,716.00	.909	18,830.84
2	24,796.00	.826	20,481.50
3	21,996.00	.751	16,519.00
4	19,996.00	.683	13,657.27
5	18,572.00	.621	11,533.21
6	18,568.00	.564	10,472.35
7	18,572.00	.513	9,527.44
8	16,784.00	.467	7,838.13
9	15,000.00	.424	6,360.00
10	21,000.00	.386	8,106.00
			123,325.74
		Less: NINV	100,000.00
		NPV	23,325.74

c.   PI = PV of cash flows / NINV
      PI = 123,325.74/100,000.00 = 1.233

d. Using trial and error, the IRR is between 15% and 16%.

Year	NCF	PVIF @ 15%	PV of NCF
1	20,716.00	.870	18,022.92
2	24,796.00	.756	18,745.78
3	21,996.00	.658	14,473.37
4	19,996.00	.572	11,437.71
5	18.572.00	.497	9,230.28
6	18.568.00	.432	8,021.38
7	18.572.00	.376	6,983.07
8	16,784.00	.327	5,488.37
9	15,000.00	.284	4,260.00
10	21,000.00	.247	5,187.00
			101,849.88
		Less: NINV	100,000.00
		NPV	1,849.88

Year	NCF	PVIF @ 16%	PV of NCF
1	20,716.00	.862	17,857.19
2	24,796.00	.743	18,423.43
3	21,996.00	.641	14,099.44
4	19,996.00	.552	11,037.79
5	18,572.00	.476	8,840.27
6	18,568.00	.410	7,612.88
7	18.572.00	.354	6,574.49
8	16,784.00	.305	5,119.12
9	15,000.00	.263	3,945.00
10	21,000.00	.227	4,767.00
			98,276.61
		Less: NINV	100,000.00
		NPV	-1,723.39

Interpolating for the IRR:

$$r = 15\% + \frac{1{,}849.88}{1{,}849.88 + 1{,}723.39}(16\% - 15\%) = 15\% + .52(1\%) = 15.52\%$$

8. Gus Kalogeras must choose between two mutually exclusive projects with differing lives. Project F requires a $20,000 outlay and produces an after-tax net cash flow of $12,000 each year over its three-year life. Project G involves a $30,000 outlay and generates $13,000 each year for four years. Both projects have no salvage value. Project G, then, involves a larger outlay than Project F, but it provides a slightly larger cash inflow over the first 3 years and then provides $13,000 in year 4 when Project F has expired. The services of either project are required more or less indefinitely, it is simply a question of which is more profitable. Assume a 10% cost of capital.

a. Calculate the net present value of a replacement chain for each project over the least common multiple of the project's lives.

b. Calculate the equivalent annual annuity for each project.

Solution:

a. The least common multiple of 3 and 4 (the lives of F and G) is 12.

The cash flows for 12 years would be:

Time	Outlay(F)	Net Cash Flow(F)	Outlay(G)	Net Cash Flow(G)
0	20,000	--	30,000	--
1		12,000		13,000
2		12,000		13,000
3	20,000	12,000		13,000
4		12,000	30,000	13,000
5		12,000		13,000
6	20,000	12,000		13,000
7		12,000		13,000
8		12,000	30,000	13,000
9	20,000	12,000		13,000
10		12,000		13,000
11		12,000		13,000
12		12,000		13,000

The net present value of each project over the 12 year period is:

$$NPV_F = 12{,}000(PVIFA_{.10,12}) - 20{,}000(PVIF_{.10,0}) - 20{,}000(PVIF_{.10,3})$$
$$- 20{,}000(PVIF_{.10,6}) - 20{,}000(PVIF_{.10,9})$$

$$NPV_F = 12{,}000(6.814) - 20{,}000(1) - 20{,}000(.751) - 20{,}000(.564)$$

$$- 20,000(.424)$$

$$NPV_F = 81,768 - 20,000 - 15,020 - 11,280 - 8,480$$

$$NPV_F = \$26,988$$

$$NPV_G = 13,000(PVIFA_{.10,12}) - 30,000(PVIF_{.10,0}) - 30,000(PVIF_{.10,4}) - 30,000(PVIF_{.10,8})$$

$$NPV_G = 13,000(6.814) - 30,000(1) - 30,000(.683) - 30,000(.467)$$

$$NPV_G = 88,582 - 30,000 - 20,490 - 14,010$$

$$NPV_G = \$24,082$$

Apparently, Project F has the superior net present value ($26,988 compared to $24,082).

b.   Find the NPV of each project over its original life:

$$NPV_F = -20,000 + 12,000(PVIFA_{.10,3})$$

$$NPV_F = -20,000 + 12,000(2.487) = \$9,844$$

$$NPV_G = -30,000 + 13,000 (PVIFA_{.10,4})$$

$$NPV_G = -30,000 + 13,000(3.170) = \$11,210$$

Find the equivalent annual annuity EAA for each project by dividing its NPV by the present value of an annuity factor for its original life:

$$EAA_F = NPV_F/(PVIFA_{.10,3})$$

$$EAA_F = \$9,844/2.487 = \$3,958$$

$$EAA_G = NPV_G/(PVIFA_{.10,4})$$

$$EAA_G = \$11,210/3.170 = \$3,536$$

Choose Project F because it provides an annuity of $3,958 per year while G provides a lesser $3,536. If a net present value of a perpetuity is desired, divide the equivalent annual annuity for each project by the cost of capital:

$$NPV_F = \$3,958/.10 = \$39,580$$
$$NPV_G = \$3,536/.10 = \$35,360$$
Project F has the greater NPV for such a long-lived chain.

9. Rework Problem 7 using the capital budgeting Excel template accompanying the text (Capbudg). The results of doing this are on the following pages. If you do this, you should notice how much faster you can do this problem, and also that you can readily do much more complicated problems with the help of a spreadsheet program.

Capital Budgeting Investment Analysis	

Information On Old Asset

Original Installed Cost Of Asset		$0
Net Working Capital Required For Asset		$0
Investment Tax Credit	0.00%	$0
At		
Economic Life Of Asset		0
Years Depreciated		0
Straight-Line Depreciation (Otherwise Enter Each Year Individually)		
Accumulated Depreciation		$0
Book Value		$0
Proceeds From Sale Of Old Asset		$0
Tax Effects		
Capital Gains Tax Rate	40.00%	
Marginal Tax Rate	40.00%	
Tax On Sale Of The Old Asset		$0
Recapture Of ITC		$0

Information On New Asset

Cost Of New Asset	$100,000
Delivery And Installation	$0
Net Working Capital Required For Asset	$0
Investment Tax Credit %	0.00%
Depreciable Class Of Asset (Under MACRS)	4

Class	Enter
3-Year	2
5-Year	3
7-Year	4
10-Year	5
15-Year	6
20-Year	7

Economic Life Of New Asset	8

   For MACRS Enter Class Life + One

For Straight-Line Enter Years Of
Depreciation

Salvage Value Of New Asset	$10,000
Depreciation Method	2
(1) - Straight-Line	
(2) - MACRS	

Information On Real Property

Original Cost Of Land		$0
Estimated Value At End Of Project		$0
Cost Of Building		$0
Class Of Property	Enter	0
27.5 (Residential Rental Property)	1	
39 (Nonresidential Real Property)	2	
Month Building Is Placed In Service (1-12)		0
Estimated Value At End Of Project		$0
Net Investment		$100,000

Life Of The Project	10

Net Cash Flow Calculation	0	1	2	3	4
Cash Inflows	Growth Rate				
Revenues With Project	0.00%	45,000	45,000	45,000	45,000
Revenues Without Project	0.00%	0	0	0	0
Incremental Revenue		45,000	45,000	45,000	45,000
Cash Outflows	Growth Rate				
Costs With Project	0.00%	20,000	20,000	20,000	20,000
Cost Without Project	0.00%	0	0	0	0
Incremental Cost		20,000	20,000	20,000	20,000
Depreciation					
Depreciation On Building		0	0	0	0
Depreciation With Project		14,290	24,490	17,490	12,490
Depreciation Without Project		0	0	0	0
Incremental Depreciation		14,290	24,490	17,490	12,490
Incremental Earnings Before Taxes		10,710	510	7,510	12,510
Taxes		4,284	204	3,004	5,004
Recapture Of Asset Salvage Value		0	0	0	0
Recapture Of Working Capital		0	0	0	0
Recapture Of Land Salvage Value		0	0	0	0
Recapture Of Building Salvage Value		0	0	0	0
Additional Investment In Working Capital		0	0	0	0
Net Cash Flow	($100,000)	$20,716	$24,796	$21,996	$19,996

	5	6	7	8	9	10
	45,000	45,000	45,000	45,000	45,000	45,000
	0	0	0	0	0	0
	45,000	45,000	45,000	45,000	45,000	45,000
	20,000	20,000	20,000	20,000	20,000	20,000
	0	0	0	0	0	0
	20,000	20,000	20,000	20,000	20,000	20,000
	0	0	0	0	0	0
	8,930	8,920	8,930	4,460	0	0
	0	0	0	0	0	0
	8,930	8,920	8,930	4,460	0	0
	16,070	16,080	16,070	20,540	25,000	25,000
	6,428	6,432	6,428	8,216	10,000	10,000
	0	0	0	0	0	6,000
	0	0	0	0	0	0
	0	0	0	0	0	0
	0	0	0	0	0	0
	0	0	0	0	0	0
	$18,572	$18,568	$18,572	$16,784	$15,000	$21,000

Summary Information	
Discount Rate	10.00%
Initial Guess For IRR	10.00%
Net Present Value	$23,340
IRR	15.51%
Profitability Index	1.2334
Payback (Years)	4.67

grocery = low beta risk.

vs

Large competitors, lack of expertise = high level of total project risk.

Beta of a firm influences the returns required by investors in that firm and hence the firms value.

Chapter

10

Capital Budgeting and Risk

In Chapter 9, investment projects were evaluated using the firm's weighted cost of capital (required rate of return). This requires that the projects under consideration exhibit the same level of risk as the firm as a whole. When a project being evaluated is more or less risky than the firm's average risk level, it is necessary to modify the analysis to account for risk differences between the project and the rest of the firm. This chapter discusses several methods to account for risk differences in capital budgeting projects.

beta (systematic) risk

I. It is important to distinguish between the *total project risk* and the *portfolio* or *beta* risk of an investment when analyzing capital expenditures.

A. Total project risk reflects the probability that the returns from a project will be less than expected. This type of risk assumes that the project is considered in isolation, however in most circumstances, some of total project risk can be diversified away.

B. Portfolio or beta risk measures the risk of the project relative to the market; portfolio or beta risk cannot be diversified away.

Beta risk

II. To adjust for portfolio or beta risk, the capital asset pricing model can be used to estimate risk-adjusted discount rates for capital budgeting. Just as the beta of a portfolio of securities is the weighted-average of the individual security betas, the firm may be considered a portfolio of assets, each having its own beta.

A. All-equity case. If a firm is financed exclusively with equity capital, the beta of the assets with be equity to the beta of the debt.. If a project of the same risk as the firm's existing assets is being considered, its beta will be the same as the firm's equity. The project's risk-adjusted discount rate is found with the SML equation.

Can have both

157

High level of total project risk (of a project) may not affect the portfolio risk of the firm at all.

$$k^* = r_f + (r_m - r_f)B$$

(financed with)

B.   **Equity and debt case.** If betas can be observed for firms in the same investment class as the proposed investment, these betas can be used to estimate risk-adjusted discount rates. A complication is that the observed firm's financing (debt and equity mix) may be different than the one you are using. An adjusted beta for the project is determined in two steps.

1.   Step 1: Calculate an unleveraged beta:

$$B_u = \frac{B_l}{1 + (1-T)(B/E)}$$

where B_u is the unleveraged beta, B_l is the leveraged beta of the proxy firm, T is the firm's tax rate, and B/E is the proxy firm's debt to equity ratio (market value of debt/market value of equity).

2.   Step 2: Calculate a new leveraged beta for your investment:

$$B_l = B_u[1 + (1-T)(B/E)]$$

— observed beta
or unleveraged beta
or pure project beta

3.   A firm's equity beta reflects its specific mix of debt and equity financing. To determine an unleveraged asset beta for the firm, use the formula for the unleveraged beta in step 1 above.

C.   The project's net present value is: *Risk adjusted NPV*

$$NPV = \sum_{t=1}^{n} \frac{NCF_t}{(1+k^*)^t} - NINV$$

where k^* is the risk-adjusted weighted cost of capital (required return).

D.   The firm is a portfolio of assets and the firm's beta is a weighted-average of the asset betas. The firm's weighted-cost of capital is based on the firm's beta. Individual projects will have a greater (or smaller) required rate of return than the weighted cost of capital if the project's beta is greater than (or less than) the firm's beta.

The weighted-cost of capital is the correct discount rate for a project only when the project beta equals the firm's beta. When the project beta is less than (or greater than) the firm's beta, the weighted cost of capital is greater than (less than) the project's risk-adjusted rate of return from the SML.

In general: the risk adjusted discount rate approach is considered preferable to the weighted cost of capital approach when the projects under consideration differ significantly in their risk characteristics.

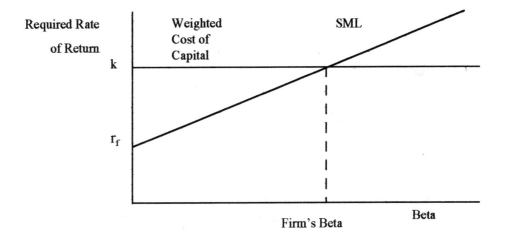

III.   A variety of techniques are used to adjust for the total project risk for an individual investment (neglecting portfolio effects).

Subjective, not related to variability of returns
Some projects more risky during startup period
may reject acceptable projects

   A.   NPV-Payback Approach. To be accepted, a project must have a positive NPV <u>and</u> a payback of less than a critical number of years (such as 4 years).

   B.   Simulation Approach. In this approach the probability distribution of the project's NPV is estimated. Based on the mean and standard deviation of the NPV distribution, one can assess the risk of the project.   *Models events*

          1.   Simulation requires that estimates of the probability distributions of each element that influences the cash flows of a project be made. These elements include the number of units sold, market price, unit production costs, unit selling costs, net investment, project life, and the cost of capital.

Considerable time & effort to gather info & formulate model.
limits feasibility for large projects
assumes variables are independent.

random variables

          2.   Net present values are calculated using numerical values chosen randomly from the relevant probability distribution. This process is repeated many times until a probability distribution of the project's NPV can be estimated.

   C.   Sensitivity analysis. Sensitivity analysis involves systematically changing relevant variables to determine the relative sensitivity of the NPV (or IRR) to these variables. It enables decision-makers to ask "what if" questions and study their impact on the NPV (or IRR).

          1.   Sensitivity curves can be created to show the impact of changes in a

(handwritten top left:) (pg 389) (10-3)

(handwritten top left margin:) Flat cost of capital-NPV curve indicates NPV is not very sensitive to changes in the firm's cost of capital.

(handwritten top right:) Steep slope of price-NPV curve indicates NPV is very sensitive to changes in the price for which the product can be sold.

variable (such as the price of the output, the cost of capital, the tax rate, etc.) on the project's NPV.

2.   Computer spreadsheets such as Lotus and Excel make sensitivity analysis relatively easy to perform.

(handwritten left margin:) changes in key variables vs. changes (individual) in key variables

D.   Scenario analysis. Scenario analysis considers the impact of simultaneous changes in several key variables on the desirability of the investment project. This is in contrast to sensitivity analysis that considers the impact of individual changes in key variables. For example, one can consider a pessimistic, most likely, and optimistic scenario with respect to the key variables and examine their joint impact on the NPV (or IRR). *(handwritten:)* · pessimistic, ← most likely → optimistic (Risk premiums are subjective)

(handwritten left margin:) RADR

E.   Risk-adjusted discount rate approach To calculate the NPV of a project, the project's cash flows are discounted at a discount rate adjusted for the relative risk of the project instead of discounting all projects at one rate (the firm's cost of capital). The firm carries a risk premium that depends on its overall risk This risk premium is:

$$q = k - r_f$$

(handwritten left margin:) The difference between the risk-free rate and the firm's required rate of return (cost of capital) is an average risk premium to compensate investors for the fact that the company's assets are risky.

where q = average risk premium for the firm, r_f = risk-free rate, and k = cost of capital (required rate of return) for projects of same risk as firm.

The risk premiums applied to individual projects usually are chosen in a subjective manner. Many firms establish risk classes (such as low, medium, high), assign individual projects to these classes, and discount all the projects in each class by a discount rate arbitrarily chosen for that class.

(handwritten left margin:) greater than average risk discounted at a higher rate - to reflect the increased riskiness. subjective.

Given a risk premium q_a for project a, the risk adjusted discount rate for the project, k^*_a, would then be

$$k^*_a = r_f + q_a$$

and the net present value for the investment project is:

$$NPV_a = \sum_{t=1}^{n} \frac{NCF_t}{(1+k^*_a)^t} - NINV$$

F.   The certainty equivalent approach involves converting expected risky cash flows to their certainty equivalents and then computing the net present value of the project.

(handwritten bottom:) Adjusts the net cash flows in the numerator of the NPV equation, in contrast to the RADR approach, which involves adjustments to the denominator of the NPV equation.
Initial outlay is known with certainty. (may be purchase price)

1.   The risk-free rate, r_f, not the firm's risky cost of capital, k, is used as the discount rate.

2.   The certainty equivalent cash flow is a certain cash flow that the decision-maker feels is equivalent to the risky cash flow. (At time t, the decision-maker would be indifferent between the risky cash flow and the certainty equivalent). The certainty equivalent factor (a_t) is the ratio of the certainty equivalent cash flow to the risky cash flow.

$$\alpha_t = \frac{certain\ return}{risky\ return}$$

Certainty equivalent factors range from 0 to 1.0. The higher the factor, the more certain the expected cash flows.

3.   The certainty-equivalent net present value is:

Certainty equivalent factors decline into the future as most cash flows are viewed as being more risky the further into the future they are projected to occur.

$$NPV = -NINV(\alpha_0) + \sum_{t=1}^{n} \frac{NCF_t \alpha_t}{(1+r_f)^t}$$

where:

α_0 = certainty equivalent factor associated with the net investment (NINV) at time 0,

α_t = certainty equivalent factor associated with expected risk cash flows (NCF_t) at time t,

r_f = risk-free rate, and

n = economic life of the project.

IV.   Multinational firms should focus on cash flows to the parent and not cash flows that accrue to the foreign subsidiary. Managers in multinational firms need to be aware of special elements of risk when investing abroad.

A.   A foreign host country might block a subsidiary from remitting funds back to the parent.

B.   A foreign government might take over the assets of your foreign subsidiary with no or inadequate compensation.

C.   Exchange rate risk is an additional risk when doing business in several currencies.

D.   Because of the complexities, some financial managers in multinational companies rely on their personal feelings about political and economic risks in foreign countries.

TRUE AND FALSE QUESTIONS

Agree with each of the statements or **reject** it and modify it so that it is acceptable.

1. T   If a project's return has a zero standard deviation, then it is considered to be risk-free.

2. T   A project's portfolio risk cannot be diversified away.

F 3.   In the risk-adjusted discount rate approach, a project's NPV is found by discounting with the weighted cost of capital.

F 4.   The certainty equivalent factor is the ratio of the present value of a risky cash flow to the expected cash flow.

F 5.   The internal rate of return is not used for capital budgeting under risk.

F 6.   Discounting all projects at the cost of capital instead of the risk-adjusted discount rate might cause the firm to reject some high-risk projects that should be accepted and to accept some low-risk projects that should be rejected.

7. T   Computer simulation can be used for evaluating risky projects.

F 8.   A project with a beta higher than the overall beta of the firm should have a required rate of return less than the firm's weighted cost of capital.

9. T   Diversified investors should use a systematic risk measure such as beta and nondiversified investors should use a total risk concept.

10. T   When portfolio effects are present, the capital asset pricing model approach is recommended to find the appropriate risk-adjusted discount rate.

F 11.   Scenario analysis is useful in studying the impact of changes in key variables, one at a time, on the profitability of capital budgeting projects.

Answers to True and False Questions

1.   True.
2.   True.
3.   The risk-adjusted discount rate, not the weighted cost of capital, is used as the discount rate.

4.   The certainty equivalent factor (a_t) is the ratio of the certainty equivalent cash flow at time t to the expected risky cash flow at time t.

5.   The IRR is compared to the risk-adjusted discount rate (k^*) instead of the cost of capital (k).

6.   The errors are the opposite of the ones named. Using the cost of capital instead of risk-adjusted discount rates might cause the firm to accept some bad high-risk projects and to reject some good low-risk projects.

7.   True.

8.   A project with a beta <u>less</u> than the overall beta of the firm should have a required rate of return less than the firm's weighted cost of capital.

9.   True.

10.   True.

11.   Scenario analysis is useful when considering the impact of simultaneous changes in several key variables on the profitability of the project. Sensitivity analysis is useful in studying the impact of changes in key variables one at a time on the profitability of the project.

MULTIPLE CHOICE QUESTIONS

1.   The total project risk of a proposed investment reflects:
   A.   Only the market risk of the project.
   B.   The average risk of the overall firm.
   C.   The weighted average risk of all of the firm's investments.
   D.   The effects of financial leverage on the project's returns.
   E.   The probability that the project returns will be less than expected.

2.   The firm's weighted average cost of capital should be used to discount the cash flows of a proposed investment if and only if:
   A.   The firm uses all equity to finance the project..
   B.   The risk of the project is the same as the overall risk of the firm.
   C.   The project's unsystematic risk can be diversified away.
   D.   The project's portfolio risk is similar to that of the overall firm.
   E.   The total project risk cannot be completely determined.

3.   An asset's unlevered beta reflects the relative risk for the asset after adjusting for:
   A.   the portfolio risk of the asset.
   B.   the total risk of the asset.
   C.   the use of debt.
   D.   the systematic risk of the asset.
   E.   the market value of a comparable asset.

4.   The use of the firm's weighted average cost of capital to evaluate proposed investments of all risk classes causes the firm to reject _____ projects that should be accepted and to accept _____ projects that it should reject.
    A.   low beta; average beta
    B.   average beta, high beta
    C.   high beta, low beta
    D.   low beta; high beta
    E.   average beta, average beta

5,   _____ involves systematically changing relevant variables to determine the relative sensitivity of the NPV (or IRR) to these variables.
    A.   Sensitivity Analysis
    B.   Simulation Analysis
    C.   NPV/Payback Analysis
    D.   Scenario Analysis
    E.   Risk adjusted discount rate approach

6.   In the risk-adjusted discount rate approach, the appropriate discount rate for a project is equal to:
    A. $R_f + B(R_m - R_f)$
    B. $R_f + q_a$
    C. q_a
    D. $q_a + B$
    E. $R_f - q_a$

7.   Scenario analysis differs from sensitivity analysis in that:
    A.   Sensitivity analysis considers the impact of changes in several key variables at once, where scenario analysis considers the impact of a change in only one variable.
    B.   Scenario analysis considers the impact of changes in the level of interest rates, where sensitivity analysis considers the impact of changes in only variables that contribute to cash flow.
    C.   Scenario analysis considers the impact of changes in several key variables at once, where sensitivity analysis considers the impact of a change in only one variable.
    D.   Scenario analysis considers the impact of changes in only variables that contribute to cash flow, where sensitivity analysis considers the impact of a change in the level of interest rates.

8.   The appropriate discount rate to use with the certainty equivalent approach to capital budgeting is:
A.   The risk-adjusted discount rate.
B.   The weighted average cost of capital.
C.   The required rate of return.
D.   The required rate of return on an unlevered project.
E.   The risk-free rate.

9.   A certainty equivalent cash flow is:
A.   the certain cash flow that the decision-maker feels is equivalent to the risky cash flow.
B.   the expected cash flow discounted at the risk-free rate.
C.   the risky cash flow that the decision-maker would be willing to exchange for the known certain cash flow.
D.   the ratio of the expected cash flow to the risky cash flow.
E.   the dollar value of the expected risky cash flow discounted at the risk adjusted discount rate.

10.   In international capital budgeting, the project's relevant cash flows are:
A.   the foreign currency cash flows generated by the foreign investment.
B.   the cash flows that are blocked by the host country government.
C.   the cash flows that accrue to the foreign subsidiary.
D.   the cash flows that accrue to the parent firm.
E.   the inflation adjusted cash flows form project net income.

ANSWERS TO MULTIPLE CHOICE QUESTIONS

1.	D	5.	B	9.	E
2.	E	6.	A	10.	B
3.	C	7.	D		
4.	A	8.	C		

PROBLEMS

1. Diaz Investments uses a combined NPV-Payback approach to capital budgeting: a project must have a payback of less than four years and a positive NPV. Which of the following projects are acceptable, if the cost of capital is 10%?

		Project A	Project B
Outlay:		200,000	100,000
Cash flow:	1 year	75,000	25,000
	2 years	50,000	25,000
	3 years	50,000	25,000
	4 years	40,000	25,000
	5 years	40,000	25,000
	6 years	20,000	25,000

Solution:

$Payback_A = 3.625$ years

		10% Present Value	
Year	NCF	PV Factor	PV of NCF
1	75,000	.9091	68,182
2	50,000	.8264	41,322
3	50,000	.7513	37,566
4	40,000	.6830	27,321
5	40,000	.6209	24,837
6	20,000	.5645	11,289
	Less: Net Investment		200,000
	NPV_A	=	$10,517

$Payback_B = 100,000/25,000 = 4.0$ years

		10% Present Value	
Year	NCF	Interest Factor	PV of NCF
1-6	25,000	4.3553	108,883
	Less: Net Investment		100,000
	$NPV_B =$		$8,883

Project A meets both the NPV and payback criteria while Project B's payback does not meet Diaz Investment's payback cutoff.

2.   Bob White estimates the outlay for a risky project to be $1,000,000. He also expects after-tax net cash flows of $400,000 for each of the first three years and $300,000 for years 4 and 5. His certainty equivalent factors are estimated to be:

$\alpha_0 = 1.00$
$\alpha_1 = .95$
$\alpha_2 = .89$
$\alpha_3 = .85$
$\alpha_4 = .75$
$\alpha_5 = .70$

The cost of capital is 18% and the risk-free rate is 6%. Use the certainty-equivalent method to obtain a net present value.

Solution:

Year	NCF_t	α_t	$NCF_t\alpha_t$	PVIF@6%	PV
0	-$1,000,000	1.00	-$1,000,000	1.000	-$1,000,000
1	400,000	.95	380,000	.9434	358,491
2	400,000	.89	356,000	.8900	316,839
3	400,000	.85	340,000	.8396	285,471
4	300,000	.75	225,000	.7921	178,221
5	300,000	.70	210,000	.7473	156,924
			NPV	=	$ 295,945

3.   Miguel Acosta is an accountant for a small oil company. He has been asked by the company's chief executive officer to estimate the required rate of return for an investment in oil storage facilities. Acosta, after two weeks of study, has found these to be very risky investments. He estimates the standard deviation of the return on oil storage facilities to be 30% per year and that the correlation between the returns on oil storage facilities and returns on investments in general to be 0.75. Current market conditions would argue for a 9% riskless rate of return, a 15% rate of return in the market for risky assets, and a 10% standard deviation for the market return.

a.   What is the beta for oil storage facilities?
b.   What is the required rate of return on this investment?

Solution:

a.

$$B = \frac{\rho_{jm}\sigma_j\sigma_m}{\sigma_m^2} = \frac{.75(.30)(.10)}{(.10)^2} = 2.25$$

b.

$$k_j = r_f + B_j(r_m - r_f)$$

$$k = .09 + 2.25(.15 - .09) = .09 + .135 = .225 \text{ or } 22.5\%$$

4.   The risk-free rate is 5%, the firm's beta is 0.8, and the required rate of return for the market is 10%. The firm is evaluating the following investment projects:

Project	Internal Rate of Return	Beta
A	7.0%	1.00
B	11.0%	1.40
C	14.0%	1.10
D	10.0%	0.70
E	7.5%	0.60
F	13.0%	1.00
G	11.0%	1.25
H	12.0%	1.70
I	8.5%	0.60
J	8.5%	0.75

a.   What is the weighted-cost of capital or required rate of return for the firm? If this is used as the hurdle rate for all projects, which projects will be selected?

b.   If a separate required rate of return is estimated for each project, which projects will be selected?

Solution:

a.   WCC $= r_f + B_j(r_m - r_f) = 5\% + .8(10\% - 5\%) = 5\% + 4\% = 9\%$

Accept all projects with IRR above 9%.
Accept: B C D F G H   Reject: A E I J

b. $k_j = r_f + B_j(r_m - r_f)$

	Required Rate of Return	Internal Rate of Return	Decision
$k_A = 5 + 1.0(5) = 10\%$		7.0%	Reject
$k_B = 5 + 1.4(5) = 12\%$		11.0%	Reject
$k_C = 1.1(5) = 10.5\%$		14.0%	Accept
$k_D = 5 + .7(5) = 8.5\%$		10.0%	Accept
$k_E = 5 + .6(5) = 8.0\%$		7.5%	Reject
$k_F = 5 + 1.0(5) = 10.0\%$		13.0%	Accept
$k_G = 5 + 1.25(5) = 11.25\%$		11.0%	Reject
$k_H = 5 + 1.7(5) = 13.5\%$		12.0%	Reject
$k_I = 5 + .6(5) = 8.0\%$		8.5%	Accept
$k_J = 5 + .75(5) = 8.75\%$		8.5%	Reject

Accept any projects with an IRR above its RRR.

Accept: C D F I   Reject: A B E G H J

Note that the two approaches select different projects. The WCC approach accepted projects B, G and H that should have been rejected and rejected project I that was a good project.

5.   Frasher Airways is considering an investment in a small commuter route. A proxy firm in that line of business has a beta of 1.5, and a debt/equity ratio of 3.0 (i.e., 75% debt, 25% equity), and a tax rate of 40%.

   a.   If Judith Frasher has a 40% tax rate and plans to finance her investment with 50% equity, what should she use as the project's beta?

   b.   If the current risk-free rate is 7% and the market return is 16%, what should Judith use as the project's cost of capital?

Solution:

a.

$$B_u = \frac{B_l}{1 + (1-T)(B/E)}$$

$$B_u = \frac{1.50}{1 + (1-.4)(3)} = .536 \;\; for \; proxy \; firm$$

$$B_l = B_u\,[1 + (1 - T)(B/E)]$$

$$B_l = .536[1 + (1-.4)(1)] = .8576 \;\; for \;\; Frasher$$

b. $k = r_f + (r_m - r_f)B$

$k = .07 + (.16 - .07).8576 = .07 + .077 = .147 = 14.7\%$

Judith should use 14.7% as her cost of capital for the commuter route investment.

Chapter

11

The Cost of Capital

One of the key variables in capital budgeting decisions is the cost of capital. The cost of capital can be thought of as what the firm must pay for capital or the return required by investors in the firm's securities. It can also be thought of as the minimum rate of return required on new investments undertaken by the firm. The cost of capital is determined in the capital markets and depends on the risk associated with the firm's activities.

I.   The weighted cost of capital is the discount rate used when computing the NPV of a project of average risk. Similarly, the weighted cost of capital is the hurdle rate used in conjunction with the internal rate of return.

   A.   The weighted cost of capital is based on the after-tax cost of capital where the cost of the next (marginal) sources of capital are weighted by the proportions of the capital components in the firm's long-range target capital structure.

   B.   The weighted, or overall, cost of capital is obtained from the weighted costs of the individual components. The weights are equal to the proportion of each of the components in the target capital structure.

      1.   The general expression for calculating the weighted cost of capital, k_a, is:

      k_a = (equity fraction)(cost of equity) + (debt fraction)(cost of debt)

      $$k_a = \frac{E}{B+E}(k_e) + \frac{B}{B+E}(k_d)(1-T)$$

$$k_a = \frac{E}{B+E}(k_e) + \frac{B}{B+E}(k_i)$$

where B = amount of debt and E = amount of equity.

2.   The appropriate component costs to use in determining k_a are the marginal costs or the costs associated with the next dollar of capital to be raised. These may differ from the historical costs of capital raised in the past.

C.   If the capital structure includes debt, preferred stock and common stock, the weighted cost of capital is:

$$k_a = \frac{E}{B+E+P_f}(k_e) + \frac{B}{B+E+P_f}(k_i) + \frac{P_f}{B+E+P_f}(k_p)$$

II.   The required return, k, on any security may be thought of as consisting of a risk-free rate of return plus a premium for the risk inherent in the security, or

Required return = r_f + Risk premium.

A.   The risk-free rate of return (r_f) is usually measured by the rate of return on risk-free securities such as short term Treasury securities. The risk-free rate consists of 2 components:

1.   A *real risk-free rate of return* determined by supply and demand for funds in the overall economy.

2.   An *inflation premium* to compensate for loss in purchasing power.

B.   There are five major risk components which determine the risk premium on a security.

1.   *Business risk* arises from the variability of the firm's operating income and is determined by the variability of sales revenues and expenses and by the amount of operating leverage the firm uses.

2.   *Financial risk* arises from the additional variability of the firm's net earnings associated with the use of financial leverage together with the increased risk of bankruptcy associated with the use of debt.

3.   *Marketability risk* refers to the ability to quickly buy and sell the securities. Securities that are widely traded have less marketability risk than those that are less actively traded.

4.   *Interest rate risk* refers to the variability in returns on securities arising from changes in interest rates. Increases in interest rates reduce the market price of the

security. Decreases in interest rates reduce the rate at which intermediate interest payments can be reinvested.

    5.   *Seniority risk* refers to the risk due to the priority of a security's claim in a firm's capital structure.

  C.   The cost of funds increases with the amount of financing required.

  D.   A risk-return trade-off exists between investors' required rate of return and various sources of funds. More risky sources of funds will have a relatively higher cost of capital: the cost of common equity is higher than that for preferred stock, the return required on preferred stock is higher than that for unsecured debt which is higher than that for secured debt.

  E.   A firm's cost of capital is equal to the equilibrium rate of return that investors demand in the capital markets for securities of that degree of risk.

III.   The weighted cost of capital depends on the *component costs* of capital and the *proportions* of the components in the target capital structure used for capital budgeting decisions. The component costs of capital are measured at the margin, i.e., what the next increment of capital from that particular source would cost.

  A.   On a before-tax basis, the cost of debt is the rate of return, k_d, that equates the present value of the future cash flows from interest and principal to P_{net}, the net proceeds of the security.

$$P_{net} = \sum_{t=1}^{n} \frac{I}{(1+k_d)^t} + \frac{M}{(1+k_d)^n}$$

    1.   The before-tax cost of debt can be found by using the methods for calculating yield-to-maturity illustrated in the chapter on bond valuation.

    2.   Interest payments on debt are deductible in arriving at taxable income. The after-tax cost of debt, k_i, is given by:

$$k_i = k_d (1 - T)$$

    3.   This method works well if the firm is in the process of issuing debt or has recently issued debt. In other situations, the firm can use the yield to maturity on currently outstanding bonds (based on their current market price). If no bonds are outstanding or they are traded infrequently, the firm could use the pretax cost of debt recently sold by other firms of similar risk to the firm under consideration.

  B.   The cost of preferred stock is the rate of return required by investors in the preferred stock of the firm adjusted for flotation costs.

    1.   The preferred stock valuation model tells us:

$$P_0 = D_p/k_p$$

where P_0 is the price, D_p is the dividend, and k_p is the investor's required rate of return.

2.   The cost of preferred stock is given by:

$$k_p = D_p/P_{net}$$

where P_{net} is the net proceeds to the firm after subtracting flotation costs.

3.   Dividends on preferred stock are not deductible in arriving at taxable income, so no tax adjustment is made. Because of this the cost to the firm of preferred stock is usually higher than that of debt, and firms prefer to obtain leverage from debt rather than from preferred stock.

C.   The basic cost of equity capital is the equilibrium rate of return required by investors in the firm's common stock. Equity capital can be raised internally through retained earnings or externally through the sale of new common stock. Use of externally generated equity capital entails flotation costs in addition to the required return.

D.   The cost of internally generated equity can be developed in several different ways.

1.   Recall the general dividend valuation model

$$P_0 = \sum_{t=1}^{\infty} \frac{D_t}{(1+k_e)^t}$$

2.   If dividends are expected to grow at a constant rate g, the price of common stock can be obtained as:

$$P_0 = D_1/(k_e - g)$$

where k_e is the required rate of return and D_1 is the next anticipated dividend which is equal to the current dividend D_0 times $(1 + g)$. By simple algebra:

$$k_e = D_1/P_0 + g$$

3.   In many cases, the non-constant dividend growth model can be used to estimate the cost of equity. If dividends are expected to grow at a rate g_1 for m years followed by perpetual growth at a rate g_2 in later years, the valuation model can be generalized to:

$$P_0 = \sum_{t=1}^{m} \frac{D_0(1+g_1)^t}{(1+k_e)^t} + \frac{1}{(1+k_e)^m} \times \frac{D_{m+1}}{k_e - g_2}$$

4. Dividend valuation models (frequently called DCF or discounted cash flow models) are frequently used to calculate a firm's cost of equity. Analysts' forecasts of future earnings rates are a superior source of information for DCF models. Individual brokerage houses and investment advisory services will give earnings and dividend forecasts. Institutional Brokers Estimate Service (IBES) and Zacks Earnings Estimates summarize analysts' forecasts for the stocks of more than 3500 firms.

5. The cost of equity capital can also be estimated using the capital asset pricing model (CAPM). In the CAPM, the required return on a stock depends on the risk-free rate, r_f, and a risk premium. The risk premium is determined by the difference between the expected return on the market as a whole and the risk-free rate, $(r_m - r_f)$ and by beta, B, which is a measure of the volatility of the stock relative to the volatility of the market index. Using the CAPM, the required return on equity is given by:

$$k_e = r_f + B(r_m - r_f)$$

6. Another method of estimating the cost of equity is to use the risk premium on debt approach. Historically, common stocks have averaged a return of 6.5 percentage points more than corporate debt. Thus for a firm with average risk (Beta = 1.0) the cost of equity capital can be assumed to be 6.5% greater than the firm's cost of debt. For a firm with a beta of 0.7, about 4 percentage points are added to the cost of debt to yield an estimate of the cost of equity.

E. The cost of external equity capital is greater than the cost of retained earnings and must be measured slightly differently.

1. The cost of new issues of common stock must include flotation costs.

2. Because a new issue increases the supply of stock, the equilibrium price of the stock can be expected to drop so that the offering price of a new issue must be lower than the market price of the stock before announcement of the new issue.

3. The cost of external equity, k_e, can be determined as:

$$k_{e'} = \frac{D_1}{P_{net}} + g$$

where P_{net} is the actual proceeds to the firm.

IV. The estimates of the cost of capital that have been discussed thus far are applicable for the firm as a whole. When some divisions of a company have higher or lower systematic risk than others, the discount rates for these divisions should be higher or lower than the discount rate for the firm as a whole.

A.   Each division could have its own beta and its own discount rate. The beta for the firm would be a weighted average of the divisional betas.

B.   In computing each divisional beta and cost of capital, many firms try to reflect both the differential risks and the differential normal debt ratios for each division.

V.   Once the component costs of capital have been determined, the weighted (marginal) cost of capital can be estimated.

A.   The weighted (marginal) cost of capital is calculated by multiplying the component costs of capital by their respective proportions in the target capital structure (for formula, see I. C.). This assumes that all common equity is internal and the all debt and preferred stock have a single cost.

B.   As larger amounts of capital are raised, the marginal cost of capital increases because of the need to raise external equity and the increased cost associated with additional increments of debt. This requires that a marginal cost of capital schedule be developed which shows the costs associated with each increment or "package" of capital throughout the range of the potential capital budget. A new package occurs when a component cost changes. The resulting schedule of marginal costs can be plotted on a graph as a marginal cost of capital curve.

VI.   The optimal capital budget is determined by comparing the expected project returns (investment opportunities curve) to the firm's marginal cost of capital schedule.

A.   The investment opportunities curve is a plot of the expected returns from proposed capital expenditures (in descending order) against the cumulative funds required to finance these projects.

B.   The optimal capital budget is the point where the investment opportunities curve and the marginal cost of capital curve intersect. This procedure is illustrated in the solved problem number 4 below.

VI.   For some firms depreciation is a major source of funds for investment.

A.   The cost of funds generated by depreciation is taken as equal to the firm's weighted cost of capital based on retained earnings and the lowest cost debt.

B.   The availability of funds from depreciation shifts the marginal cost of capital curve to the right.

VII.   Multinational firms have a more complex cost of capital than purely domestic firms.

    A.   Some host countries offer preferential (subsidized) financing terms as an incentive for a firm to locate some of its operations in that country.

    B.   Some evidence reflecting (perhaps temporary) differences in the real cost of capital between countries has been found. Multinational firms will shop the world for the lowest available capital costs.

    C.   Most multinationals raise all, or the vast majority, of their equity capital in their home country. Multinationals raise a substantial portion of their debt capital in the countries where they maintain significant operations. There are two reasons for this. First, foreign debt may hedge the balance sheet risk associated with changes in the value of assets due to changes in exchange rates. Second, this may insulate the firm from the risk of expropriation.

VIII.   Small, entrepreneurial firms have a difficult time attracting capital to support their investment programs.

    A.   The issuance costs of selling common stock may exceed 20 percent of the issue size.

    B.   Small firms often issue two classes of stock, Class A and Class B, where the Class A stock is sold to outsiders and usually pays a higher dividend and the Class B stock is held by the company's founders and has greater voting power.

    C.   Sources of debt capital are also limited. Small firms may have to rely on:

- the owners' own funds and loans from friends,
- loans from banks and savings and loan associations,
- Small Business Administration loans,
- commercial finance company loans,
- leasing companies,
- venture capital firms, and
- private placement of debt with insurance companies and large corporations.

        Small firms use creative financing, with equity sweeteners such as warrants and convertible debt being commonplace.

TRUE AND FALSE QUESTIONS

Agree with each of the statements or **reject** it and modify it so that it is acceptable.

1.   Business risk does not depend on the capital structure of the firm so it does not affect the firm's cost of capital.

2.   Marketability risk refers to the ability to buy and sell the firm's securities quickly and easily.

3.   Secured debt has a higher cost than unsecured debt.

4.   The component cost of debt sold at its par value is equal to the coupon rate of interest on the debt.

5.   The component cost of preferred stock must be adjusted for taxes which the stockholders must pay on the dividends.

6.   Using the dividend model, the cost of equity capital is given by

$$k_e = (D_0/P_0) + g.$$

7.   The cost of external equity is higher than the cost of retained earnings.

8.   If a firm uses preferred stock, the expression for the weighted cost of capital is

$$k_a = \frac{E}{B+E+P}(k_e) + \frac{B}{B+E+P}(k_i) + \frac{P}{B+E+P}(k_p)$$

where P is the amount of preferred stock.

9.   All potential capital investment projects are evaluated using a single cost of capital.

10.   Marginal cost of capital refers to the cost of the next dollar of capital to be raised.

11.   Funds derived from depreciation are free.

Answers to True and False Questions

1.   Business risk is a component of the risk of the firm and the cost of capital depends on this risk.
2.   True..
3.   Secured debt has a <u>lower</u> cost than unsecured debt.
4.   True.
5.   Preferred dividends are not deductible in arriving at the taxable income of the firm so no adjustment is needed. Stockholders' taxes do not directly affect the cost of preferred stock to the firm.

6.   Using the dividend model, the cost of equity capital is given by $k_e = (D_1/P_0) + g$.
7.   The cost of external equity is higher than the cost of retained earnings because of flotation costs.
8.   True.
9.   The optimal capital budget and determination of the cost of capital must be integrated.   The marginal cost of capital increases as the package of sources of capital changes with the amount of capital to be raised. High risk projects should be evaluated at a cost of capital that is consistent with project risk.
10.   True.
11.   Since the funds could be returned to the stockholders or used to retire debt, the appropriate opportunity cost is the firm's weighted cost of capital.

MULTIPLE CHOICE QUESTIONS

1.   The cost of capital represents:
    A.   The return required on the firm's outstanding securities.
    B.   The minimum required rate of return on new investments.
    C.   The rate that the firm must pay for capital.
    D.   The appropriate discount rate on an average risk project.
    E.   All of the above.

2.   The appropriate component costs to use in determining k_a are the _____ of the firm's individual security issues.
    A.   historical costs
    B.   marginal costs
    C.   average costs
    D.   current costs
    E.   overall costs

3.   _____ refers to the risk due to the priority of a security's claim in a firm's capital structure.
    A.   Interest rate risk
    B.   Marketability risk
    C.   Financial risk
    D.   Seniority risk
    E.   Business risk

4.   The before-tax cost of debt can be determined in each of the following ways except:
    A.   The interest payments on recently issued debt.
    B.   The yield-to-maturity on currently outstanding bonds.
    C.   The interest rate on long-term treasury bonds.
    D.   The pretax cost of debt recently sold by similar risk firms.
    E.   All of the above are appropriate means of determining the before-tax cost of debt.

5.   The cost of external equity capital is greater than the cost of internal equity due to:
    A.   The flotation costs associated with new equity
    B.   The higher dividends associated with new equity.
    C.   The higher risk associated with new equity.
    D.   The dilution of ownership rights associated with new equity.
    E.   The priority risk associated with new equity issues.

6.   Which of the following is not an appropriate manner in which to develop the cost of internally generated equity?

    A. $k_{e'} = \dfrac{D_1}{P_{net}} + g$

    B. $k_e = D_1/P_0 + g$

    C. $k_e = r_f + B(r_m - r_f)$

    D. $P_0 = \sum\limits_{t=1}^{m} \dfrac{D_0(1+g_1)^t}{(1+k_e)^t} + \dfrac{1}{(1+k_e)^m} \times \dfrac{D_{m+1}}{k_e - g_2}$

7.   As larger amounts of capital are raised, the marginal cost of capital _____.
    A.   declines
    B.   remains constant.
    C.   increases.

8.   The optimal capital budget is the point where the marginal cost of capital intersects with the:
    A.   Capital asset pricing model.
    B.   Weighted cost of capital.
    C.   Security market line.
    D.   Investment opportunities curve.
    E.   Internal rate of return.

9.   The two reasons that multinational firms raise a substantial portion in the countries where they maintain significant operations are to insulate the firm from the risk of expropriation and:
    A.   To hedge exchange rate risk.
    B.   To reduce the cost of operations.
    C.   To satisfy local funding requirements.
    D.   To diversify overall funding costs.
    E.   To remove local criticism.

10.   The cost of capital for small, entrepreneurial firms tends to exceed the cost of capital for larger firms. Which of the following is not a reason for this difference?
    A.   Limited sources of debt capital for small firms
    B.   The use of creative financing by small firms
    C.   The use of multiple classes of stock by small firms
    D.   The issuance costs of common stock for small firms.
    E.   All of the above are reasons for this difference

Answers to Multiple Choice Questions

1.	E	5.	A	9.	A
2.	B.	6.	A	10.	E
3.	D	7.	C		
4.	C	8.	D		

PROBLEMS

1. The Sweet Pea Produce Company is planning to issue $25 million of 7- 1/4% preferred stock at a price of $85 per share. Flotation costs will be $5 per share. Sweet Pea's tax rate is 40%. Calculate the after tax cost of the preferred stock assuming:

   a. The stock is a perpetuity.

   b. The stock is callable in 7 years at $99 per share and is expected to be called at that time.

Solution:

   a. The cost of perpetual preferred stock is given by $k_p = D/P_{net}$. No adjustment for taxes is required.

   $$D = 7\text{-}1/4\% \text{ of } \$85 = \$6.06$$

   $$P_{net} = \$85 - \$5 = \$80$$

   $$k_p = 6.06/80 = .0757 \text{ or } 7.57\%$$

   b. The general principle is that the cost of a component of capital is equal to the discount rate that equates the present value of expected cash flows to the proceeds from the issue. Here we want

   $$P_{net} = \sum_{t=1}^{7} \frac{D}{(1+k_p)^t} + \frac{Call\ Price}{(1+k_p)^7} \quad \text{or,}$$

   $$Pnet = Div\ (PVIFA_{kp,7}) + Call\ Price\ (PVIF_{kp,7})$$

   $$\$80 = \$6.06\ (PVIFA_{kp,7}) + \$99\ (PVIF_{kp,7})$$

   $$k_p = 10.07\%$$

2.   The following information is available concerning the Blazer and Sons Company.

Per share current market price	$15.00
Per share current dividend	0.60
Per share current earnings	2.00
Expected growth rate in EPS	10%
Beta	1.2
Risk-free rate	6.0%
Expected market return	13.5%

The dividend payout ratio is expected to remain constant. Earnings are expected to grow at a constant rate for the foreseeable future. Calculate the cost of retained earnings using:

a.   The dividend capitalization approach

b.   The CAPM approach

Solution:

a.   The dividend capitalization approach uses the formula: $k_e = (D_1/P_0) + g$.

The constant payout ratio implies that dividends will grow at the same rate as EPS, so $g = 10\%$.

We are given that $D_0 = .60$, $D_1 = D_0(1 + g)$, so $D_1 = .60(1 + .1) = .66$.

Since $P_0 = \$15$, $k_e = (.66/15) + .10 = 14.\%4$

b.   The CAPM approach uses

$$k_e = r_f + B(r_m - r_f), \text{ so}$$

$$k_e = .06 + 1.2(.135 - .06) = .15.$$

3.   The Webster Links Company has a target capital structure of 60% long-term debt and 40% equity. Long-term debt will cost 12% before taxes and the cost of retained earnings is 18%. The firm's tax rate is 40%. Calculate the weighted cost of capital.

Solution:

The weighted cost of capital is given by

$$k_a = (\text{equity fraction})(k_e) + (\text{debt fraction})(k_d)(1\text{-}T)$$

$$k_a = (0.40)(0.18) + (0.60)(0.12)(0.60) = 0.1132 = 11.32\%$$

4.   The Parr Golf Company is working on their capital budget. Four projects have been identified with the following characteristics:

Project	Investment	IRR
A	$2 million	11%
B	$5 million	10%
C	$4 million	12%
D	$3 million	13%

The company can issue up to $5 million of debt at a cost of 9% and any reasonable additional amount at 12%. The target capital structure calls for equal amounts of debt and equity. Anticipated net income from which earnings will be retained for reinvestment in the business is $7,025,000. The current stock price is $55 and there are 1.1 million shares outstanding. The most recent dividend was $2.50 per share. Dividends are expected to grow at 10% per year. Additional shares can be issued at $53 before a $3 per share flotation cost. The firm's marginal tax rate is 40%.

Determine the following:
a.   The marginal cost of capital schedule
b.   The investment opportunities schedule
c.   The size of the optimal capital budget and the projects it contains.

Solution:

a.   The first step in finding the MCC schedule is to find the costs of the individual components. The before tax costs for debt are given, but the costs of retained earnings and new equity must be found.

Based on the nature of the information provided, the cost of retained earnings must be found using the dividend capitalization approach. This is $k_e = (D_1/P_0) + g$.

We are given that $P_0 = \$55$, $D_0 = \$2.50$ and $g = .10$.
From this, we have $D_1 = 2.50(1.1) = 2.75$.

$$k_e = (2.75/55) + .10 = .15$$

The cost of new equity capital is calculated similarly except that we use P_{net} rather than P_0.

$$P_{net} = \text{Issue cost - flotation costs} = 53 - 3 = \$50$$

$$k_e' = (D_1/P_{net}) + g = (2.75/50) + .10 = .155$$

To complete the gathering of information regarding the individual components, we must determine the amount of retained earnings to be available. Net income is expected to be $7,025,000 out of which we expect to pay dividends of $2.75 per share on 1.1 million shares. This represents total dividends of $3,025,000 leaving retained earnings of $4 million.

We can now summarize the component costs and the amounts available at those amounts as follows.

Debt	Equity
1st $5 million: 9%	1st $4 million: 15.0%
any additional: 12%	any additional: 15.5%

We now examine the composition of the marginal packages of capital. To do this we first find the break points in the MCC schedule.

Break points occur as successively higher cost debt or equity are used.

We will have "used up" the 9% debt when the $5 million available represents 50% of the capital raised. This occurs when

$5 million = .5 x capital raised
capital raised = $5 million/.5 = $10 million

We will have "used up" the 15% equity when the $4 million available represents 50% of the capital raised. This occurs when

$4 million   = 0.5 x capital raised
capital raised = $8 million

Ordering these break points, they occur at $8 million and $10 million. From these calculations we know that the following packages are to be considered.

Total Capital $(w_e)(k_e) + (w_d)(k_d)(1 - T) = k_a$

less than 8 million (.5)(.150) + (.5)(.09)(.6) = .1020
8 million-10 million (.5)(.155) + (.5)(.09)(.6) = .1045
more than 10 million (.5)(.155) + (.5)(.12)(.6) = .1135

This is a schedule of the MCC from which a graph can be drawn.

b.   Determination of the investment opportunities schedule consists of organizing the information about the potential investments. This is done by ordering the rates of return in descending order and determining the total amount of the capital budget for projects at each rate of return or higher.

Total Capital Budget	IRR
$ 3 million	13%
$ 7 million	12%
$ 9 million	11%
$ 14 million	10%

c.   To determine the optimal capital budget, we can either graph the marginal cost of capital and investment opportunities schedules and determine where they cross or we can accomplish the same thing in a table as follows:

Total Capital Budget	IRR	MCC
$ 3 million	13%	10.20%
$ 7 million	12%	10.20%
$ 9 million	11%	10.45%
$ 14 million	10%	11.35%

The optimal capital budget will be for $9 million since that is the last point where the IRR exceeds the MCC. This capital budget will include those projects with IRR's of 11% and above. They are A, C, and D. Graphically, this solution is found as follows:

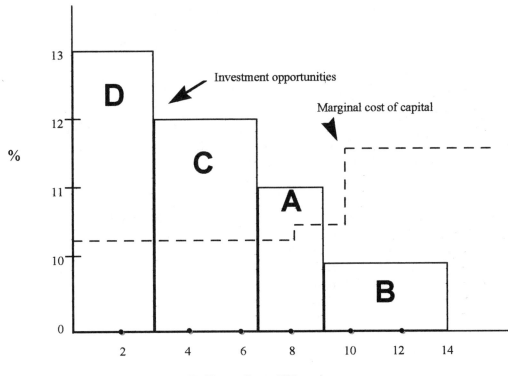

Dollars (in millions)

5.   The Kinky Rope Company is determining their MCC schedule. They expect to generate $3 million from depreciation. Their target capital structure consists of 40% debt and 60% equity. Debt and equity capital can be raised according to the following schedule:

Debt		Equity	
1st $2 million	8%	1st $1.5 million	18%
next $4 million	10%	next $4.5 million	20%
any additional	13%	any additional	23%

Find the breakpoints in their MCC.

Solution:

To find the breakpoints, we look at the cumulative amounts of debt and equity available in successively higher cost increments and determine the total capital that can be raised with these amounts of debt and equity under the target capital structure. The breakpoints thus found are then adjusted for the funds available from depreciation.

Cumulative debt levels	Total capital raised
$2 million	$2 million/.4 = $5 million + $3 million = $8 million
$2 million + 4 million	$6 million/.4 = $15 million + $3 million = $18 million

Cumulative equity levels	Total capital raised
$1.5 million	$1.5 million/.6 = $2.5 million + $3 million = $5.5 million
$6.0 million	$6 million/.6 = $10 million + $3 million = $13 million

Sorting these into order we find breakpoints at $5.5 million, $8 million, $13 million, and $18 million. Each of these breakpoints has been increased by the $3 million available from depreciation resulting in the following packages:

Amount raised ($)	Component Costs	
0 - 5.5 million	8% debt	18% equity
5.5 - 8.0 million	8% debt	20% equity
8.0 -13.0 million	10% debt	20% equity
13.0 -18.0 million	10% debt	23% equity
over 18.0 million	13% debt	23% equity

6.   Determine the marginal cost of capital in problem 4 using the Excel template (Costcap). The results should look as follows:

Marginal Cost Of Capital Worksheet

Target Capital Structure:	Percentages
Long-term Debt	50.00%
Preferred Stock	0.00%
Common Equity	50.00%
	100.00%

Summary of Financing Information:	
Common Stock Current Market Price	$55.00
Per-Share Common Stock Proceeds	$50.00
Current Common Stock Dividend (Do)	$2.50
Constant Growth Rate (g)	10.00%
Retained Earnings	$4,000,000
Per-Share Preferred Stock Proceeds	0.00%
Preferred Stock Dividend	0.00%
Marginal Tax Rate	40.00%

Terms of Financing and Component Costs:

Debt:

Principal	Before Tax Interest Rate	After-tax Cost
$5,000,000	9.00%	5.40%
$0	12.00%	7.20%
$0	0.00%	0.00%
$0	0.00%	0.00%

Preferred Stock:			Internal Equity:	
Amount	Dividend ($)	After-tax Cost	Amount	After-tax Cost
$0	$0.00		$4,000,000	15.00%

External Equity:

Amount	Dividend ($)	After-tax Cost
$1,000,000	$2.50	15.50%

	Amount of Lowest Cost Financing Available	Financing Available Supports an Increment of	Break Point	Increment Sources	Remaining Amount of Lowest Cost Financing	After-tax Cost	Marginal Cost of Capital
			Marginal Cost of Capital Schedule				
1st Increment							
Debt	$5,000,000	$10,000,000		$4,000,000	$1,000,000	5.40%	
Equity	$4,000,000	$8,000,000	$8,000,000	$4,000,000	$0	15.00%	10.20%
Preferred	$0			$0	$0		
2nd Increment							
Debt	$1,000,000	$2,000,000		$1,000,000	$0	5.40%	
Equity	$1,000,000	$2,000,000	$10,000,000	$1,000,000	$0	15.50%	10.45%
Preferred	$0			$0	$0	0.00%	
3rd Increment							
Debt	$0	$0		$0	$0	7.20%	
Equity	$0	$0	$10,000,000	$0	$0	15.50%	11.35%
Preferred	$0			$0	$0	0.00%	

Chapter

12

Capital Structure Concepts

Capital structure is the relative amount of permanent short-term debt, long-term debt, preferred stock, and common stock used to finance the firm. This chapter summarizes some basic concepts and theories of capital structure.

I.   Capital structure is one of the fundamental topics in financial management. Some important terms are:

    A.   *Capital structure*--the relative amounts of permanent short-term debt, long-term debt, preferred stock, and common stock used to finance a firm.

    B.   *Financial structure*--the relative amounts of total current liabilities, long-term debt, preferred stock, and common stock used to finance a firm.

    C.   *Optimal capital structure* -- the capital structure that minimizes a firm's weighted cost of capital and, therefore, maximizes the value of the firm.

    D.   *Target capital structure* -- the capital structure at which the firm plans to operate.

    E.   *Debt capacity* -- the amount of debt in the firm's optimal capital structure.

    F.   The optimal capital structure (and debt capacity) are determined by factors including: the business risk of the firm, the tax structure, bankruptcy potential, agency costs, and signaling effects.

II.   The discussion of capital structure is based on important assumptions.

    A.   Assume that the firm's investment policy is held constant. The capital structure changes the distribution of the firm's operating income (EBIT) among the firm's claimants, including debtholders, preferred stockholders, and common stockholders.

    B.   With a constant investment policy, investments are assumed to leave the debt capacity of the firm unchanged.

III.   Business risk is the variability or uncertainty of a firm's operating income (EBIT).

    A.   A firm's business risk is influenced by many factors, including:

- the variability of sales volume;
- the variability of selling prices;
- the variability of costs;
- the degree of market power (the absence of present or future competition reduces the firm's risk);
- the extent of product diversification;
- the firm's growth rate; and
- the *degree of operating leverage* (DOL). Operating leverage involves the use of assets having fixed costs. The DOL is defined as the percentage change in EBIT resulting from a given percentage change in sales.

    B.   Business risk has elements of both systematic risk and unsystematic risk. Some of the variability of operating income that results from business risk can be diversified away (the unsystematic portion) and some of the variability cannot be diversified away (the systematic part).

IV.   Financial risk refers to the additional variability of earnings per share and the increased probability of bankruptcy that result when the firm uses fixed cost sources of funds such as debt and/or preferred stock.

    A.   The use of fixed cost sources of financing is known as financial leverage.

    B.   Financial leverage can increase the returns to common shareholders, but the increased returns are achieved at the expense of increased risk.

    C.   Financial ratios that can indicate financial risk are the debt-to-assets ratio, the debt-to-equity ratio, the times interest earned ratio, and the fixed charge coverage ratio. Another financial risk measure is the degree of financial leverage, (DFL). Recall that the degree of financial leverage is defined as the percentage change in EPS resulting from a given percentage change in EBIT.

D.   The probability distribution of profits also indicates the nature of financial risk.

E.   EBIT-EPS diagrams show the relationship between EBIT and earnings per share. These diagrams, covered in more detail in the next chapter, show how the firm with more financial leverage has EPS that is more sensitive to changes in EBIT. At low levels of income, the highly levered firm has lower EPS and at high levels of income, the levered firm has higher EPS. The change in EPS for a given change in EBIT is greater for the highly levered firm.

V.   Capital structure theory studies the relationship between capital structure (the ratio of debt to assets) and the cost of capital (and the value of the firm). Capital structure models help to show the role of personal and corporate taxes, financial distress costs, and agency costs on the determination of an optimal capital structure.

A.   Franco Modigliani and Merton Miller (MM) showed that, under certain assumptions, the firm's overall cost of capital (and the firm's value) is independent of capital structure. Their classic article was published in 1958.

1.   MM assumed the following perfect capital market conditions:

a.   No transactions costs for buying and selling securities;

b.   Large numbers of buyers and sellers in the market;

c.   Relevant information costless and readily available to all investors;

d.   All investors can borrow or lend at the same rate;

e.   Investors are rational and have homogeneous expectations of a firm's earnings; and,

f.   Firms can be put into homogeneous risk classes, i.e., they have the same degree of business risk.

2.   In their model, the cost of debt, (k_d), and the cost of capital, (k_a), are constant as capital structure changes. If leverage increases, the cost of equity, (k_e), increases to exactly offset the benefit of more debt financing, leaving the cost of capital constant.

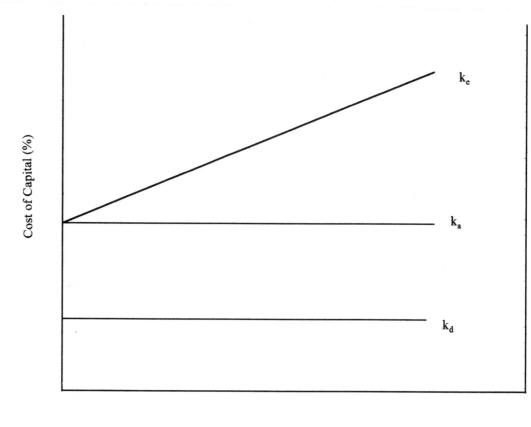

0

Debt/Total Assets

If the overall cost of capital is independent of capital structure, it follows that the firm's value is independent of capital structure.

3.   MM showed their theory to be correct using an *arbitrage* argument.

    a.   Suppose that there are two unlevered firms of identical business risk. If one of the firms issues some debt, then some people argue that its value would increase (and MM would argue the firm is overvalued relative to the unlevered firm).

    b.   Investors would sell the stock of the overvalued (levered) firm and take on personal debt of an amount similar to the debt behind the levered shares.

    c.   With the proceeds of the stock sale and personal borrowing, investors will buy enough of the unlevered firm's shares to service the debt and replace the income lost from the sale of the levered firm's shares. Because the unlevered firm is undervalued, some of the proceeds will be left over and the investor will have an arbitrage profit.

d.   The selling of the overpriced (levered) stock drives its price down and the buying of the underpriced (unlevered) stock drives its price up until their values are in line and arbitrage profits are no longer possible. Assuming no taxes, the values of the two firms are easily given. The value of the unlevered firm is:

$$Value\ of\ U\ =\ \frac{D}{k_e}$$

The value of the levered firm is:

$$Value\ of\ L\ =\ \frac{D}{k_e}\ +\ \frac{I}{k_d}$$

The dividends paid to L's stockholders are reduced by the amount of interest paid on the debt and k_e is higher for L because of the additional leverage-induced risk. The values of U and L are identical due to arbitrage.

B.   With corporate income taxes, the value of the levered firm will be more than the value of the unlevered firm. MM established this in 1963.

1.   The values of U and L are still given by the same two equations

$$Value\ of\ U\ =\ \frac{D}{k_e}$$

$$Value\ of\ L\ =\ \frac{D}{k_e}\ +\ \frac{I}{k_d}$$

2.   The dividends distributed to U's stockholders are reduced by the taxes paid on operating income, so the value of U drops. However, for L, dividends paid are operating income minus interest and taxes. Since interest is tax deductible, so the levered firm realizes a tax saving relative to U. This is shown as:

$$Tax\ shield\ =\ iBT$$

where i = interest rate, B = value of debt, and T = tax rate.

3.   The value of the tax shield to L is capitalized at the interest rate on the debt, so the present value of the tax shield equals the tax rate times the amount of debt (shown below).

$$Present\ value\ of\ tax\ shield\ =\ \frac{iBT}{i}\ =\ BT$$

4.   The value of the levered firm equals the value of the unlevered firm plus the value of the tax shield. The value of the firm will increase with the amount of debt.

Value of levered firm = Value of unlevered firm + Value of tax shield

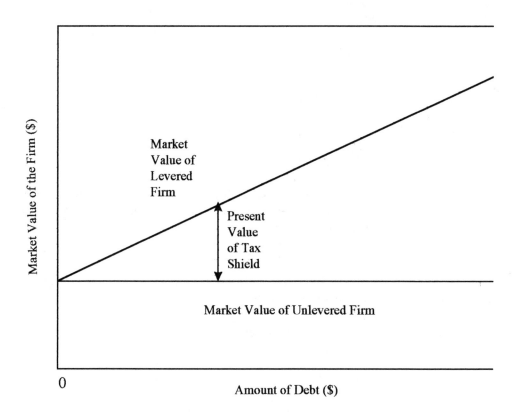

The cost of capital, k_a, decreases with the amount of debt:

5.   According to this result, the firm maximizes its value by choosing a capital structure that is all debt.

C.   The analysis of capital structure can be extended by including financial distress costs and agency costs.

1.   Increasing a firm's leverage can increase the potential costs of financial distress. Financial distress costs include the costs incurred to avoid bankruptcy as well as direct and indirect costs incurred if the firm files for bankruptcy. Some examples of financial distress costs are:

a.   As the firm increases its debt level, lenders may demand higher interest rates.

b.   Lenders may decline to lend at all, which imposes an opportunity cost on the firm from lost investment opportunities.

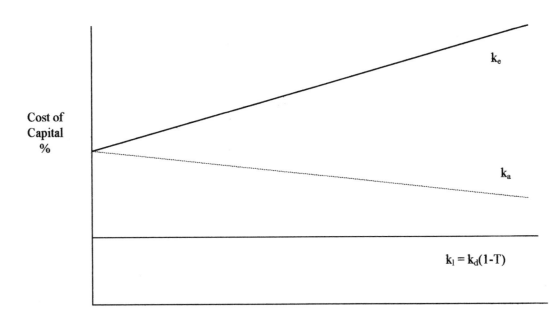

Financial Leverage

c.   Customers may doubt the firm's ability to continue in existence and shift their business to other firms they feel are more likely to remain.

d.   A company facing financial distress incurs extra accounting and legal costs.

e.   Finally, if a firm is forced to liquidate, its assets may have to be sold for less than their market values.

2.   Agency costs arise in any agency relationship. In the stockholder-bondholder relationship, the bondholders are the principals and the stockholders are the agents. There are conflicts of interests between these two parties.

a.   Investing in projects with high risk and low returns can shift wealth from bondholders to stockholders.

b.   The stockholders may forego some profitable investments in the presence of debt.

c.   Stockholders might issue high quantities of new debt and diminish the protection afforded to earlier bondholders.

d.   Monitoring and bonding costs may be incurred to reduce the incidence of agency costs. Bondholders will shift these costs back to the agents through charging higher interest rates.

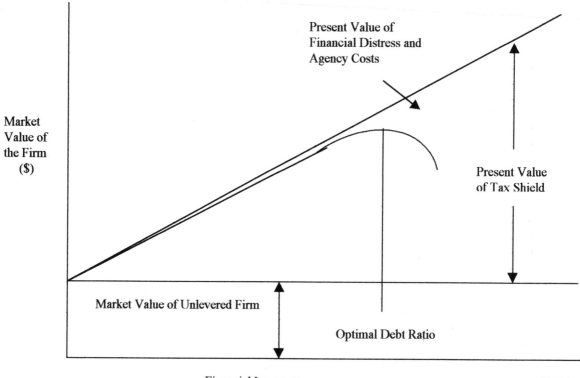

3.   Because financial distress costs and agency costs increase with the amount of leverage, they can eventually offset the marginal benefits from the value of the tax shield. This is illustrated in the following conceptual formula:

Market value of levered firm   =   Market value of unlevered firm
                                +   Present value of tax shield
                                -    Present value of bankruptcy costs
                                -    Present value of agency costs

With corporate income taxes and no agency or bankruptcy costs, the optimal capital structure is a corner solution with 100% debt financing. With the inclusion of agency and financial distress costs, the optimal capital structure will be an interior solution with a mixture debt and equity in the capital structure. The figure below illustrates this important result.

D.   The relationship between the cost of capital and optimal capital structure is shown in the graph below. In the presence of corporate taxes, financial distress costs and agency costs, it can be shown that the cost of capital will be U-shaped with the optimal capital structure occurring at the point where the cost of capital is minimized. The graph on the next page illustrates the important relationships of capital structure theory.

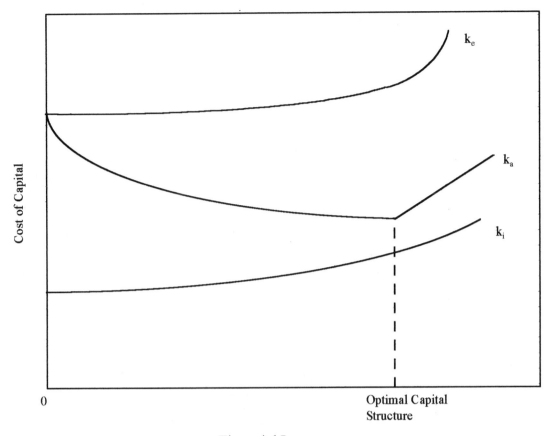

Financial Leverage

1.   The greater the proportion of debt used, the greater the risk of financial distress and the higher interest costs on the debt will be.

2.   The greater the proportion of debt used, the greater the variability of earnings per share and the higher the risk premium required by common stockholders.

3.   The after tax cost of debt is less than the cost of equity.

4.   The precise relationship between cost of debt and the debt ratio is difficult to determine. It is generally argued that the cost of debt increases rather slowly at moderate levels of debt. However, beyond some level of debt, depending on industry and business risk, the markets view additional debt to be very risky and require increasingly higher rates of return.

5.   For similar reasons to the cost of debt, the cost of equity rises slowly at first and then more rapidly.

6.   For any level of B/(B + E) (except 0), the weighted cost of capital is between k_e and $k_d(1 - T) = k_i$:

$$k_a = \frac{E}{B+E}k_e + \frac{B}{B+E}k_i$$

7.   The resulting relationships yield a cost of capital that is saucer shaped.

8.   If the firm's cash flows from operations are taken as given, discounting them at the lowest possible cost of capital maximizes the value of the firm. Hence the least cost capital structure is optimal.

E.   Personal tax effects, industry effects, signaling effects, and managerial preferences also impact the optimal capital structure.

1.   Miller (half of MM) in 1977 showed that if *personal tax*es rates are higher for interest income from debt than for equity income, this would reverse some or all of the tax benefit corporations receive from issuing debt instead of equity.

2.   Industry profitability and bankruptcy patterns tend to be reflected in different amounts of leverage across industries.

3.   Managers have superior information about the firm compared to outsiders. This is referred to as *asymmetric information*. Given that managers know more about the firm than do outside investors, changes in a company's investment, financing, or dividend decisions can give a *signal* to investors concerning management's assessment of expected future returns, and hence the market value of the company. When firms issue new equity securities, negative stock price responses frequently occur. Stock repurchases have had positive responses, and leverage increasing decisions have been received positively while leverage decreasing decisions have been received negatively.

4.   According to the *pecking order theory*, there may be no particular target or optimal capital structure for a firm. Capital structure changes whenever there is an imbalance between internal cash flows and profitable investment opportunities. Managers seem to have a preference for internal financing. When external financing is used, debt financing seems to be preferred over equity. Profitable firms with limited needs for investment funds will tend to build up *financial slack* (in the form of cash and marketable securities and unused debt capacity). These preferences may reflect a desire by management to avoid the floatation costs of external financing and to avoid the discipline and monitoring that occurs when new securities are sold publicly. The pecking order of financing is internal financing first, and then if external financing is used, debt securities are issued before new external equity.

F.   Capital structure theory and related empirical research provide important implications for managers.

1.   Capital structure is a centrally important management decision.

2.   The benefits of the tax shield from debt provide an incentive to use debt financing to the point that increasing agency and financial distress costs offset the debt advantage.

3.   The optimal capital structure is heavily influenced by business risk.

4.   Changes in capital structure signal important information to investors.

VI.   Many recent mergers and acquisitions have been financed by leveraged buyouts (LBOs) in which a small group of investors uses a large amount of debt to acquire ownership and control of a large firm with a relatively small equity investment.

A.   By concentrating ownership and control, the equity agency problems of separation of ownership and control are largely eliminated.

B.   Increased operating efficiencies are often achieved by eliminating jobs, reducing other payroll expenses, and closing inefficient plants. This obviously affects many employees and communities.

C.   Bondholders of the acquired firm typically realize a loss in the value of their bonds when the LBO is announced.

D.   Ethical questions arise with LBOs.

1.   Is it in the long-run interest of employees when firms maintain staffing levels that are inefficient and reduce the firm's ability to compete?

2.   Are bondholders harmed in LBO transactions? To the extent that they did not protect themselves (through bond covenants) when they bought their bonds, they presumably were rewarded through higher interest payments while they owned the bonds.

3.   When managers are on the LBO team, they are acting as both the buyers and the sellers of the firm. Will they extract full value for outside shareholders when they sell the firm to themselves?

VII.   Multinational firms have a more complex capital structure decision than purely domestic firms.

A.   Exchange rate risk should lead firms to finance investments in a country with funds from that country's capital markets.

B.   Some countries use more financial leverage than others.

C.   Some host country governments restrict foreign investments in their countries.

D.   There is risk of expropriation in some countries.

E.   Some host countries provide low-cost financing to stimulate investment.

TRUE AND FALSE QUESTIONS

Agree with each of the statements or **reject** it and modify it so that it is acceptable.

1.   Capital structure refers to the composition of the right hand side of the balance sheet.

2.   Financial structure refers to the amount of long-term debt, preferred stock, and common equity of the firm.

3.   The optimal capital structure minimizes the weighted-average cost of capital.

4.   In their 1958 article, Modigliani and Miller showed that (in the absence of taxes, market imperfections) the use of debt will increase the value of a firm.

5.   The introduction of corporate income taxes had no impact on the optimal capital structure of a firm.

6.   An example of a bankruptcy cost imposed on highly levered firms is the reluctance of customers to do business with the firm if the customers doubt the continued existence of the firm.

7.   Firms should try to minimize their cost of capital.

8.   All other things equal, investors in debt consider the debt less risky if the firm is less leveraged rather than more leveraged.

9.   The cost of equity capital decreases as the financial leverage increases because of the potential for higher EPS.

10.   The lower the cost of capital, the higher the value of the firm.

11.   An example of an agency cost in the shareholder-bondholder relationship would be a decision to invest in very risky projects that cause the value of the bonds to drop and the value of common stock to rise.

12.   The existence of bankruptcy and agency costs causes the firm to choose more leverage.

Answers to True and False Questions

1. Capital structure refers to the composition of the long-term portion of the right hand side of the balance sheet.

2. Financial structure refers to the composition of the right hand side of the balance sheet including the proportion of current liabilities.

3. True.

4. In their 1958 article, Modigliani and Miller showed that (in the absence of taxes, market imperfections) two firms of the same operating risk class and different capital structures would have the same overall cost of capital.

5. Assuming no agency or bankruptcy costs, the introduction of corporate income taxes creates a tax shield to debt such that the optimal capital structure is a corner solution with all debt financing.

6. True.

7. True.

8. True.

9. The cost of equity capital increases as financial leverage increases because of the increased volatility of EPS.

10. True.

11. True.

12. Since bankruptcy and agency costs increase with leverage, they cause the firm to use less debt financing.

MULTIPLE CHOICE QUESTIONS

1. A firm's business risk includes each of the following factors except:
    A.   Variability of sales volume
    B.   Degree of market power
    C.   Financial leverage
    D.   Operating leverage
    E.   Extent of product diversification

2. The use of financial leverage _____ expected returns to shareholders and _____ the variability of returns to shareholders.
    A.   increases;   decreases
    B.   increases;   increases
    C.   decreases;   decreases
    D.   decreases;   increases
    E.   increases;   does not affect

3. The general conclusion of Modigliani and Miller's arbitrage argument to capital structure theory is:
    A.   The moderate use of debt will increase the firm's value.
    B.   The firm will maximize its value by choosing a capital structure that is all debt.
    C.   The precise relationship between firm value and capital structure is impossible to determine.
    D.   The firm's optimal use of debt depends on the general level of interest rates.
    E.   The firm's value is independent of its capital structure.

4.   The present value of a firm's tax shield from the use of debt is equal to:
A.   Value of the outstanding debt divided by the tax rate (B/T)
B.   Value of the outstanding debt times the tax rate divided by the interest rate (BT/i).
C.   The interest rate on debt times the value of the outstanding debt times the tax rate (iBT).
D.   Value of the outstanding debt times the tax rate (BT).
E.   The interest rate on debt divided by the value of the outstanding debt times the tax rate (i/BT).

5.   If corporate taxes are included in Modigliani and Miller's arbitrage argument to capital structure theory, then the theory's general conclusion is:
A.   The moderate use of debt will increase the firm's value.
B.   The firm will maximize its value by choosing a capital structure that is all debt.
C.   The precise relationship between firm value and capital structure is impossible to determine.
D.   The firm's optimal use of debt depends on the general level of interest rates.
E.   The firm's value is independent of its capital structure.

6.   _____ include the costs incurred to avoid bankruptcy as well as direct and indirect costs incurred if the firm files for bankruptcy.
A.   Financial distress costs
B.   Agency costs
C.   Accounting costs
D.   Monitoring costs
E.   Bonding costs

7.   When corporate taxes and agency and bankruptcy costs are included, the general conclusion of capital structure theory is:
A.   The moderate use of debt will increase the firm's value.
B.   The firm will maximize its value by choosing a capital structure that is all debt.
C.   The precise relationship between firm value and capital structure is impossible to determine.
D.   The firm's optimal use of debt depends on the general level of interest rates.
E.   The firm's value is independent of its capital structure.

8.   Each of the following sentence completions is not true. As the proportion of debt in a firm's capital structure increases:
A.   The greater the risk of financial distress.
B.   The greater the variability of earning per share.
C.   The greater the present value of the tax shield.
D.   The greater the market value of the unleveled firm.
E.   All of the above sentence completions are correct.

9.   Changes in a firm's investment, financing, or dividend decision conveys additional to investors concerning management's assessment of expected future returns. This economic concept is known as:
A.   Pecking order theory
B.   Financial slack
C.   Signaling
D.   Inside information
E.   Conveyance

10.   The pecking order theory suggests that managers have a specific preference as to the means of raising capital. This order of preference is:
   A.   New debt issues, internal equity and then new equity.
   B.   Internal equity, new debt issues, and then new equity.
   C.   Internal equity, new equity, and then new debt issues.
   D.   New debt issues, new equity issues and then internal equity.
   E.   New equity issues, internal equity, and then new debt issues

Answers to Multiple Choice Questions

1.	C	5.	B	9.	C
2.	B	6.	A	10.	B
3.	E	7.	A		
4.	D	8.	D		

PROBLEMS

1.   The No Debt Company and the High Debt Company are identical in every respect except that the No Debt Company is unlevered while the High Debt Company has $1,000 in 6 percent perpetual bonds outstanding (on which $60 of interest is paid each year). Both firms have expected net operating income of $300 (forever). Both firms distribute as dividends all income available to stockholders. There are no taxes. Assume no agency costs or bankruptcy costs. The cost of equity is 10 percent for the No Debt Company and 12 percent for the High Debt Company.

   a.   Calculate the market value of each firm.

   b.   Calculate the cost of capital for each firm.

   c.   What is the total income available annually to the firm's security holders?

Solution:

   a.   Value of firm = Value of equity + Value of debt
          Value of firm = $D/k_e + I/k_d$
          Value of No Debt = 300/0.10 + 0 = $3,000

          Dividends for High Debt = 300 - 60 = $240
          Value of High Debt = 240/0.12 + 60/0.06
          Value of L = 2000 + 1000 = $3,000

b.

$$k_a = \frac{E}{B+E}k_e + \frac{B}{B+E}k_d$$

For No Debt: $K_a = (3000/3000)(.10) + 0 = 10\%$

For High Debt: $K_a = (2000/3000)(.12) + (1000/3000)(.06) = 10\%$

c.   For No Debt, income distributed to security holders is $300 of dividends and $0 of interest. For High Debt, the income distribution is $300, composed of $240 of dividends and $60 of interest.

Summary of results for Problem 1:

	No Debt Company	High Debt Company
Value of equity	$3000	$2000
Value of debt	0	1000
Value of firm	$3000	$3000
Cost of equity	.10	.12
Cost of debt	--	.06
Cost of capital	.10	.10
Net operating income	$ 300	$ 300
Less: Interest	0	60
Income available to stockholders	$ 300	$ 240
Total income available to security holders	$ 300	$ 300

2.   Assume a 40 percent corporate income tax (with interest paid as a tax-deductible expense). Reevaluate your answers to Problem 1.

Solution:

a.   Dividends for No Debt are $300(1 - .40) = 180$ since taxes paid were $300(.40) = 120$
Value of No Debt = $180/.10 + 0 = \$1,800$

Dividends for High Debt are $(300-60)(1 - .40) = \$144$ and taxes paid were $(300 - 60)(.40) = \$96$
Value of High Debt = $144/.12 + 60/.06 = 1,200 + 1,000 = \$2,200$

The value of L can also be equal to the value of the unlevered firm plus the present value of the tax shield.

Value of L = Value of U + BT
Value of L = $1,800 + 1,000(.40) = 1,800 + 400 = \$2,200$

b.   The cost of capital is:

$$k_a = \frac{E}{B+E} k_e + \frac{B}{B+E} k_d(1-T)$$

For No Debt: $K_a = (1800/1800)(.10) + 0 = 10\%$
For High Debt: $K_a = (1200/2200)(.12) + (1000/2200)(.06)(1-.4) = 8.18\%$

c.   For No Debt, income distributed to security holders is $180 of dividends to stockholders.

For High Debt, income distributed to security holders is $144 of dividends plus $60 of interest, which is a total of $204. Notice that the extra income distributed to L's security holders, 204 - 180 = $24, is equal to the tax saving on interest charges, 60(.40) = $24.

Summary of Results for Problem 2:

	No Debt Company	High Debt Company
Value of equity	$1800	$1200
Value of debt	0	1000
Value of firm	$1800	$2200
Cost of equity	.10	.12
Cost of debt (after-tax)	--	.06(1-.4)=.036
Cost of capital	.10	.0818
Net operating income	$ 300	$ 300
Less: Interest	0	60
Taxable Income	$ 300	$ 240
Less: Taxes (40%)	120	96
Income available to stockholders	$ 180	$ 144
Total income available to security holders	$ 180	$ 204

3.   The Adams Manufacturing Company has determined the following costs of debt and equity capital for various capital structures.

Debt Fraction	k_e	$k_d(1 - T)$
0.00	13.0	---
.10	13.1	6.0
.20	13.2	6.2
.30	13.4	6.4
.40	13.6	6.6
.50	14.0	7.0
.60	16.0	9.0

Determine the company's optimum capital structure and the associated cost of capital.

Solution:

To determine the optimum capital structure, we find the weighted cost of capital at each capital structure and choose the capital structure with the minimum weighted cost.

(Debt Fraction) x $k_d(1-T)$) +		(Equity Fraction)	x	(k_e)	=	k_a
.00		1.00		13.0		13.00
.10	6.0	.90		13.1		12.39
.20	6.2	.80		13.2		11.80
.30	6.4	.70		13.4		11.30
.40	6.6	.60		13.6		10.80
.50	7.0	.50		14.0		10.50
.60	9.0	.40		16.0		11.80

The minimum cost of 10.5% occurs with a capital structure consisting of 50% debt and 50% equity.

13

Capital Structure Management
in Practice

Chapter 13 focuses on several tools of analysis that assist managers in making capital structure decisions. The first part of the chapter covers operating leverage and financial leverage, which are important components of a firm's business risk and financial risk. EBIT-EPS analysis and cash insolvency analysis are additional tools that aid management in assessing their risk-reward tradeoffs. The appendix to the chapter discusses breakeven analysis, a tool that provides additional insight into the business risk facing a firm.

I. Operating and financial leverage result from fixed operating costs or fixed capital costs. Leverage magnifies shareholders' potential losses as well as potential gains.

    A. With reference to the income statement, costs can be classified into operating costs, capital costs, and taxes.

        1. Operating costs can be fixed, variable, or semi-variable.

            a. Fixed operating costs are costs that do not vary directly with sales. Examples of fixed operating costs are rent, insurance, lighting and heating bills, and property taxes.

            b. Variable costs are costs that vary directly with sales. Examples include, cost of raw materials used in production, direct labor costs and sales commissions.

            c. Semi-variable costs are the costs that increase in a step-wise fashion as output is increased. An example is management salaries—a decrease in sales may be accompanied by a cut in management staff.

2.   Capital costs are costs associated with capital sources such as interest on debt and dividends on preferred stock that are considered fixed.

3.   Income taxes are considered to be variable as they are a function of income and earnings.

B.   Operating leverage results from fixed operating costs such that a change in sales revenue is magnified into a relative larger change in earnings before interest and taxes (EBIT).

1.   The firm's *degree of operating leverage* (DOL) at a given level of sales, X, can be measured as the percentage change in earnings before interest and taxes (EBIT) resulting from a given percentage change in sales (or output).

a.   The formula for the DOL is

$$DOL \ at \ X = \frac{Percentage \ change \ in \ EBIT}{Percentage \ change \ in \ sales}$$

$$DOL \ at \ X = \frac{\Delta EBIT \ / \ EBIT}{\Delta Sales \ / \ Sales}$$

$$DOL \ at \ X = \frac{(EBIT_1 - EBIT_0) \ / \ EBIT_0}{(Sales_1 - Sales_0) \ / \ Sales_0}$$

where $EBIT_0$ and $Sales_0$ are the original values of EBIT and sales and $EBIT_1$ and $Sales_1$ are the new values.

b.   Economists term the percentage change in one variable with respect to another variable its *elasticity*. For example, the DOL is the elasticity of EBIT with respect to sales.

c.   If the breakeven model assumptions apply (see the appendix), the degree of operating leverage for sales level X or output level Q can also be found as:

$$DOL \ at \ X = \frac{Sales \ - \ Variable \ costs}{EBIT}$$

$$DOL \ at \ Q = \frac{(P-V)Q}{(P-V)Q-F}$$

C.   Financial leverage occurs when the firm employs funds with fixed costs, such as debt with fixed interest payments and preferred stock with fixed preferred stock dividends.

1.   The use of debt or preferred stock financing changes the returns to common shareholders (earnings per share) and also affects the magnitude of change in earnings per share in response to a given change in EBIT.

2.   The *degree of financial leverage* (DFL) at a given level of earnings before interest and taxes, X, can be measured as the percentage change in earnings per share (EPS) resulting from a given percentage change in earnings before interest and taxes (EBIT).

   a.   The formula for DFL is

$$DFL \ at \ X \ = \ \frac{Percentage \ change \ in \ EPS}{Percentage \ change \ in \ EBIT}$$

$$DFL \ at \ X \ = \ \frac{\Delta EPS \ / \ EPS}{\Delta EBIT \ / \ EBIT}$$

$$DFL \ at \ X \ = \ \frac{(EPS_1 - EPS_0) \ / \ EPS_0}{(EBIT_1 - EBIT_0) \ / \ EBIT_0}$$

   where EPS_0 and $EBIT_0$ are the original values and EPS_1 and $EBIT_1$ are the new values.

   b.   An alternative formula for the DFL is calculated is:

$$DFL \ at \ X \ = \ \frac{EBIT}{EBIT - I - D_p \ / \ (1 - T)}$$

   where

> I = interest payments,
> D_p = preferred dividend payments, and
> T = the marginal tax rate.

   To convert the effects of the use of preferred stock to a before-tax basis, the preferred dividend is divided by (1 - T). Since interest payments are tax-deductible, no such adjustment is made to I.

   c.   A firm with a high fixed capital cost relative to EBIT will have a high DFL, i.e., financial risk. The amount of fixed capital costs depends on the mix of debt and equity in that firm's capital structure. The firm's capital structure is the makeup of its permanent long-term debt, preferred stock, and common stock equity.

D.   Combined leverage is the effect of both operating leverage (fixed operating costs) and financial leverage (fixed capital costs) on the returns to a firm's common stockholders.

1.   The *degree of combined leverage* (DCL) at a given level of sales, X, is the percentage change in earnings per share (EPS) resulting from a given percentage change in sales.

a.   The basic formula for the DCL is

$$DCL \ at \ X = \frac{Percentage \ change \ in \ EPS}{Percentage \ change \ in \ Sales}$$

$$DCL \ at \ X = \frac{\Delta EPS / EPS}{\Delta Sales / Sales}$$

$$DCL \ at \ X = \frac{(EPS_1 - EPS_0) / EPS_0}{(Sales_1 - Sales_0) / Sales_0}$$

where EPS_0 and $Sales_0$ are the original values and EPS_1 and $Sales_1$ are the new values.

b.   The degree of combined leverage is the product of the degree of operating leverage and the degree of financial leverage,

$$DCL \ at \ X = DOL \ x \ DFL$$

c.   The DCL also equals

$$DCL \ at \ X = \frac{Sales - Variable \ costs}{EBIT - I - D_p / (1-T)}$$

2.   A firm can trade off operating and financial leverage to control its degree of combined leverage. For example, a firm with a high DOL may choose a capital structure with a low DFL to avoid a high DCL. Business risk and financial risk account for the total variability of the firm's earnings per share.

E.   The use of leverage has an impact on shareholder wealth and cost of capital.

1.   Firms are limited in the amount of combined leverage (operating and financial leverage together) that can be used to seek higher EPS and shareholder wealth.

2.   Higher combined leverage results in increased risk of financial distress.

3.   Higher financial distress possibility will increase capital costs that will tend to offset the returns gained from leverage. Thus excessive use of combined leverage may result in a decline in firm value and a rise in the firm's cost of capital.

II.   The probability of a loss is a good intuitive risk measure. The probability of negative (or positive) earnings per share can be found if the distribution of EBIT is known. If EBIT is normally distributed, then:

$$Z = \frac{\textit{Loss level EBIT - Expected EBIT}}{\textit{Standard deviation of EBIT}}$$

The loss level EBIT is the amount of EBIT needed to cover interest charges and preferred dividends (on a before-tax basis). This Z value can be found on a standard normal table to find the probability of a negative EPS.

III.   EBIT-EPS is another technique commonly used to analyze the desirability of alternative capital structure. EBIT-EPS analysis can be performed graphically or algebraically. In either case the intent is to determine the level of EBIT where EPS would be identical under either debt or equity financing.

A.   EBIT-EPS analysis can be performed algebraically by use of the relationship

EPS(debt financing) = EPS(equity financing)

$$\frac{(EBIT - I_d)(1-T) - D_p}{N_d} = \frac{(EBIT - I_e)(1-T) - D_p}{N_e}$$

where I_d and I_e represent the amount of interest to be paid under the debt and equity financing plans, respectively, and N_d and N_e represent the number of shares of common stock under each plan.

B.   For graphical analysis of EBIT-EPS indifference points, we calculate earnings per share at each of two levels of EBIT for each of the financing plans. Lines constructed through the pairs of points provides a graphical representation of the effects of the different levels of debt on EPS. The point where the lines intersect indicates the indifference point.

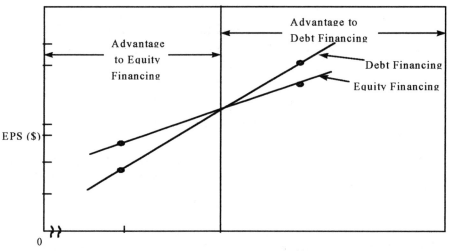

EBIT (in millions of dollars)

C.   If it is reasonable to expect that EBIT will be to the right of the indifference level, increased leverage is favorable in the sense that higher EPS results.

D.   Managers assess the riskiness of their capital structure using EBIT-EPS analysis:

Step 1:   Compute the expected level of EBIT after an expansion.
Step 2:   Estimate the variability of operating income.
Step 3:   Compute the indifference point between two financing plans.
Step 4:   Estimate the probability that EBIT will exceed the indifference point.
Step 5:   Examine the market evidence to see if the capital structure
               is too risky in relation to the firm's level of business risk,
               industry norms for leverage and coverage ratios, and
               recommendations of the firm's investment bankers.

E.   Because leverage can increase earnings to stockholders and financial risk (the firm's P/E ratio often drops), the firm's management must assess the tradeoff between higher earnings per share for its stockholders and its higher costs of equity capital.

IV.   Cash insolvency analysis also helps managers choose their capital structure. In the case of a recession, liquidity is important.

A.   Liquidity ratios like the current and quick ratio show the ability of the firm to pay its maturing short term debt.

B.   The projected cash balance in a recession is also critical. The firm needs cash (or access to cash) to survive a recession. This analysis provides an estimate of these cash requirements and is shown as:

$$CB_R = CB_0 + FCF_R$$

where CB_R = cash balance in a recession,
        CB_0 = cash balance at the beginning of a recession, and
        FCF_R = free cash flow during the recession.

V.   Managers also consider several other factors in deciding the firm's capital structure policy.

A.   While there are exceptions, financial analysis, investment bankers, bond rating agencies, investors, and commercial bankers compare a firm's debt ratios and coverage ratios to *industry norms*. There is a tendency for firms to cluster around its industry average.

B.   The *need for fund*s can force a firm to deviate temporarily from its target capital structure.

C.   Lenders and bond rating agencies will have benchmark leverage ratios that they try to impose on bond issuers.

D.   *Managerial risk aversion* can be a factor when some managers have a strong preference for unusually risky or unusually low-risk capital structures.

E.   In order to retain *control*, the management of some firms use debt or preferred stock financing to avoid the dilution of the control position of existing common shareholders that would occur if common stock were issued.

VI.   (Appendix to Chapter 13)   Breakeven analysis (also known as cost-volume-profit analysis) is used to show the relationship between revenues, costs, and operating profits at various output levels.

A.   If the firm sells its output at a constant price per unit (P), has a constant variable cost per unit (V), and has fixed costs (F), its profit is a function of the level of output (Q).

Total operating cost = TC = V(Q) + F
Total revenue = TR = P(Q)
Profit = EBIT = TR - TC
EBIT = P(Q) - V(Q) - F

B.   The breakeven point is defined as the output level at which total revenues equal total operating costs. It is found by dividing fixed operating cost F, by the difference between the price, P, and variable cost per unit.

$$Q_b = \frac{F}{P-V}$$

The difference between the selling price per unit and the variable cost per unit, P - V, is called the contribution margin per unit.

C.   The break-even dollar sales volume (S_b) is easily found in one of two ways:
V/P is the variable cost ratio, i.e., the variable costs per dollar of sales. 1 - (V/P) is the contribution margin per dollar of sales.

$$S_b = P(Q_b), \; or$$

$$S_b = \frac{F}{1-(V/P)}$$

D.   The sales volume necessary to achieve some profit level other than zero (breakeven) is

$$Target\ volume = \frac{Fixed\ cost + Target\ profit}{Contribution\ margin\ per\ unit}$$

E.   Breakeven analysis is easy to see graphically.

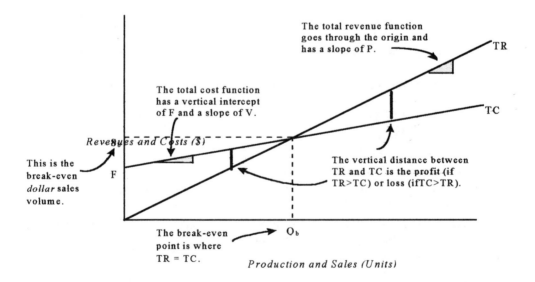

F.   If the distribution of sales is known, the probability of an operating profit or loss can be determined. If sales are normally distributed, let

$$Z = \frac{Breakeven\ point\ -\ Expected\ (mean)\ sales}{Standard\ deviation\ of\ sales}.$$

Z is the number of standard deviations the breakeven point differs from expected sales. This Z value can be looked up in a normal table to find the probability of an operating loss or profit.

G.   Breakeven analysis has a number of limitations that arise from the assumptions that are made in constructing the model and in developing the data used in the analysis.

1.   The selling price and variable cost per unit are assumed to be constant.

2.   Costs are classified as fixed or variable. In fact, whether costs are fixed or variable depends on the time period involved and the output range under consideration.

3.   Breakeven analysis assumes the firm is producing or selling either (a) a single product or (b) a constant mix of different products. This is unrealistic when the output mix is changing.

4.   All of the parameters used are subject to uncertainty.

5.   Breakeven analysis is usually performed for a short-term planning horizon, which ignores benefits and costs that might not be realized until future periods.

TRUE AND FALSE QUESTIONS

Agree with each of the statements or **reject** it and modify it so that it is acceptable.

1.   A firm is breaking even when total revenues equal total costs.

2.   If the sales forecast is $10,000,000, the net profit margin is 12 percent and dividends are planned to be $500,000, the addition to retained earnings for the period should be $700,000.

3.   The cash breakeven point is usually greater than the breakeven point.

4.   An increase in fixed interest expenses increases financial leverage while an increase in preferred dividends does not affect financial leverage.

5.   The degree of combined leverage is equal to the product of the degrees of operating leverage and financial leverage.

6.   An increase in the variable cost per unit increases the breakeven point.

7.   Business risk is unsystematic risk while financial risk is systematic.

8.   Variable costs are costs that vary in close relationship with the level of a firm's output.

9.   EBIT-EPS analysis can be used to determine when debt financing is advantageous.

10.   EBIT-EPS analysis implies that debt financing should be used when the expected level of EBIT is less than the indifference level of EBIT.

Answers to True and False Questions

1.   True.
2.   True.
3.   The cash breakeven point is usually <u>less</u> than the breakeven point.
4.   Interest and dividend expenses both affect financial leverage.
5.   True.
6.   True.
7.   Both business risk and financial risk include elements of unsystematic (firm-specific) risk and systematic (market-related) risk.
8.   True.
9.   EBIT-EPS analysis alone is not sufficient basis. The effect of a change in leverage on the P/E multiple must also be considered in order to determine the effect on the stock price.
10.   EBIT-EPS analysis implies that debt financing should be used when the expected level of EBIT is more than the indifference level of EBIT.

MULTIPLE CHOICE QUESTIONS

1.   _____ are costs that do not vary directly with sales. Examples of these costs are rent, insurance and property taxes.
    A.   Variable costs
    B.   Fixed operating costs
    C.   Semi-variable costs
    D.   Capital costs
    E   Semi-fixed operating costs

2.   A firm's degree of operating leverage (DOL) at a given level of sales can be measured as the percentage change in _____ resulting from a given percentage change in _____.
    A.   Sales;   EBIT
    B.   EBIT;   EPS
    C.   EPS,   Sales
    D.   EBIT;   Sales
    E.   Sales,   EPS

3.   A firm's degree of financial leverage (DFL) at a given level of EBIT can be measured as the percentage change in _____ resulting from a given percentage change in _____.
    A.   Sales;   EBIT
    B.   EBIT;   EPS
    C.   EPS,   Sales
    D.   EBIT;   Sales
    E.   EPS;   EBIT

4.   _____ occurs when firms employ funds with fixed csots, such as debt with fixed interest payments and preferred stock.
    A.   Financial leverage
    B.   Operating leverage
    C.   Semi-variable costs
    D.   Capital costs
    E   Semi-fixed operating costs

5.   A firm's degree of combined leverage (DCL) at a given level of sales can be measured as the percentage change in _____ resulting from a given percentage change in _____.
    A.   Sales;   EBIT
    B.   EBIT;   EPS
    C.   EPS,   Sales
    D.   EBIT;   Sales
    E.   Sales,   EPS

6.   A firm with a high _____ should choose a capital structure with a low _____ to avoid a high _____.
    A.   DFL;   DCL;   DOL
    B.   DCL;   DFL;   DOL
    C.   DOL;   DCL;   DFL
    D.   DOL;   DFL;   DCL
    E.   DFL;   DOL;   DCL

7.   EBIT-EPS analysis is commonly used to:
    A.   Determine the degree of combined leverage that a firm should employ.
    B.   Determine the degree of financial leverage that a firm should employ.
    C.   Determine the degree of operating leverage that a firm should employ.
    D.   Determine the level of assets that the firm should employ.
    E.   Determine the level of fixed assets that the firm should employ.

8.   The motive for cash insolvency analysis is to:
    A.   Prepare a cash budget under recessionary conditions.
    B.   Prepare an estimate of cash requirements under insolvency.
    C.   Prepare an estimate of long-term fixed capital outlays.
    D.   Prepare a cash budget under bankruptcy conditions.
    E.   Prepare an estimate of annual cash requirements.

9.   One factor in selecting an appropriate capital structure for a firm is the control issue. What does control mean in the capital structure context?
    A.   Managers tend to use large amounts of debt to take control of firms through LBOs.
    B.   Firms issue common equity to avoid the restrictions that may be imposed by the use of debt.
    C.   Firms use debt or preferred stock instead of common equity to avoid dilution of existing shareholders.
    D.   Capital structure decisions are really outside the control of managers.

10.   In breakeven analysis, the slope of the total cost function is the:
    A.   Fixed costs per unit.
    B.   Quantity produced and sold..
    C.   Sales price.
    D.   Total cost per unit.
    E.   Variable cost per unit.

Answers to Multiple Choice Questions

1.	B	5.	C	9.	C
2.	D	6.	D	10.	E
3.	E	7.	B		
4.	A	8.	A		

PROBLEMS

1.   As a community service, the local YWCA runs Saturday afternoon movies for children, charging fifty cents admission per child. The fixed costs are $100 per weekend for film rental and cleanup. The YWCA also sells candy, drinks, and popcorn with a variable cost ratio (variable costs divided by selling price) of 0.50. The average child buys $2.00 of junk food.

    a.   What is the breakeven number of children?

    b.   How many children are necessary to make a profit of $200?

Solution:

    a.   Revenue per child = 0.50 + 2.00 = $2.50
        Variable cost per child = 0.5(2.00) = $1.00

$$Q_b = \frac{F}{P-V} = \frac{100.00}{2.50-1.00} = \frac{100.00}{1.50} = 66.7 \, children$$

b.

$$Target\ volume\ (units) = \frac{Fixed\ cost + Target\ profit}{Contribution\ margin\ per\ unit}$$

$$Target\ volume = \frac{100 + 200}{1.50} = \frac{300}{1.50} = 200.0\ children$$

2. AquaCrafts Inc. makes inflatable rafts that they sell for $600 each. Their fixed costs are $100,000 and variable costs are $200 per dinghy.

   a. What is the breakeven point in units and in dollars?

   b. If the fixed costs include $25,000 of noncash depreciation charges, what is the cash breakeven point in units and in dollars?

   c. If their sales level is 1,200 units, what is the percentage increase in EBIT and the degree of operating leverage if sales increase 10 percent?

   d. What is the degree of operating leverage at a sales level of 800 dinghies?

Solution:

   a.

$$Q_b = \frac{F}{P-V} = \frac{100,000}{600-200} = \frac{100.000}{400} = 250\ dinghies$$

$$S_b = 600(250) = \$150,000$$

   b.

$$Q_b = \frac{100,000 - 25,000}{600 - 200} = \frac{75,000}{400} = 187.5\ units$$

$$S_b = 600(187.5) = \$112,500$$

   c. At 1,200 units, EBIT = PQ - VQ - F
$$= 600(1200) - 200(1200) - 100,000$$
$$= 720,000 - 240,000 - 100,000 = \$380,000$$

   At 1320 units, EBIT = 600(1320) - 200(1320) - 100,000
$$= 792,000 - 264,000 - 100,000 = \$428,000.$$

   Increase in EBIT = 428,000 - 380,000 = $48,000.

Percentage increase in EBIT = 48,000/380,000 = 0.1263 = 12.63%

$$DOL = \frac{Percentage\ change\ in\ EBIT}{Percentage\ change\ in\ sales} = \frac{12.63\%}{10.00\%} = 1.263$$

This can also be calculated with the alternate formula

$$DOL = \frac{(P-V)Q}{(P-V)Q - F}$$

$$DOL = \frac{(600 - 200)(1200)}{(600 - 200)(1200) - 100,000} = \frac{480,000}{380,000} = 1.263$$

d. $$DOL = \frac{(600 - 200)(800)}{(600 - 200)(800) - 100,000} = \frac{320,000}{220,000} = 1.545$$

3.   The Widget Maker has operating profits of $150,000 and a degree of operating leverage of 4.5. Forecast the Brass Monkey's operating profits if sales increase by 10%.

Solution:

$$DOL = \frac{Percentage\ change\ in\ EBIT}{Percentage\ change\ in\ Sales}$$

Percentage change in EBIT = 4.5(10%) = 45%
Increase in EBIT = 45%($150,000) = $67,500
New EBIT level = $150,000 + $67,500 = $217,500

4.   Use the Excel leverage and breakeven analysis template (Levb-e)for this problem.   Sales are $400,000, fixed costs are $100,000, and variable costs are 50% of sales. The firm has $150,000 of debt on which it pays 12% interest. The tax rate is 40%. The firm has 5,000 outstanding common shares.

    a.   What is the firm's EPS?
    b.   What is the DOL, DFL AND DCL?
    c.   What happens to EPS if sales increase 10%?

Leverage And Breakeven Analysis

Summary Of Input

Total Sales	$400,000
Fixed Operating Costs	$100,000
Variable Cost Ratio	50.00%
Number Of Common Shares	5,000
Number of Preferred Shares	0
Preferred Stock Dividend per Share	$0.00
Marginal Tax Rate	40.00%
Analysis Of % Change In Sales	10.00%

Summary Of Current Financial Obligations:

	Principal	Interest Rate	Interest
	$150,000	12.00%	$18,000
	$0	0.00%	$0
	$0	0.00%	$0
	$0	0.00%	$0
	$0	0.00%	$0
Total Interest Obligation			$18,000

Income Statement

Sales	$400,000
Variable Costs	200,000
Fixed Costs	100,000
Operating Income (EBIT)	$100,000
Interest Expense	18,000
Income Before Taxes (EBT)	$82,000
Income Tax	32,800
Net Income	$49,200
Preferred Dividends	0
Earnings Available To Common	$49,200

Breakeven Sales Level And Summary Of Leverage Measures		
Breakeven Dollar Sales		$200,000
Degree Of:		
Operating Leverage		2.000
Financial Leverage		1.220
Combined Leverage		2.439
Forecasted Earnings Per Share		
If Sales Change By	10.00%	$12.24

5.   The Even Break Glass Company is planning to raise $100 million of new capital. They currently have $20 million of 5% debt outstanding together with 5 million shares of common stock. They can raise the additional funds by using either 10% debt or issuing an additional 5 million shares at $20 per share. Their marginal tax rate is 40%.

a.   Algebraically determine the indifference level of EBIT.

b.   Graphically determine the indifference level of EBIT. (HINT: To get EPS results that graph easily, use EBIT levels of $16 million and $26 million).

Solution:

a.   The indifference point occurs when EPS is the same under either plan. This occurs when we have

$$EPS(debt\ financing) = EPS(equity\ financing)$$

$$\frac{(EBIT - I_d)(1-T) - D_p}{N_d} = \frac{(EBIT - I_e)(1-T) - D_p}{N_e}$$

If we issue new equity, interest is $1 million on the existing debt and the number of shares increases to 10 million. If new debt is issued, interest increases by 10% of $100 million to $11 million and the number of shares remains at 5 million.

Thus we have:

$$\frac{(EBIT - 11,000,000)(1-.4)}{5,000,000} = \frac{(EBIT - 1,000,000)(1-.4)}{10,000,000}$$

Solving gives EBIT = $21 million.

b.   To determine the breakeven level of EBIT graphically, we first determine EPS at each of two levels of EBIT for each of the plans.

	Equity Alternative		Debt Alternative	
EBIT	16,000,000	26,000,000	16,000,000	26,000,000
- Interest	-1,000,000	-1,000,000	-11,000,000	-11,000,000
Taxable Income	15,000,000	25,000,000	5,000,000	15,000,000
Tax @ 40%	6,000,000	10,000,000	2,000,000	6,000,000
Net Income	9,000,000	15,000,000	3,000,000	9,000,000
Shares	10,000,000	10,000,000	5,000,000	5,000,000
EPS	.90	1.50	.60	1.80

The EBIT-EPS pairs are now graphed and used to establish straight lines for each of the plans.

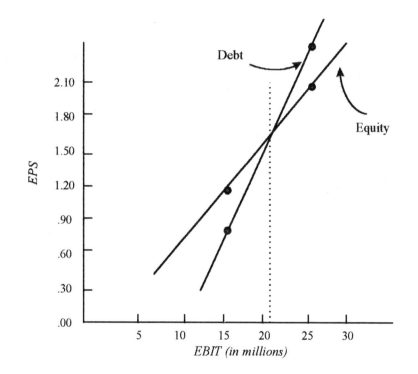

The breakeven point is seen to be at $21 million EBIT.

6.   For the Even Break Glass Company in Problem 5, which plan is riskier?

Solution:

Riskiness is measured by the variability of returns. Returns are more variable if the debt financing is used.

7.   The Wacky Tabakky Company needs $40 million for expansion. They currently have 10 million shares outstanding and $20 million of 5% long-term debt. They can raise the new capital by issuing an additional 4 million shares at $10 per share or by issuing $40 million of long-term debt at an interest cost of 10%.

a.   Determine the indifference level for EBIT.

b.   If the expected level of EBIT is $18 million and the standard deviation for EBIT is $5 million, what is the probability that equity financing will be preferred to the debt financing?

Solution:

a.   Using the formula for the indifference level for EBIT, we find indifference EBIT = $15,000,000.

b.   Equity financing is preferred if EBIT is less than $15 million. Using the normal distribution, we are looking for the shaded area shown below.

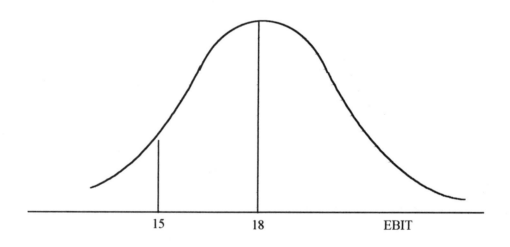

Transforming to the standard normal distribution we get:

$$Z = \frac{\$15,000,000,000 - \$18,000,000}{\$5,000,000} = -0.6$$

Using a Normal Table, we find the probability of being more than 0.6 standard deviations below the mean is 0.2743.

8.   Charles Mims has two financing plans for his new business:

Plan I   All equity (ten thousand shares sold for $10 per share).

Plan II 50% equity, 50% debt (five thousand shares sold for $10 per share plus $50,000 of debt paying 12% interest).

The business is in the 40% tax bracket.

a.   If EBIT is $20,000, what is the earnings per share for each financing plan?

b.   If EBIT is 20% greater, what is the EPS for each plan? What is the degree of financial leverage?

c.   Construct an EPS-EBIT graph for each plan (plot both of the EPS-EBIT functions on the same graph). What is the level of EBIT when the two functions intersect?

Solution:

a.	Plan I	Plan II
EBIT	$20,000	$20,000
Interest	0	6,000
EBT	$20,000	$14,000
Taxes (@ 40%)	8,000	5,600
EAT	$12,000	$ 8,400
Number of Shares	10,000	5,000
EPS	$ 1.20	$ 1.68

b.   If EBIT increases by 20%, EBIT = $24,000.

	Plan I	Plan II
EBIT	$24,000	$24,000
Interest	0	6,000
EBT	$24,000	$18,000
Taxes (@ 40%)	9,600	7,200
EAT	$14,400	$10,800
Number of Shares	10,000	5,000
EPS	$ 1.44	$ 2.16

With Plan I, the percentage increase in EPS is

$$(1.44-1.20)/1.20 = .24/1.20 = 20\%$$

With Plan II, the percentage increase in EPS is

$$(2.16-1.68)/1.68 = .48/1.68 = 28.56\%$$

The degree of financial leverage is the percentage change in EPS divided by the percentage change in EBIT.

For Plan I, $DFL_I = 20\%/20\% = 1.00$. For Plan II, $DFL_{II} = 28.57\%/20\% = 1.43$.

c.

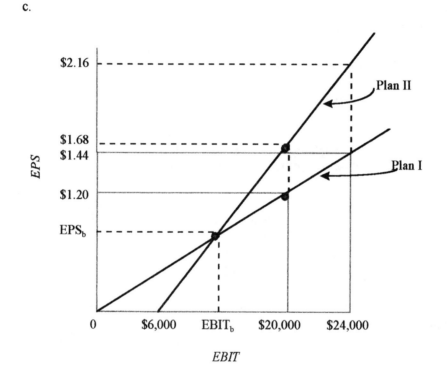

For Plan I, EPS will be zero if EBIT = 0, so the graph goes through the origin. If EBIT increases $1,000, net income increases $600 (taxes are $400), so earnings per share increase $.06 per $1,000 increase in EBIT. ($.06 = $600/10,000 shares).

For Plan II, EPS will be zero if EBIT equals the interest charge, or $6,000. If EBIT increases $1,000, net income increases $600 (taxes are $400 again, interest charges are unchanged), so earnings per share increase $.12 per $1,000 increase in EBIT. ($.12 = $600/5,000 shares). Because there are fewer shares with Plan II, a given EBIT change has a larger impact on EPS than with Plan I.

Notice that EPS will be greater with Plan II as long as EBIT is above the level where the two EPS-EBIT functions intersect. When they intersect, the EPS is the same for both plans. We can find this EBIT level easily.

$$EPS(debt\ financing)\ =\ EPS(equity\ financing)$$

$$\frac{(EBIT - I_d)(1 - T) - D_p}{N_d} = \frac{(EBIT - I_e)(1 - T) - D_p}{N_e}$$

$$\frac{(EBIT - 6,000)(1 - .4)}{5,000} = \frac{(EBIT - 0)(1 - .4)}{10,000}$$

Solving, we get EBIT = $12,000

When EBIT is $12,000, $EPS_I = EPS_{II}$ (When EBIT = $12,000, EPS = $.72)

An important relationship is to compare the ratio EBIT/Assets to the interest rate. The assets in this business are $100,000, so

$$\frac{EBIT}{Assets} = \frac{\$12,000}{\$100,000} = 12\%$$

when both plans have the same EPS. Of course, the interest rate on the debt is equal to 12%. Leverage will increase earnings per share only if the operating rate of return, EBIT/Assets, exceeds the interest rate. If EBIT/Assets are less than 12%, Plan II would have a lower EPS than Plan I.

9.   Rework Problem 8 using the Excel template for indifference point analysis (Indiffpt) accompanying the text. In addition to the questions and answers for Problem 8, assume that EBIT is normally distributed with a mean of $20,000 and a standard deviation of $10,000. What is the probability that Plan II results in higher EPS? What is the probability of a loss under Plan I and plan II? The output from the template is as follows:

Indifference Point Analysis

Before Financing:

Current Interest Payments	$0
Preferred Dividends	$0
Number of Common Shares	0

Financing Proposals:

	Option 1	Option 2
Amount of Debt Financing (1st Source)	$0	$50,000
Cost of Debt Financing (1st Source)	0.00%	12.00%
Amount of Debt Financing (2nd Source)	$0	$0
Cost of Debt Financing (2nd Source)	0.00%	0.00%

Cost of Debt Financing (2nd Source)	0.00%	0.00%
Amount of Preferred Stock Financing	$0	$0
Number of Preferred Shares	0	0
Preferred Dividend Per Share ($)	$0.00	$0.00
Additional Shares of Common Stock	10,000	5,000
Net Common Stock Proceeds (Per Share)	$10.00	$10.00
Amount of Equity Financing	$100,000	$50,000
Total - Proposed Financing	$100,000	$100,000
Marginal Tax Rate	40.00%	

Impact of Financing Proposals:

Interest Payments		$0	$6,000
Preferred Dividends		$0	$0
Number of Common Shares		10,000	5,000
Indifference Point (EBIT)	$12,000		
Earnings Per Share at EBIT		$0.72	$0.72
Expected EBIT	$20,000		
Standard Deviation	10,000		
Earnings Per Share		$1.20	$1.68

Probability of Operating Income Less Than Indifference Point	21.19%
Probability of Operating Income Greater Than Indifference Point	78.81%

Probability of Operating Income Less Than The Interest Payment:
(Earnings Per Share Negative)

Under Option 1	2.28%
Under Option 2	8.08%

Chapter

14

Dividend Policy

This chapter deals with the process and procedures that firms employ in the determination of an appropriate dividend policy. Of chief concern is how much of the firm's earnings should be distributed to the shareholders. In evaluating potential dividend policies, managers must also consider its capital budgeting decisions and its capital structure decisions. The interaction of these three decisions determines the value of the firm. The size of the capital budget is affected by the amount and cost of capital available; the capital structure and cost of capital are affected by the amount of earnings retained in the business; and retained earnings and dividends are alternative uses of available net income. These decisions must be made jointly to choose a set of decisions that will maximize shareholder wealth.

I.   Dividend payout ratios vary considerably across industries and even within an industry. Dividend decisions are affected by consideration of a number of issues concerning legality, bond indenture provisions, tax aspects, liquidity considerations, borrowing capacity, earnings prospects, growth requirements, the inflation outlook, shareholder preferences, and dilution effects.

   A.   Most states impose three types of regulations on the payment of dividends by firms that are chartered in that state.

      1.   The *capital impairment restriction* stipulates that dividends cannot be paid out of capital. Depending on the state, capital is defined as either the common stock account or that account together with other contributed capital in excess of the par value of the common stock.

      2.   The *net earnings restriction* stipulates that dividends must be paid only out of present and past net earnings.

      3.   The *insolvency restriction* states that dividends cannot be paid when a firm is insolvent, when the firm's liabilities exceed its assets. This is to protect the creditors of the firm.

B.   Restrictive covenants in bond indentures, loan agreements, lease contracts, and preferred stock agreements may prohibit or limit dividend payments.

C.   The Tax Reform Act of 1986 equalized the personal marginal tax rates on dividend income and long-term capital gains for many individuals. Prior to the TRA of 1986, capital gains were taxed at lower rates, which favored the retention of earnings (and, hopefully, future capital gains) over distributing cash dividends. Under the Revenue Reconciliation Act of 1993, the maximum capital gains tax rate is 28 percent, while the marginal tax rate on dividend income can be 39.6%, 35%, and 31% for certain high income individuals. For these persons, the tax code favors distributions from capital gains rather than cash dividends. Another tax advantage of capital gains is that dividends are taxed in the year they are received, but capital gains (and corresponding taxes) can be deferred indefinitely.

D.   The IRS code prohibits excessive accumulation of profits for the purpose of protecting stockholders from paying taxes on the dividends that they would otherwise receive. A tax is imposed on these excessive accumulations.

E.   Payment of dividends requires liquidity, i.e., cash. Firms with substantial cash flow and liquidity are more able to pay dividends.

F.   Available investment opportunities together with the availability of capital may dictate that earnings be retained in the business rather than paid out as dividends.

G.   Firms are often reluctant to lower their dividend payments once they are established. Firms with stable earnings are able to pay higher dividends without risk of cutting them than are firms with unstable earnings.

H.   Firms in rapid growth industries with a substantial need for capital must frequently retain earnings for investment or face the higher cost of external equity capital.

I.   Inflation may decrease a firm's ability to pay high dividends because funds generated by depreciation will not be adequate for the firm to maintain its productive capability in the face of rising equipment costs.

J.   Inflation may decrease a firm's liquidity because of the rising dollar investment in inventories and accounts receivable for the same volume level of business.

K.   In closely-held corporations, shareholder preference plays a more important role in the dividend decision.. If the majority of shareholders are in the high marginal tax bracket, they may favor a policy of high earnings retention over a policy of high dividend payout.

L.   For broadly-held firms, dividend policies attract investor groups with preferences for those payout policies. Thus, the *clientele effect* theory of dividends suggests that maintaining a steady policy will account for the preferences of a firm's stockholders. In other words, high payout firms will attract investors desiring high dividend yields while low payout firms will appeal to shareholders that prefer earnings retention and greater price appreciation.

M.   If payment of large dividends results in the need to raise external equity capital and existing shareholders cannot maintain their proportionate share of ownership, their control in the company may be diluted.

II.   There are two schools of thought regarding the effect of dividend policy on a firm's value. One school, led by Miller and Modigliani, argues that dividend policy is irrelevant, that dividend policy does not affect firm value. The other school, led by Gordon, Durand, and Lintner obviously disagrees.

A.   The Miller and Modigliani (MM) group contends that the value of a firm is based on its investment decisions. The payment of a particular dividend is only a mere financing detail since a dividend policy can be offset by other forms of financing, such as selling new shares of common stock.

1.   The MM irrelevance of dividends argument is based on several assumptions:

- No taxes
- No transactions costs
- No issuance costs on new securities
- A fixed investment policy

2.   When the issue of new common shares is used to finance a cash dividend, the value of the old shares will be diluted and will fall by the amount of the dividend received. Conversely, if stockholders forego a dividend, their stock does not realize the drop that would have occurred if a dividend were paid. The wealth of a shareholder (cash received from dividends plus the value of shares owned) is not affected by dividend policy.

3.   MM suggest that empirical evidence documenting the influence of dividend policy on stock price may be due to the fact that dividends may contain informational content regarding the firm's future earnings prospects. Thus changes in dividend payments represent a *signal* to investors concerning the future earnings and cash flows of the company.

4.   MM claim that the existence of clienteles of investors favoring a particular firm's dividend policy should have no effect on share value. Some investors may sell a company's stock after a dividend policy change, but others will buy, and no net change in the stock's value should result.

B.   A second school asserts that the MM argument is reasonable, but that MM's restrictive assumptions would cause dividend policy to be important if the assumptions were relaxed.

1.   Risk-averse investors prefer cash dividends now over the promise of more income later.

2.   Brokerage costs make it expensive for stockholders to sell part of their holdings to substitute for cash dividends.

3.   Removal of the no tax assumption may make a difference. Shareholders in the high marginal tax bracket may prefer low (or no) dividends, preferring that the firm reinvest the earnings within the firm resulting in a capital gain (from price appreciation) that is taxed a lower rate when the stock is finally sold in the future.

4.   High issuance costs make it expensive for a firm to sell external equity (sell new shares of stock) to finance a cash dividend payment.

5.   The payment of dividends can reduce agency costs between shareholders and management. Paying cash dividends causes a firm to raise more capital in external markets, which subject the firm to scrutiny by regulators and potential investors. This serves as a monitoring function of managerial performance.

III.   A number of alternative dividend strategies are frequently used as the basis for a dividend policy. The actual choice of a policy is influenced by the practical considerations above.

A.   The passive residual policy integrates the dividend decision with the optimal capital budget--marginal cost of capital decision discussed in Chapter 11.

1.   If the optimal capital budget can be financed with a package that does not fully utilize available earnings, the earnings not required for retention are paid out in dividends.

2.   If the optimal capital budget fully uses the available earnings, no dividend is paid.

3.   Under this policy, dividends can fluctuate significantly from year to year depending on the firm's investment opportunities.

4.   In practice, the dividends can be smoothed by recognizing that it is acceptable for the actual capital structure to vary around the target by borrowing more in years with a high demand for funds and using more equity in years with less demand for funds.

5.   The residual theory suggests that "growth" firms will normally have lower dividend payout ratios than non- growth firms.

B.   Much evidence indicates that most firms and stockholders prefer reasonably stable dividend policies.

1.   Stable dividends are characterized by a reluctance to reduce the dollar level of dividends from one period to the next.

2. Under a policy of stable dividends, increases in dividends tend to lag behind increases in earnings to insure against a need to decrease them in the future.

3. Stable dividends are desirable for a number of reasons.

 a. Dividends are often interpreted as an indication of the firm's longer run profit potential.

 b. Many shareholders depend on dividends for their cash income requirements.

 c. Stability of dividends may be taken as an indication of the riskiness of the firm and affect the capitalization rate and cost of capital.

 d. Many financial institutions such as banks, pension funds, and insurance companies are restricted in the types of common stock that they can own. Some are restricted to firms that have a record of continuous and stable dividends.

C. Some firms attempt to maintain a fairly constant payout ratio. If a firm's earnings fluctuate substantially, a constant payout ratio causes dividends to fluctuate also.

D. Some firms follow a policy of paying a small regular dividend plus year-end extras.

1. Stockholders can depend on the regular payout.

2. The policy can accommodate changing earnings and investment requirements.

E. Small firms typically differ from larger, more mature firms in the dividend policies that they follow. Small firms tend to pay out a smaller percentage of their earnings than larger firms because small firms tend to be growing rapidly and have limited access to the capital markets.

F. For multinational firms, dividend payments from foreign subsidiaries are the primary means of transferring funds to the parent company. Tax effects, exchange risk, political risk, the availability of funds, the financing needs of the subsidiary, and exchange controls can all influence these dividend payments.

IV. Corporations generally pay dividends quarterly.

A. The board of directors holds quarterly or semi-annual meetings to decide the amount of dividends to be paid. The declaration and payment procedure follows the sequence given below:

1. *Declaration date*--the board of directors announces a dividend to be payable to shareholders of record on the record date. (for example, February 1)

2. *Record date*--the firm takes its list of shareholders from its stock transfer books. (for example, February 15) These shareholders of record will receive dividend checks mailed on the payment date.

3. *Ex-dividend date*--the major stock exchanges require two business days prior to the record date. (for example, February 13) Persons buying the stock on February 13 or later are buying the stock ex-dividend, meaning without the dividend.

4. *Payment date*--the date the dividend checks are actually mailed. (for example, March 1)

B. Many firms have *dividend reinvestment plans*.

1. Under these plans, shareholders can elect to have their cash dividends reinvested automatically in additional shares.

2. Some plans purchase existing shares on the open market (through a trustee) and other plans purchase newly issued shares. The latter plan raises new equity capital for the firm.

3. Brokerage commissions are not charged for these plans.

4. Investors are still liable for income taxes on dividends reinvested even though they received no cash.

V. Dividends are usually taken to mean cash dividends. Sometimes firms declare stock dividends that result in the payment of additional shares of stock to common stockholders.

A. Stock dividends are usually stated as a percent of shares outstanding.

B. Stock dividends increase the number of shares outstanding.

C. An accounting transaction transfers the pre-dividend market value of the dividend from retained earnings to the capital accounts.

1. The par value of the new shares is credited to common stock.

2. Any additional value is credited to contributed capital in excess of par.

D. Because each shareholder's proportionate claim on the firm's net worth and earnings is unchanged, the market price of each share of stock should decline in proportion to the number of new shares issued.

$$Post\text{-}stock\ dividend\ price\ =\ \frac{Pre\text{-}stock\ dividend\ price}{1+Percentage\ stock\ dividend\ rate}$$

A 10% stock dividend would reduce the stock price by 9.09%.

E.   Even though the theoretical value of a stock dividend is zero, firms declare them for several reasons.

     1.   A stock dividend may broaden the ownership of the firm's shares since many stockholders sell the stock from the dividend.

     2.   If the firm pays a cash dividend, a stock dividend results in an effective increase in cash dividends provided that the level of the cash dividend is not reduced.

     3.   The reduction in share price may broaden the appeal of the stock to investors resulting in a real increase in market value.

VI.   Stock splits are similar to stock dividends. They increase the number of shares and reduce the price of each share.

VII.   Some firms distribute funds to investors through repurchasing shares of the stock rather than paying dividends.

A.   Stock may be repurchased by a tender offer, in the open market, or by negotiation with larger holders.

B.   Repurchased stock is known as treasury stock.

C.   Stock repurchases reduce the number of shares outstanding and hence increase the EPS.

D.   Plans for a repurchase are usually announced so that investors know the reason for the additional trading in the stock and can wait for the anticipated price increase before selling their shares.

E.   Ignoring taxes, transactions costs, and other market imperfections it can be shown that cash dividends and share repurchases are equivalent. Therefore, investors should be indifferent between the two methods of cash distribution.

F.   From a tax perspective, share repurchases are preferred because capital gains may be taxed at a lower rate than dividend income.

G.   Repurchases allow the stockholder to exercise his/her preference for current income or longer term capital gains.

H.   The IRS will not permit a firm to regularly repurchase a stock as an alternative to paying cash dividends because repurchases convert ordinary income to capital gains which receive preferential tax treatment. Regular stock repurchases are viewed as equivalent to cash dividends and taxed accordingly.

I.   Share repurchases, like cash dividend increases, can represent a signal that management expects higher future earnings. The market often responds favorably to such positive signals.

J.   Substituting discretionary stock repurchases for regular cash dividends provides the firm flexibility of deferring stock buyback programs when competing uses for the cash flow exist.

TRUE AND FALSE QUESTIONS

Agree with each of the statements or **reject** it and modify it so that it is acceptable.

1.   Dividends may be paid only out of current earnings.

2.   Inflation causes dividends to increase because of the increased revenues from higher prices.

3.   MM's theory of dividend irrelevance assumes a low tax rate.

4.   The clientele theory of dividends suggests that dividend policy should be changed often to attract new clientele.

5.   The residual theory of dividends integrates the dividend decision with the capital budgeting and cost of capital decisions.

6.   Growth firms often must retain a larger portion of their earnings in order to meet their investment needs.

7.   A policy of stable dividends means the firm always pays a stable percentage of earnings.

8.   Individuals who buy a stock any time before the record date receive the dividend.

9.   Stock dividends are more valuable to shareholders than cash dividends because the value of the stock received is usually much more than the amount of a typical cash dividend.

10.   Regular repurchases are a good way to help stockholders avoid income taxes.

11.   Stock repurchases reduce the number of shares outstanding and hence increase EPS.

Answers to True and False Questions

1.   Dividends may be paid only out of current or past earnings.
2.   Inflation may limit the ability to pay dividends because of the need to invest funds in higher priced inventory, larger accounts receivable, and the replacement of equipment not adequately covered by depreciation.
3.   MM assume no taxes in their proof of the dividend irrelevance argument.
4.   The clientele theory of dividends suggests that dividend policy should seldom be changed.
5.   True.
6.   True.
7.   A policy of stable dividends means that a firm attempts to pay a dividend which will not need to be reduced.
8.   Individuals who buy the stock before the ex-dividend date will receive the dividend.
9.   Unless a stock dividend results in an effective increase in cash dividends or in a higher market price for the firm because of the increased attractiveness of the lower share price, it is worthless.
10.   The IRS views regular repurchases as equivalent to cash dividends and taxes them accordingly.
11.   True.

MULTIPLE CHOICE QUESTIONS

1.   The capital impairment rule stipulates that:
      A.   Dividends must be paid from present and past earnings.
      B.   Dividends can not be paid out of equity capital.
      C.   Dividends can not exceed the total capital of the firm.
      D.   Dividends can not be paid if this payment impairs the growth of capital.
      E.   Dividends can only be paid if cash is readily available.

2.   If capital gains are taxed at a lower rate than ordinary income:
      A.   Individual investors would prefer dividends instead of retention and future capital appreciation.
      B.   Individual investors would have no preference between dividends and future capital appreciation.
      C.   Individual investors would prefer retention and future capital appreciation instead of dividends
      D.   Individual investors would prefer an equal distribution of profits through dividends and capital appreciation.

3.   Which of the following conditions would promote the payment of a higher dividend all other things held constant?
      A.   Restricted access to capital markets
      B.   Restricted cash flows and low liquidity
      C.   An inflationary environment
      D.   Restrictive covenants in bond indentures
      E.   Restricted investment opportunities

4.   Wealthy shareholders of closely held firms have a preference for:
    A.   A payout policy that includes stock splits and stock dividends.
    B.   A payout policy that balances expected growth and current dividends.
    C.   A high payout dividend policy.
    D.   A low payout dividend policy.

5.   If a firm suddenly changes its low payout dividend policy to a high dividend policy, its shareholders may choose to sell their shares. The reason for this sell of assets can be attributed to the:
    A.   Consistency Effect.
    B.   Capital Impairment Rule.
    C.   Clientele Effect.
    D.   Revenue Reconciliation Act of 1993
    E.   Tax Reform Act of 1986.

6.   In regards to dividends, Modigliani and Miller suggest that:
    A.   A firm's dividend policy does not affect the value of the firm.
    B.   Risk-averse investors prefer current cash dividends over the promise of future capital appreciation.
    C.   A progressive tax system creates preferences for low payout policies by some investors.
    D.   If the optimal capital budget uses all available earnings, no dividends should be paid.
    E.   Changes in a firm's dividend policy may provide additional information to investors on the future prospects for the firm.

7.   The passive residual dividend policy suggests:
    A.   A firm's dividend policy does not affect the value of the firm.
    B.   Risk-averse investors prefer current cash dividends over the promise of future capital appreciation.
    C.   A progressive tax system creates preferences for low payout policies by some investors.
    D.   If the optimal capital budget uses all available earnings, no dividends should be paid.
    E.   Changes in a firm's dividend policy may provide additional information to investors on the future prospects for the firm.

8.   Which of the following answers provides the correct sequence of events in the dividend process?
    A.   Declaration date; Record date; Ex-dividend date
    B.   Payment date; Declaration date; Record date
    C.   Record date; Ex-dividend date; Payment date
    D.   Ex-dividend date; Record date; Declaration date
    E.   Ex-dividend date; Record date; Payment date

9.   Which of the following statements concerning stock dividends is not true?
    A.   Stock dividends increase the liquidity of the outstanding common shares.
    B.   Theoretically, stock dividends should increase shareholder wealth.
    C.   Stock dividends redistribute the retained earnings to the higher common stock accounts.
    D.   The par value of the outstanding shares remain unchanged after a stock dividend.
    E.   The market price of each share of stock should decline in proportion to the number of new shares issued.

10.   Which of the following statements concerning stock repurchase is not true?
    A.   Repurchased common stock is known as treasury stock.
    B.   Stock repurchases reduce the number of outstanding shares and increase the firm's earnings per share.
    C.   The IRS will not permit a firm to regularly repurchase its stock as an alternative to cash dividends.
    D.   Share repurchases often indicate that a firm's investment alternatives are limited and often the market responds unfavorably.
    E.   From a tax perspective, share repurchases are preferred over cash dividends.

Answers to Multiple Choice Questions

1.	B	5.	C	9.	B
2.	C	6.	A	10.	D
3.	E	7.	D		
4.	D	8.	E		

PROBLEMS

1.   The City Street Paving Company has the following equity accounts on its balance sheet:

Common stock ($1 par, 10 million shares)	$10,000,000
Contributed capital in excess of par	12,000,000
Retained earnings	36,000,000
Total Common Equity	$58,000,000

    a.   If the capital impairment laws of the state define capital as the par value of the common stock, what is the maximum dividend that can be paid?

    b.   If capital is defined as common stock and contributed capital in excess of par, what is the maximum dividend that can be paid?

Solution:

    a.   If capital is defined as the par value of the common stock, then dividends can be paid out of retained earnings and contributed capital in excess of par for a total of $48,000,000.

    b.   If capital is defined as the par value of the common stock and contributed capital in excess of par, then up to $36,000,000 of dividends may be paid out of retained earnings.

2.   The Angel Management Company has EBIT of $250,000. Annual depreciation is $100,000 and interest expense is $40,000. They must make a payment of $50,000 annually into a sinking fund for retirement of the debt. What is the maximum per share dividends they can pay on their 500,000 shares of common stock if the bond indenture requires that cash flow must be at least equal to dividends, interest, and sinking fund requirements? Their tax rate is 40%.

Solution:

The first step is to determine available cash flow.

EBIT	$250,000
- Interest Expense	40,000
Taxable Income	$210,000
x (1 - T)	0.60
Net Income	$126,000
+ Depreciation	100,000
Cash Flow	$226,000

The maximum total dividend is equal to the available cash flow less the interest and sinking fund requirements:

Cash Flow	$226,000
- Interest Expense	40,000
- Sinking Fund Requirements	50,000
Available for Dividends	$136,000
divide by 500,000 Shares	
Maximum per share dividend	$ 0.272

3.   The Wholly Tire Company believes in the residual theory of dividends. Their target capital structure calls for equal amounts of debt and equity. Anticipated earnings amount to $3 million. The after tax cost of debt is 6%, the cost of retained earnings is 20%, and the cost of new equity is 24%.

      a.   If their investment opportunities include $5 million worth of projects with a return greater than 13%, what amount of dividends should they pay?

      b.   If their investment opportunities include $7 million worth of projects with a return greater than 15%, what amount of dividends should they pay?

Solution:

      a.   The first step is to determine the marginal cost of capital schedule. The target package of capital consists of equal amounts of retained earnings and debt. Potential retained earnings of $3 million permit financing up to $6 million of projects with this package. The weighted cost is given by
$$.5(.06) + .5(.20) = .13$$

The next increment of capital must contain equal amounts of new equity with a cost of 24% and debt with an after tax cost of 6%. The weighted cost of this package is

$$.5(.06) + .5(.24) = .15$$

The optimal capital budget will use a total of $5 million of capital at a cost of 13%. This $5 million consists of $2.5 million of debt and $2.5 million of retained earnings leaving $3.0 - 2.5 = $.5 million of earnings available for dividends.

b.   All $7 million of investment opportunities will be taken and the entire first package of capital will be used along with $1 million of the second package. All earnings are retained and no dividends are paid.

4.   The C-Thru Glass Company has the following equity accounts on its balance sheet:

Common Stock ($2 par, 100,000 shares)	$200,000
Contributed capital in excess of par	$100,000
Retained Earnings	$700,000

The current price of stock is $10 per share. If C-Thru declares a 5% stock dividend, what is the effect on the firm's capital accounts?

Solution:

A 5% stock dividend involves creation of an additional 5,000 shares. The market value of these shares is transferred from retained earnings to the common stock account and the contributed capital in excess of par account. Market value of the dividend is 5,000 shares x $10 = $50,000. $2 per share, the par value, is transferred to the common stock account and the remaining $40,000 to the contributed capital in excess of par amount. The resulting capital accounts appear as follows:

Common Stock ($2 par, 105,000 shares)	$210,000
Contributed capital in excess of par	$140,000
Retained Earnings	$650,000

5.   Theoretically, to what level will the stock price drop if the following stock dividends are declared? Assume that the pre-stock dividend stock price is $60.

A.   10% stock dividend
B.   20% stock dividend
C.   50% stock dividend
D.   100% stock dividend

Solution:

Use the following formula:

$$Post\text{-}stock\ dividend\ price = \frac{Pre\text{-}stock\ dividend\ price}{1 + Percentage\ stock\ dividend\ rate}$$

a. $= (\$60 / (1 + .1)) = \$54.55$

b. $= (\$60 / (1 + .20)) = \$50.00$

c. $= (\$60 / (1 + .5)) = \$40.00$

d. $= (\$60 / (1 + 1)) = \$30.00$

Chapter

15

Financial Forecasting
and Working Capital Management

This chapter has two parts. The first part discusses various techniques for forecasting future cash flows and the firm's need for funds. The second part of the chapter deals with overall management of working capital. In this section we focus on the optimal level of current assets and the optimal level of short term and long term funds needed to finance the current assets.

I.   Financial forecasting is used to estimate the additional financing that may be required in an upcoming period. Pro forma financial statements play an important part in the financial forecasting process. Pro forma financial statements project the results of an assumed or planned event.

   A.   *Percentage of sales forecasting* assumes that most balance sheet items vary directly with sales and that the firm's profit margin (EAT/Sales) is constant. This approach uses the sales forecast to obtain estimates of changes in the other balance sheet accounts.

      1.   Total financing required can be tied to a sales increase (ΔS):

$$
\begin{array}{ccccc}
\textit{Total} & & \textit{Forecasted} & & \textit{Forecasted} \\
\textit{financing} & = & \textit{asset} & - & \textit{current liability} \\
\textit{needed} & & \textit{increase} & & \textit{increase}
\end{array}
$$

$$
\textit{Total financing needed} \; = \; \frac{A}{S}(\Delta S) \; - \; \frac{CL}{S}(\Delta S)
$$

2.   The portion of total required financing that can be generated internally:

$$\begin{matrix} \textit{Increased} & & \textit{Forecasted} & & \\ \textit{retained} & = & \textit{earnings after} & - & \textit{Dividends (D)} \\ \textit{earnings} & & \textit{tax (EAT)} & & \end{matrix}$$

$$\textit{Increased retained earnings} \; = \; EAT - D$$

3.   The total additional financing required is the difference between the total financing needed and the internal financing provided.

$$\begin{matrix} \textit{Additional} & & \textit{Total} & & \textit{Increased} \\ \textit{financing} & = & \textit{financing} & - & \textit{retained} \\ \textit{needed} & & \textit{needed} & & \textit{earnings} \end{matrix}$$

$$\textit{Additional financing needed} \; = \; \left[\frac{A}{S}(\Delta S) - \frac{CL}{S}(\Delta S) \right] - [EAT - D]$$

B.   Cash budgeting can estimate more precisely both the amount of financing required by the firm and the timing of those financing requirements.

1.   A budget is simply a financial plan. Budgets are used to plan, coordinate, and control a firm's operations.

2.   The cash budget projects the firm's cash receipts and disbursements over future periods of time.

a.   Many cash receipts and disbursements are tied to projected sales. Receipts on credit sales will lag projected sales. Payments for purchases (of raw materials, merchandise, or supplies) to accommodate projected sales depend on how long the purchase precedes the sale and on credit terms received from suppliers.

b.   Other expected receipts and disbursements of cash such as long-term loans, capital expenditures, dividend payments, wages and salaries, rent, etc., must be scheduled. Total disbursements are subtracted from total receipts and beginning cash to obtain an ending balance.

C.   Pro forma statements of cash flows can also be used to determine how much additional financing firms will need in a future period.

D.   Computerized forecasting and financial planning models are also used as financial planning tools.

    1.   A deterministic model uses single-value forecasts of each financial variable. These values may not be optimal and nothing is specified about their probabilities. Management can perform sensitivity analyses, rerunning the model to see the sensitivity of the result to changes in forecasts or assumptions.

    2.   Probabilistic models utilize probability distributions for input data instead of single point estimates and provide probabilistic output.

E.   Optimization models choose the optimal levels of some variables rather than having them specified beforehand.

E.   Financial ratios incorporated into sophisticated statistical techniques can be used to forecast a firm's financial events.

    1.   Traditional ratio analysis is limited in that it looks at only one ratios at a time.

    2.   Statistical techniques such as discriminant analysis use multiple variables (several different ratios) simultaneously to forecast future events.

    3.   Discriminant analysis has been used successfully to predict bankruptcy using the following ratios:

        Net working capital / Total assets
        Retained earnings / Total assets
        EBIT / Total assets
        Market value of total equity / Book value of total debt
        Sales / Total assets

II.   Working capital management is concerned with current assets and current liabilities and their relationship to the rest of the firm.

A.   *Working capital* refers to the total investment in current assets while *net working capital* refers to the difference between current assets and current liabilities. The two terms are frequently used interchangeably.

B.   Working capital policies affect the future returns and risk of the company; consequently, they have an ultimate bearing on shareholder wealth.

C.   Working capital management involves a number of types of decisions:

    1.   The level of investment in current assets.

2.   The proportion of short-term versus long-term debt the firm uses to finance its assets.

3.   The investment in each type of current asset.

4.   The specific sources and mix of current liabilities.

D.   Working capital represents assets that flow through the business at a relatively rapid rate. Working capital is needed because of the asynchronous nature of cash receipts and disbursements.

E.   The *operating cycle* of a manufacturing firm can be characterized by the time intervals between the following dates:

- Date 1   (Sept 1)   Purchase of resources
- Date 2   (Oct 1)   Pay for resource purchases
- Date 3   (Oct 15)   Sell product on credit
- Date 4   (Dec 1)   Collect receivables

1.   The time interval from the purchase of resources until the collection of receivables is the *operating cycle*. This interval from Date 1 to Date 4 in the example above is 90 days long.

2.   The *inventory conversion period* is the period between the purchase of resources and sale of the product (from Date 1 to Date 3 - 45 days). The *receivables conversion period* is the period between the sale of the product on credit and the receivable collection (between Date 3 and Date 4 - 45 days).

3.   The *payables deferral period* is the period between the purchase of resources and the payment for these resources (from Date 1 to Date 2 - 30 days). The *cash conversion cycle* is the period between when the firm pays for its resources and when the firm collects on its own sales (from Date 2 to Date 4 - 60 days).

4.   The relationship between these time periods also can be seen as:

$$Operating\ cycle\ =\ Inventory\ conv.\ pd.\ +\ Receivables\ conv.\ pd.$$

$$Inventory\ conversion\ period\ =\ \frac{Average\ inventory}{Cost\ of\ sales\ /\ 365}$$

$$Receivables\ conversion\ period\ =\ \frac{Accounts\ receivable}{Annual\ credit\ sales\ /\ 365}$$

$$Cash\ conversion\ cycle\ =\ operating\ cycle\ -\ payables\ deferral\ pd.$$

F.   The net working capital position of a firm is a measure of the firm's riskiness in terms of its ability to pay its bills on time.

G.   The size and nature of a firm's investment in current assets depend on a number of factors:

     1.   The type of products manufactured

     2.   The length of the operating cycle

     3.   Requirements for inventory to support sales

     4.   Inventory policies regarding safety stock and probabilities of running out of goods

     5.   Credit policies affecting levels of accounts receivable

     6.   Efficiency of current asset management.

H.   Determination of the appropriate level of working capital involves a tradeoff between risk and profitability.

     1.   More conservative policies involve holding a greater amount of current assets relative to sales. More aggressive policies hold less.

     2.   More conservative working capital policies have lower expected profitability (measured as return on total assets) since more assets are used to produce a given level of income.

     3.   More conservative working capital policies have a lower risk of insufficient cash to pay bills and insufficient inventory to meet demand. More conservative policies often result in lost sales due to restrictive credit policies.

     4.   The optimal level of working capital investment is the level that is expected to maximize shareholder wealth.

III.   In addition to the level of current assets, the firm must consider the proportions of short-term and long-term financing used to support them. This decision involves tradeoffs between profitability and risk.

A.   Recall that the relationship between debt maturity and interest rates is known as the term structure of interest rates. The term structure may be displayed as a graph called a yield curve.

     1.   The yield curve is generally upward sloping.

2.   Sometimes the yield curve is downward sloping or approximately flat.

3.   Even if the yield curve is downward sloping, the cost of financing working capital with long-term debt may be higher than that of short-term debt because long-term debt is less flexible and may require payment of interest on funds which are needed only part of the time.

B.   The risk associated with financing working capital with short-term debt is greater than that for long-term debt.

1.   There is a risk the firm will not be able to refund the short-term debt.

2.   Short-term interest rates tend to fluctuate more than long-term rates so that the cost is less certain.

C.   Current assets can be divided into permanent current assets and fluctuating current assets.

1.   Fluctuating current assets are those which are affected by seasonal or cyclical demand.

2.   Permanent current assets are those which are affected by seasonal or cyclical demand.

3.   One approach to financing working capital is to attempt to match the maturity of the debt to the maturity of the assets. Under this approach, permanent working capital is financed from long-term sources while fluctuating working capital is financed with short-term debt.

a.   A more conservative approach uses a higher proportion of long-term financing. This usually involves higher cost and lower profitability, with reduced risk of unavailable funding and interest rate changes.

b.   A more aggressive approach uses a higher proportion of short-term debt.

D.   The optimal combination of long- and short-term financing for working capital is the combination that maximizes shareholder wealth. This varies from firm to firm depending on other factors affecting risk and profitability.

TRUE AND FALSE QUESTIONS

Agree with each of the statements or **reject** it and modify it so that it is acceptable.

1.   If the sales forecast is $10,000,000, the net profit margin is 12 percent and dividends are planned to be $500,000, the addition to retained earnings for the period should be $700,000.

2.   One advantage of a cash budget is that the cash budget can identify a cash shortage that may be covered by short-term borrowing.

3.   Optimization models find the optimal levels of variables rather than specifying them beforehand.

4.   Deterministic planning models utilize probability distributions for input data and provide probabilistic output.

5.   If planned uses of cash flow exceed planned sources and long-term external financing cannot make up the difference, the firm may need to reduce dividends or planned capital expenditures.

6.   Budgets cannot be coordinated with the firm's projected financial statements.

7.   Once a budget is agreed upon, managers should not attempt to change the document during the budget period.

8.   Net working capital = working capital - current liabilities.

9.   If a firm finances its working capital entirely with short-term debt, it will have no net working capital.

10.   The amount of working capital needed is determined by the amount of the firm's current liabilities.

11.   The amount of working capital required increases faster than sales.

12.   Working capital policies that hold larger amounts of working capital for a given level of sales are more aggressive.

13.   The optimal level of working capital is that which gives a current ratio equal to the industry average.

14.   Inventory is a part of permanent working capital.

15.   A given working capital policy can be made more conservative by either increasing the proportion of long-term debt relative to short-term debt or by increasing the level of working capital relative to sales.

Answers to True and False Questions

1.   True.
2.   True.
3.   True.
4.   This statement is true for probabilistic models. Deterministic values use single-valued forecasts for input data.
5.   True.
6.   They can and should be coordinated.
7.   A budget is a financial plan, and plans should be flexible to accommodate changes through time.
8.   True
9.   True.
10.   The amount of working capital is determined by the nature of the firm's business, length of the operating cycle, level of sales, and attitudes toward risk.
11.   The amount of working capital required usually increases slower than sales.
12.   Working capital policies that hold smaller amounts of working capital for a given level of sales are more aggressive..
13.   The optimal level of working capital is that which maximizes stockholder wealth.
14.   Only current assets are included in working capital. Permanent working capital consists of the minimum long-term level of current assets.
15.   True.

MULTIPLE CHOICE QUESTONS

1.   The chief assumption of the percentage of sales forecasting method is:
        A.   The level of sales always increases.
        B.   The income statement items vary directly with the level of sales.
        C.   That all required financing arises internally.
        D.   The balance sheet accounts vary directly with the level of sales.
        E.   That all external funding requirements are met with debt.

2.   For a given level of sales, if a firm increases its dividend payout ratio, then:
        A.   The additional financing needed will increase.
        B.   The additional financing needed will decline.
        C.   The additional financing needed will be unchanged.

3.   For a given level of sales, if a firm's profit margin increases, then:
        A.   The additional financing needed will increase.
        B.   The additional financing needed will decline.
        C.   The additional financing needed will be unchanged.

4.   For a given level of sales, if the market price of a firm's stock increases, then:
        A.   The additional financing needed will increase.
        B.   The additional financing needed will decline.
        C.   The additional financing needed will be unchanged.

5.   Working capital refers to the total investment in _____.
        A.   Total assets.
        B.   Current liabilities.
        C.   Cash and marketable securities.
        D.   Current assets minus current liabilities.
        E.   Current assets.

6.   The period between the purchase of a firm's resources and the sale of the finished product is the:
        A.   Operating cycle
        B.   Inventory conversion cycle
        C.   Receivables conversion cycle
        D.   Payables deferral period
        E.   Cash conversion cycle

7.   The period between the payment for its resources and the collection for its own sales is the:
        A.   Operating cycle
        B.   Inventory conversion cycle
        C.   Receivables conversion cycle
        D.   Payables deferral period
        E.   Cash conversion cycle

8.   The operating cycle is equal to _____ plus _____.
        A.   Inventory conversion cycle; Receivables conversion cycle
        B.   Receivables conversion cycle; Payables deferral period
        C.   Payables deferral period; Inventory conversion cycle
        D.   Inventory conversion cycle; Cash conversion cycle
        E.   Cash conversion cycle; Payables deferral period

9.   More conservative working capital policies involve holding more:
        A.   Long-term debt relative to short-term debt.
        B.   Short-term debt relative to long-term debt.
        C.   Current assets relative to current liabilities.
        D.   Current assets relative to sales.
        E.   Current assets relative to long-term debt.

10.   Which of the following statements concerning working capital management is not true?
        A.   Financing working capital with short-term debt is riskier than financing it with long-term debt.
        B.   More conservative working capital policies have a higher risk of insufficient cash to pay bills.
        C.   More conservative working capital policies can result in lost sales due to restrictive credit policies.
        D.   More conservative working capital policies uses a higher portion of long-term financing.

Answers to Multiple Choice Questions

1.	D	5.	E	9.	D
2.	A	6.	B	10.	B
3.	B	7.	E		
4.	C	8.	A		

PROBLEMS

1.   Acme Diversified Products, Inc. has the following balance sheet and income statement for 1999:

BALANCE SHEET

Cash	$ 600,000	Accounts payable	$ 1,050,000
Accounts receivable	1,800,000	Salaries payable	250,000
Inventories	2,100,000	Other current liabilities	1,500,000
Fixed assets, net	2,400,000	Long-term debt	1,600,000
	$ 6,900,000	Stockholders' equity	2,500,000
			$6,900,000

INCOME STATEMENT

Net sales	$ 8,500,000
Cost of sales	5,000,000
Selling, general and administrative expenses	1,100,000
Other expenses	1,200,000
Earnings after tax	$ 1,200,000

Calculate the following:

a.   the inventory conversion period.
b.   the receivables conversion period.
c.   the length of the operating cycle.
d.   the payables deferral period.
e.   the length of the cash conversion cycle.

Solution:

a.

$$Inventory\ conversion\ period = \frac{Average\ inventory}{Cost\ of\ sales\ /\ 365}$$

$$Inventory\ conversion\ period = \frac{2,100,000}{5,000,000/365} = 153.3\ days$$

b.

$$\text{Receivables conversion period} = \frac{\text{Accounts receivable}}{\text{Annual credit sales} / 365}$$

$$\text{Receivables conversion period} = \frac{1{,}800{,}000}{8{,}500{,}000/365} = 77.29 \text{ days}$$

c.

$$\text{Operating cycle} = \text{Inventory conv. pd.} + \text{Receivables conv. pd.}$$

$$\text{Operating cycle} = 153.3 \text{ days} + 77.3 \text{ days} = 230.6 \text{ days}$$

d.

$$\frac{\text{payables}}{\text{deferral}} = \frac{\text{accts.payable} + \text{sal., benefits \& payroll taxes payable}}{(\text{Cost of sales} + \text{Selling, gen., admin.exp.})/365}$$
$$\text{period}$$

$$\frac{\text{payables}}{\text{deferral}} = \frac{1{,}050{,}000 + 250{,}000}{(5{,}000{,}000 + 1{,}100{,}000)/365} = 77.79 \text{ days}$$
$$\text{period}$$

e.

$$\text{Cash conversion cycle} = \text{Operating cycle} - \text{Payables deferral period}$$

$$\text{Cash conversion cycle} = 230.6 \text{ days} - 77.79 \text{ days} = 152.81 \text{ days}$$

2.   The Eraser Dust Company is considering three levels of working capital. Because of expected lost sales from low levels of working capital, expected sales and EBIT depend on the level of working capital. The company currently has $30 million of fixed assets. The alternative policies and the associated expected operating results are as follows:

Policy	Working Capital	Sales	EBIT
A	$30 million	$48 million	$18 million
B	35 million	50 million	20 million
C	40 million	52 million	22 million

a.   Which alternative is the most aggressive and which is the most conservative?

b.   For each alternative, find EBIT/Total assets.

Solution:

a.   A has the least investment in working capital and is the most aggressive. C is the most conservative.

		A	B	C
b.	Current Assets	$30 million	$35 million	$40 million
	Fixed Assets	30 million	30 million	30 million
	Total Assets	60 million	65 million	70 million
	EBIT	18 million	20 million	22 million
	EBIT/Tot Assets	18/60 =.300	20/65 =.308	22/70 =.314

For this case, an examination of the risk and return indicates that because of the relationship between EBIT, sales, and working capital, the most conservative is also the most profitable. Generally, however, higher risk working capital policies tend to be associated with higher returns.

3.   Eraser Dust Company in Problem 2 currently has $30 million of working capital. Because of the analysis in Problem 1, they wish to increase this to $40 million. Currently their liabilities and capital consist of:

Current liabilities (short-term debt)	$20 million
Long-term debt	$10 million
Common equity	$30 million

They are considering financing the additional working capital in three different ways; interest costs depend on the method of financing chosen. Relevant facts are summarized as:

Policy	Increase STD	Increase LTD	Cost STD	Cost LTD
A	$2 million	$8 million	10.5%	12.5%
B	5 million	5 million	10.0%	12.0%
C	8 million	2 million	9.5%	11.5%

a.   Which policy is the most conservative?

b.   For each policy determine the return on equity and the current ratio. Assume a tax rate of 40%.

Solution:

a.   Policy A is the most conservative.

b.

	A	B	C
Current Assets	$40 million	$40 million	$40 million
Fixed Assets	30 million	30 million	30 million
Total Assets	70 million	70 million	70 million
Current Liabilities	22 million	25 million	28 million
Long-term Debt	18 million	15 million	12 million
Common Equity	30 million	30 million	30 million
EBIT	22 million	22 million	22 million
Interest on STD	2,310,000	2,500,000	2,660,000
Interest on LTD	2,250,000	1,800,000	1,380,000
Taxable Income	17,440,000	17,700,000	17,960,000
Net Income	10,464,000	10,620,000	10,776,000
Return on Equity	34.9%	35.4%	35.9%
Current Ratio	1.82	1.60	1.43

4.   Lori Franz needs a quick estimate of her financing needs. Briefly, the facts are these.

Sales are forecasted to increase by $450,000
Assets will increase by 80% of the sales increase
Current liabilities will increase by 30% of the sales increase
Projected operating cash flow is $125,000
The dividends paid should be $65,000

How much additional financing is needed?

Solution:

Total	Forecasted		Forecasted
financing	*asset*	-	*current liability*
needed	*increase*		*increase*

$$\text{Total financing needed} = \frac{A}{S}(\Delta S) - \frac{CL}{S}(\Delta S)$$

Total financing needed = .80(450,000) - .30(450,000)

Total financing needed = 360,000 - 135,000 = $225,000

$$\begin{matrix} Increased \\ retained \\ earnings \end{matrix} = \begin{matrix} Forecasted \\ earnings\ after \\ tax\ (EAT) \end{matrix} - Dividends\ (D)$$

Increased retained earnings = $EAT - D$

Increased retained earnings = 125,000 - 65,000 = \$60,000

Additional financing needed
     = Total financing needed - Increased retained earnings

Additional financing needed = 225,000 - 60,000 = \$165,000

5.   Paula Revere, financial analyst for the Austin Boston Corporation, needs a rough estimate of next year's external financing needs. She has the following information:

(1)   Current sales of \$10,000,000 are expected to increase 20 percent next year.

(2)   The net profit margin is 9 percent.

(3)   Dividends will be \$500,000.

(4)   Last year's balance sheet was:

BALANCE SHEET

Cash	$ 400,000	Payables	$1,500,000
Accounts receivable	2,000,000	Short-term bank loan	1,000,000
Inventory	3,000,000	Mortgage	2,500,000
Long-term assets	3,600,000	Net Worth	4,000,000
Total Assets	$9,000,000	Total Liabilities and Net Worth	$9,000,000

(5)   The ratios of cash to sales, receivables to sales, inventory to sales, and payables to sales will remain constant.

(6)   The sales increase can be handled by the existing amount of net long-term assets (and gross investment will equal depreciation).

(7)   The principal amounts due on the short-term bank loan and mortgage will be unchanged.

Given these assumptions, Paula has only 15 minutes to predict external financing needs.

Solution:
Use ratio forecasting to construct a pro-forma balance sheet.

(a)   Cash, receivables, inventories, and payables maintain the same ratio to sales. This ratio is multiplied by new sales to find the new level of each account.

$$\text{Cash} = \frac{400,000}{10,000,000}(12,000,000) = .04(12,000,000)$$

$$= \$480,000$$

$$\text{Accounts Receivable} = \frac{2,000,000}{10,000,000}(12,000,000) = .20(12,000,000)$$

$$= \$2,400,000$$

$$\text{Inventory} = \frac{3,000,000}{10,000,000}(12,000,000) = .30(12,000,000)$$

$$= \$3,600,000$$

$$\text{Payables} = \frac{1,500,000}{10,000,000}(12,000,000) = .15(12,000,000)$$

$$= \$1,800,000$$

(b)   Next year's net income should be 9 percent of sales, or .09(12,000,000) = $1,080,000. The addition to retained earnings is net income less dividends, or 1,080,000 - 500,000 = $580,000. Net worth will be 4,000,000 + 580,000 = $4,580,000.

(c)   The pro-forma balance sheet should be

Cash	$ 480,000	Payables	$1,800,000
Accounts receivable	2,400,000	Short-term bank loan	1,000,000
Inventory	3,600,000	Mortgage	2,500,000
Long-term assets	3,600,000	Net Worth	4,580,000
Total Assets	$10,080,000	Subtotal	$9,880,000
		External Funds Needed	200,000
		Total Liabilities	$10,080,000
		and Net Worth	

Total assets are forecasted to be $10,080,000 and total liabilities and net worth should be $9,880,000 prior to raising additional external financing. $200,000 of external funds are required to finance the firm next year.

6.   The managers must prepare a cash budget for Brigham Jeans for the second quarter of 199X. The sales forecast is:

	Total Sales	Credit Sales
March 199X	$400,000	$300,000
April 199X	500,000	375,000
May 199X	700,000	525,000
June 199X	600,000	450,000
July 199X	500,000	375,000

Twenty percent of BJ's credit sales are collected in the month of the sale, and the remaining 80 percent is collected in the following month. The company's purchases are 70 percent of sales, and the purchases are made and paid for one month before the expected sales. Wages and salaries are estimated to be 9 percent of sales and are paid during the same month. Rent is $20,000 per month, and the company has forecasted additional cash operating expenses to be $50,000 in April, $60,000 in May, and $20,000 in June. A $40,000 tax payment and $40,000 dividend are expected in May. Brigham Jeans on April 1 expects a $125,000 cash balance and wishes to maintain a minimum balance of at least $100,000. BJ may borrow (or repay) needed funds from the bank in multiples of $5,000.

If no other receipts or expenditures are anticipated, prepare a monthly cash budget for April, May, and June.

Solution:

Brigham Jeans
Cash Budget, Second Quarter 199X

	April	May	June
Sales	$500,000	$700,000	$600,000
Cash balance, beginning of month	$125,000	$100,000	$102,000
Receipts*			
Cash sales	125,000	175,000	150,000
Collection of current month credit sales	75,000	105,000	90,000
Collection of prior month credit sales	240,000	300,000	420,000
Total Cash Available	$565,000	$680,000	$762,000
Disbursements			
Payment for purchases**	$490,000	$420,000	$350,000
Wages and salaries	45,000	63,000	54,000
Rent	20,000	20,000	20,000
Other expenses	50,000	60,000	20,000
Dividends	--	40,000	--
Taxes	--	40,000	--
Total Disbursements	$605,000	$643,000	$444,000
Excess of available cash over disbursements	$(40,000)	$ 37,000	$318,000
Borrowing	140,000	65,000	--
Loan repayments	--	--	205,000
Cash balance, end of month	$100,000	$102,000	$113,000
Cumulative borrowing	$140,000	$205,000	-0-

*Cash sales are the current month's total sales less credit sales. Collections of credit sales are 20 percent of the amount in the current month and 80 percent one month after the credit sale.

**Purchases are 70 percent of the next month's total sales, and cash payment is made at the time of the purchase.

7.   Rework problem 6 using the Excel template for cash budgeting (Cashbudg). The results are as follows:

	Cash Budgeting Worksheet		Cash Budgeting Worksheet			
	Month 1	Month 2	Month 3	Month 4	Month 5	Month 6
Estimated Total Sales	$0	$0	$400,000	$500,000	$700,000	$600,000
Estimated Credit Sales	0.00% $0	$0	$300,000	$375,000	$525,000	$450,000
Bad-Debt Loss Percentage	0.00%					

Credit Policy

Cash Discount (%)	0.00%	
Percent Taking Discount	0.00%	
Discount Period (Days)	0	
Credit Period (Days)	0	

Estimated Cash Receipts:

Cash Sales			$125,000	$175,000	$150,000
Collection On Credit Sales:	Percentage				
Current Month (Discount Takers)	0.00%		$0	$0	$0
Current Month (No Discount Taken)	20.00%		$75,000	$105,000	$90,000
One Month Prior	80.00%		$240,000	$300,000	$420,000
Two Months Prior	0.00%		$0	$0	$0
Three Months Prior	0.00%		$0	$0	$0
Total Receivable Collections(Must = 100%)	100.00%		$315,000	$405,000	$510,000

		Month 1	Month 2	Month 3	Month 4	Month 5
Estimated Credit Materials Purchases (%)	0.00%	$0	$0	$0	$0	#REF!
Purchases Based On Next Month's Sales Or One After Next Month's Sales (1)	1					

Month After Next Month's
Sales (2)

		Month 4	Month 5	Month 6
Payments On Credit Purchases		$0	$0	$0
% Of Previous Month's Purchases	0.00%			
% Of Purchases Two Month's Prior	0.00%			

Cash Budget				Cash Budget		

	Month 1	Month 2	Month 3	Month 4	Month 5	Month 6
Sales	$0	$0	$400,000	$500,000	$700,000	$600,000
Beginning Of Month Projected Cash Balance				$125,000	$100,000	$100,000

Receipts

	Month 4	Month 5	Month 6
Cash Sales	$125,000	$175,000	$150,000
Receivables Collections	$315,000	$405,000	$510,000
Non-Operating Cash Receipts	$0	$0	$0
Cash From Sale Of Assets	$0	$0	$0
Cash From Financing Operations	$0	$0	$0
Total Cash Available	$565,000	$680,000	$760,000

Disbursements

	Month 4	Month 5	Month 6
Payment On Credit Purchases	$0	$0	$0
Cash Purchases	$490,000	$420,000	$350,000
Labor	$45,000	$63,000	$54,000
General And Administrative Salaries	$0	$0	$0
Rent And Utilities	$20,000	$20,000	$20,000
Other Expenses	$50,000	$60,000	$20,000
Taxes	$0	$40,000	$0
Purchase Of Assets	$0	$0	$0
Interest	$0	$0	$0

Dividends Paid	$0	$40,000	$0
Repayment Of "Other" Loans	$0	$0	$0
Sinking Fund Payments	$0	$0	$0
Total Disbursements	$605,000	$643,000	$444,000
Excess Available Cash Over Disbursements	($40,000)	$37,000	$316,000
Desired Cash Balance	$100,000		
Loan (Payment) Required To Maintain Cash Balance	$140,000	$63,000	($203,000)
End Of Month Projected Cash Balance	$100,000	$100,000	$113,000

Chapter

16

The Management of Cash and Marketable Securities

Cash and marketable securities are the most liquid of a company's assets. Cash is the sum of the firm's currency and checking account deposits. Marketable securities consist of the short-term investments that a firm makes with its temporarily idle cash. The cash management function involves: (1) determining the optimal liquid asset balance to maintain, (2) efficient collection and disbursement of cash, and (3) determining the appropriate level of short term investments. Different cash management policies have implications for the risk-return trade-off.

I.   Firms hold liquid asset balances for several main reasons including day-to-day *transactions needs*, *precautionary balances* against unexpected cash requirements, balances to meet *future requirements*, balances held for *speculative reasons*, and *compensating balances* required by banks.

        A.   Cash inflows and outflows are seldom synchronized.

                1.   The first step in cash management is development of a cash budget showing the forecasted receipts and disbursement as well as a forecast of any cumulative shortages or surpluses expected during the budget period.

                2.   Many firms prepare a series of cash budgets with maturities ranging from one day to monthly intervals.

        B.   Banks provide a variety of tangible and intangible services. These institutions also charge for these services. Requirements for compensating balances are a common means for banks to receive a portion of their payment for their services. Service charges and fees frequently are used in conjunction with compensating balances to compensate banks for these services.

1.   Significant services include the maintenance of disbursement and payroll checking accounts, collection of deposits, lines of credit, term loans, handling of dividend payments, and the registration and transfer of the firm's stock.

2.   Less tangible services include supplying credit information and consulting advice.

3.   Compensating balance requirements may be stated in terms of absolute minimum balances or minimum average balances.

4.   Firms should occasionally shop around and determine whether the fee schedule and compensating balance requirements offered by their bank are competitive with those offered by other banks.

II.   A major concern in cash management is the determination of the optimal size of liquid asset balances. This involves weighing the costs and benefits of holding liquid assets.

A.   Compensating balance requirements establish a lower limit on the liquid assets which must be held.

B.   Holding of excess liquid assets results in an opportunity cost resulting from the income that the firm could earn if these funds were invested in other productive assets.

C.   Inadequate liquid balances result in "shortage" costs such as missing cash discounts, deterioration of the firm's credit rating, higher interest costs on borrowed funds, and the risk of insolvency.

III.   The processes of cash collection and disbursement provide the firm with opportunities to increase the available cash balance without additional total investment.

A.   *Float* is the difference between the checking account balances shown in the firm's books and those of the bank.

1.   Positive or disbursement float occurs when the balance on the bank's books exceeds that on the firm's books. This occurs because of the delays caused by mailing disbursement checks and the clearing process.

2.   Negative or collection float occurs when the firm shows a higher balance than the bank. This depends on the time it takes for deposited checks to clear.

3.   Management of collections and disbursements consists of attempts to maximize the net balance of positive and negative float through speeding collections and slowing disbursements.

B.   Components of float include (1) mail float, (2) processing float, and (3) check clearing float. A number of systems are available to reduce the time involved in one or more of the components.

    1.   A decentralized collection system consists of several strategically located collection centers which receive payments, deposit checks, and report information to the firm's headquarters.

        a.   Decentralized collection systems reduce mailing time and check clearing time by being closer to customers.

        b.   The decentralized banks regularly forward funds to a small number of larger accounts at concentration banks.

        c.   Use of a larger number of collection centers may decrease collection time but involve larger fees and compensating balances because of the larger number of banks involved.

    2.   A *lock-box* system consists of post office boxes maintained by local banks to receive deposits for the firm.

        a.   In a lock-box system, the local bank empties the box and deposits payments in the firm's accounts and sends the firm a report of payments received.

        b.   Funds in excess of required compensating balances are sent to a concentration bank from which the firm makes disbursements.

        c.   Lock-box systems involve significant fees and are usually more beneficial for relatively small numbers of larger deposits than for large numbers of small deposits.

        d.   Evaluation of a lock-box collection system involves comparison of the costs of the system versus the benefits of faster collection.

    3.   *Wire transfers* are funds sent electronically from one bank to another through the Federal Reserve System or a private wire system.

        a.   Wire transfers are the fastest way of moving funds between banks since no mail or clearing time is involved.

        b.   Wire transfers are used extensively in moving funds from local collection centers and lock-box banks to concentration banks.

    4.   Mail *depository transfer checks* (DTC) are unsigned, nonnegotiable checks drawn on the local collection bank and payable to the concentration bank. Each day, a

DTC in the amount of the deposits at the local collection bank will be mailed to the concentration bank. A DTC is cheaper than a wire transfer. An electronic depository transfer check (EDTC) can also be used to forward funds electronically through the Automated Clearing House (ACH) System.

5. Very large remittances may justify the use of a courier service to pick up checks and present them for collection at the bank on which they are drawn.

6. Pre-authorized checks (PAC) resemble ordinary checks except that they do not require the signature of the person (or firm) on whose account it is being drawn. Insurance companies, utilities, and savings and loans used PACs to collect amounts due from their customers.

C. Several means are available by which a firm can slow disbursements. These do not include late payment that can impair the firm's credit rating and cost the firm in lost cash discounts.

1. A zero-balance system involves the use of a master or concentration account together with a number of disbursement accounts.

a. Transfers are made from the concentration account to the disbursement accounts as checks clear through the disbursement accounts.

b. The disbursements accounts are called zero- balance accounts because transfers to them are in the exact amount required for the cleared checks so that the balance at the end of the day is always zero.

c. Use of zero-balance accounts minimizes the balances kept in disbursement accounts.

2. The use of drafts rather than checks permits a firm to keep smaller balances in its disbursement accounts.

a. A draft is similar to a check but is not payable on demand.

b. When drafts are used, funds do not have to be deposited until the draft is presented for payment.

c. Drafts are usually more expensive than checks because of the lower account balances and increased processing costs on the part of the bank.

3. With accurate estimates of disbursement float, a firm can synchronize deposits in disbursement accounts with expected check clearings.

D. Electronic funds transfer (EFT) can replace the paper (check) systems.

1. Electronic funds transfer eliminate disbursement float and collection float.

2.   Large payments are commonly made by means of wire transfers or through an automated clearinghouse (ACH).

E.   There are some ethical (and sometimes legal) issues associated with systems that delay payments and accelerate collections. A large (or sophisticated) firm might be able to exploit smaller (or less sophisticated) firms in its cash management policies.

F.   Cash management is very important for small, entrepreneurial firms.

1.   Small businesses have less extensive access to the capital markets than large firms.

2.   A cash shortage may be more expensive to rectify for a small business than a large one.

3.   Many small businesses are rapidly growing.

4.   Small businesses may have lower balances of cash resources in addition to the above problems.

IV.   Investments in marketable securities provide a means for a firm to earn interest on cash in excess of daily requirements as well as liquid assets kept for precautionary reasons or being accumulated for later investment.

A.   In choosing marketable securities, a firm should consider the default risk, marketability, maturity, and rate of return.

1.   *Default risk* is lowest on U.S. Treasury securities followed by other Federal agency securities and finally by corporate and municipal securities. Default risk and expected return are usually inversely related.

2.   *Marketability* requires that a security be able to be sold without undue loss or delay.

3.   Investment in marketable securities is usually limited to those with fairly *short maturities* that have less risk of price fluctuation due to changing interest rates. The firm may have needs for a specific maturity when it buys marketable securities.

4.   *Rate of return* is often less important than the above considerations.

B.   Purchases of marketable securities are usually confined to money market instruments which are high-grade, short-term debt instruments having original maturities less than 1 year. A number of money market instruments are available.

1.   U.S. Treasury Bills (T-Bills) are the most popular marketable securities.

    a.   T-Bills are sold at weekly auctions through Federal Reserve banks. T-Bills are issued at a discount and then redeemed for the full face amount at maturity.

    b.   T-Bills have standard maturities of 91 days, 182 days, and 1 year.

    c.   Treasury securities offer the advantages of ready marketability and are virtually default-free.

    d.   Because of their safety and marketability, Treasury bills usually offer the lowest yield of the available instruments.

2.   Other Federal agency issues that are not a legal obligation of the U.S. Government provide a slightly higher yield and very low risk.

3.   Short-term municipal securities are a suitable investment. Municipal yields are lower than other issues because municipal interest is free of Federal income tax. The yields on municipals will vary with the credit-worthiness of the particular state or local government issuer.

4.   Negotiable certificates of deposit (CDs) are issued by commercial banks.

    a.   Negotiable CDs differ from the smaller non-negotiable CDs usually purchased by individuals.

    b.   CDs offer a higher return than Federal agency issues.

    c.   Negotiable CDs have initial maturities ranging from 30 days to 18 months and are highly marketable.

5.   Commercial paper consists of short-term promissory notes issued by large corporations and finance companies.

    a.   Maturities range from 2 or 3 days to 270 days.

    b.   Commercial paper is not highly marketable.

    c.   Low marketability and high default risk result in higher yields than most other money market instruments.

6.   Repurchase agreements are arrangements in which investors acquire short-term securities subject to a commitment from the selling bank or security dealer to repurchase them on a specified date.

7.   A banker's acceptance is a short-term debt instrument issued by a firm and guaranteed by a commercial bank. They often originate in international trade.

8. Eurodollar deposits are dollar-denominated deposits in banks or bank branches located outside the United States.

9. Auction rate preferred stock has a dividend that is adjusted regularly so that the price of this security stays close to par. The advantage of money market preferred stock is that its dividends are eligible for the 70 percent inter-corporate dividend exemption.

10. Smaller firms that do not have the funds to invest in the relatively large denomination securities may invest in a money market mutual fund that pools the funds of smaller investors to obtain larger denomination investments.

11. Commercial banks also have money market accounts that pay competitive interest rates.

V. There are some unique elements of cash management for a multinational corporation (MNC).

   A. Three differences in cash management for MNCs are:

      1. It is sometimes difficult and costly to convert cash from one currency to another.

      2. Some less developed countries lack integrated international cash transfer facilities.

      3. There are a greater variety of investment opportunities for excess cash balances.

   B. MNCs usually have a centralized cash management function that tracks the firm's cash balances around the world and identifies the best sources for short-term borrowing and lending.

   C. MNCs use a process called multilateral netting. Cross-border transactions are netted off to minimize costly transactions. Funds that cross a border unnecessarily are called misdirected funds.

TRUE AND FALSE QUESTIONS

Agree with each of the statements or **reject** it and modify it so that it is acceptable.

1. Firms hold liquid assets for transaction purposes, precautionary motives, and compensating balances.

2. Cash budgets are seldom used in managing liquid assets.

3. A firm should never hold more cash than that required for compensating balances.

4.   The opportunity cost of holding excess liquid assets includes forgone cash discounts.

5.   Positive float is usually associated with the collection process.

6.   A lock-box should be maintained by a bank expecting night deposits.

7.   A zero-balance account is likely to result in a notice of insufficient funds from the bank.

8.   Generally, interest rate risk increases as the length of maturity increases.

9.   Long-term government bonds are usually an acceptable investment for idle cash.

10.   Only a weak secondary market exists for commercial paper.

11.   Federal funds are the most popular marketable security.

12.   Smaller firms can invest idle cash in money market mutual funds.

Answers to True and False Questions

1.   True.
2.   Cash budgets are fundamental to the management of cash.
3.   Compensating balance requirements establish the minimum cash that a firm can hold.
4.   The opportunity cost of excess liquid assets is the return the firm could earn on these assets in their next best use, such as expansion of other current or fixed assets.
5.   Positive float is associated with the disbursement process and arises from the mailing time, processing time by the recipient, and the check clearing time.
6.   A lock-box is a means of speeding up collections.
7.   A zero-balance account is used in conjunction with a concentration account to minimize idle balances by depositing funds as checks clear.
8.   True.
9.   Long-term bonds involve significant risk of price fluctuations due to interest rate changes. They become acceptable only when close enough to maturity to be effectively short-term instruments.
10.   True.
11.   Treasury bills are the most popular marketable security.
12.   True.

MULTIPLE CHOICE QUESTIONS

1. The cash management function the firm involves all of the below except:
    A.   Determining the optimal liquid asset balance to maintain.
    B.   Efficient collection and disbursement of cash.
    C.   Determining the appropriate level of short-term investments.
    D.   Oversight of long-term assets/

2. Which of the following is an appropriate reason for businesses to hold liquid assets?
    A.   Transactions needs
    B.   Precautionary requirements
    C.   Speculative reasons
    D.   Compensating balances
    E.   All of the above are appropriate motives for holding liquid assets.

3. _____ occurs when the balance on the bank's books exceed that on the firm's book's.
    A.   Disbursement float
    B.   Collection float
    C.   Compensating balances
    D.   Negative float
    E.   Process float

4. _____ represents the delay between the receipt of payment from a payer and the deposit of that receipt in the payee's account
    A.   Mail float
    B.   Processing float
    C.   Check-clearing float
    D.   Collection float
    E.   Disbursement float

5. _____ are funds sent electronically form one bank to another through the Federal Reserve System or a private wire system.
    A.   Wire transfers
    B.   Depository transfer checks
    C.   Pre-authorized checks
    D.   Compensating balances
    E.   Lock-box systems

6. _____ are unsigned, non-negotiable checks drawn on the local collection bank and payable to the concentration bank.
    A.   Wire transfers
    B.   Depository transfer checks
    C.   Pre-authorized checks
    D.   Compensating balances
    E.   Lock-box systems

7. U.S. Treasury securities have the lowest _____ and securities with _____ have less risk of price fluctuation due to changes in interest rates.
    A. marketability; low default risk
    B. rates of return; low marketability
    C. default risk; short maturities
    D. default risk; low rates of retun
    E. marketability; short maturity

8. _____ are short-term debt instruments issued by firms and guaranteed by commercial banks. They often originate in international trade.
    A. Banker's acceptances
    B. Negotiable certificates of deposit
    C. Commercial paper
    D. Eurodollar deposits
    E. Repurchase agreements

9. _____ are short-term promissory notes issued by large corporations or finance companies.
    A. Banker's acceptances
    B. Negotiable certificates of deposit
    C. Commercial paper
    D. Eurodollar deposits
    E. Repurchase agreements

10. _____ are the most popular marketable securities. These securities are readily marketable and are virtually default-free.
    A. Banker's acceptances
    B. Negotiable certificates of deposit
    C. Commercial paper
    D. Eurodollar deposits
    E. U.S. Treasury Bills

Answers to Multiple Choice Questions

1.	D	5.	A	9.	C
2.	E	6.	B	10.	E
3.	A	7.	C		
4.	B	8.	A		

PROBLEMS

1.   The Street Manufacturing Company has found that 12 days pass between the time payment is received from a customer and the funds become collected and available for use by the firm. The firm's annual sales are $660.5 million.

      a.   If Immobile could reduce the 12-day interval to 8 days, what would be the increase in the firm's average cash balance?

      b.   Suppose that the additional cash were used to reduce outstanding debt that has a cost of 9%. Determine the annual pre-tax savings in interest.

Solution:

      a.   Assuming that receipts are spread evenly over a 365-day year, receipts amount to $1.81 million per day. A reduction of 4 days in the amount outstanding would increase the cash balance by 4 x $1.81 million = $7.24 million.

      b.   If the $7.24 million is used to reduce outstanding debt costing 9%, pre-tax earnings would increase by 9% x $7.24 million = $651,600.

2.   The Pacific Coast Construction Company in Oakland receives large progress payments on contracts. These checks are deposited in the local bank and the funds become available 4 days later. PCCC is considering the value of receiving the use of the funds sooner by sending a messenger to the Seattle bank on which they are usually drawn. A trip to Seattle by courier costs $200. If PCCC can earn 8% on the funds in the money market, what size check will justify the use of a courier?

Solution:

If PCCC uses a courier, they will earn 4 days of interest at an annual rate of 8%. They wish to find the size of the payment for which (4/365)(.08)(payment) = $200. Solving, we find the minimum payment size is $228,125.

3.   Vista Card, a major bank credit card, processes all its payments through its main office in Saint Paul. They are considering establishing a lock-box collection system through a bank in Jamestown, North Dakota.. Under this arrangement, average mailing time for customers east of the Mississippi will be reduced from 17 days to 15 days. Check processing and clearing time would be reduced by 2 days. Annual collections from the East average $325 million from a total of 5 million payments. The Jamestown bank will process the payments for an annual fee of $95,000 plus $.06 per payment. The Saint Paul processing center will save $60,000 per year. If Vista can invest the funds for 12%, should they undertake the lock-box arrangement?

Solution:

Using a 365-day year, average daily collections amount to 325,000,000/365 = $890,411 per day. A saving of 4 days in the collection process would make available 4 x 890,411 = $3,561,644. Invested at 12%, these funds would earn .12 x 3,561,644 = $427,397 per year. The net value would be:

Annual earnings earned on released funds	$427,397
Annual savings at San Francisco office	60,000
- Cost of lock box arrangement	
(95,000 + .06 x 5,000,000)	-395,000
Net increase in pre-tax earnings	$ 92,397

The lock-box arrangement would result in an increase of $92,397 in pre-tax earnings and should be undertaken.

4.   The True-Balance Scale Company is considering establishing a zero-balance system for its payroll account. Total payroll amounts to $1.44 million per month paid on the last Friday of the month. The firm currently deposits the entire amount on Friday, but most checks do not clear until the following week. True-Balance can earn 8% on funds which are released from the payroll account. The typical distribution of check clearings is as follows:

Day	Amount Clearing
Friday	$ 300,000
Monday	444,000
Tuesday	350,000
Wednesday	200,000
Thursday	146,000
Total	$1,440,000

Determine the monthly pre-tax returns the firm would realize from use of the zero-balance system.

Solution:

To determine the annual pre-tax returns, we examine the daily balance under the present system and the lost interest on that balance. Saturday and Sunday must be included. Interest at 8% amounts to .08/365 = .000219 per day.

To be explicit, we assume that the funds needed for Monday clearings would earn interest for Friday through Sunday; Tuesday's deposit will earn interest for Friday through Monday; and so on.

Day	Clearings	No. of Days	Interest Earned
Friday	$300,000	0	0
Monday	444,000	3	291.71
Tuesday	350,000	4	306.60
Wednesday	200,000	5	219.00
Thursday	146,000	6	191.84

Total pre-tax earnings: $ 1,009.15

5.   Rework problem 3 using the Excel template for lockbox arrangement analysis (Lockbox). The results look as follows:

Lockbox Analysis

Current Collection Policy

Annual Credit Sales In Region	$325,000,000
Number Of Checks Processed Per Year	5,000,000
Pre-Tax Rate Of Return	12.00%
Average Mailing Time (Days)	17
Average Processing Time (Days)	2
Average Clearing Time (Days)	0

Forecast Of Lockbox Collections

Average Mailing Time (Days)	15
Average Processing Time (Days)	0
Average Clearing Time (Days)	0

Forecasted Reduction In Collection Time (Days)	4

Terms Of Lockbox Agreement

Compensating Balance Requirement	$0
Unit Processing Cost ($ per Check)	$0.06
Fixed Fee	$95,000.00

Impact Of Lockbox Agreement On Current Operations

Reduction In Compensating Balance	$0.00
Annual Savings In Home Office Costs	$60,000.00

Net Impact On Pre-Tax Profits

Funds Released	$3,561,643.84
Pre-Tax Earnings On Funds Released	$427,397.26
Annual Cost Of Lockbox Agreement	$395,000.00
Annual Savings In Home Office Costs	$60,000.00
Net Impact On Pre-Tax Profits	$92,397.26

Chapter

17

Management of Accounts Receivable and Inventories

Accounts receivable and inventories constitute important investments for most companies. They represent sizable proportions of the total assets in a wide variety of industries.

I. Accounts receivable are created whenever businesses extend credit to their customers. *Trade credit* is credit extended by a company to another company while *consumer credit* is credit extended by a company to its ultimate consumers. Credit management consists of: (1) establishing credit and collection policies and (2) evaluating individual credit applicants.

II. Extension of credit is essentially an investment decision as it results in an investment in accounts receivable, a current asset.

   A. Shareholder wealth is maximized by investing in accounts receivable as long as expected marginal returns from the investment exceed expected marginal cost of funds invested.

   B. Marginal returns consist of gross profits from additional sales.

   C. Marginal costs include opportunity cost of capital invested in accounts receivable, bad debt losses, cost of checking new credit accounts, and collection expenses.

III. A credit policy includes as its major variables the firm's credit standards, credit terms, and collection efforts.

   A. Credit standards are the criteria the firm uses to screen credit applications and assess whether credit should be extended. This allows the firm to control the quality of accounts that are accepted. Quality has two important facets.

1. One facet is the time a customer takes to repay given that the credit is repaid.

2. Another facet is the probability that the customer will fail to repay which is known as default risk.

3. Overall measures of the quality of accounts accepted are the average collection period and the bad-debt loss ratio.

4. The net change in pretax profits associated with granting credit to a customer can be summarized in four steps:

   A: Marginal profitability of additional sales
   = Profit contribution ratio x Additional sales

   B: Cost of additional investment in receivables
   = Additional investment in receivables x Pretax required return

   (Additional investment = Additional average daily sales x Average collection period)

   C: Additional bad-debt loss
   = Bad-debt loss ratio x Additional sales

   D: Cost of additional investment in inventory
   = Additional investment in inventory x Pretax required return

   E: Net change in pretax profits
   = Marginal returns - Marginal costs = A - (B + C + D)

B. Credit terms specify the conditions under which credit extended must be repaid.

   1. The *credit period* is the time allowed for payment.

   2. *Cash discounts* are discounts allowed if payment is made within a specified period of time. Cash discounts are usually specified as a percentage of the invoiced amount and are granted to speed up collection of accounts receivable.

   3. Seasonal datings are special terms sometimes offered to retailers on seasonal merchandise. The retailer is encouraged to order and accept delivery of merchandise well ahead of the peak season and to pay shortly after the peak sales. This assists retailers in financing inventory and allows producers to smooth their production and distribution over a longer period of time.

C. The collection effort consists of the methods employed to attempt to collect payment on past due accounts.

1.   The collection effort must be a balance between excessive leniency and the risk of alienating customers.

2.   An important part of managing accounts receivable is *monitoring* their status.

    a.   Aging of accounts is a useful means of monitoring them.

    b.   An aging analysis consists of classifying accounts into categories according to the number of days that they are past due.

    c.   Changes in the age composition of accounts may reveal changes in the quality of the firm's accounts receivable.

D.   Analysis of a change in credit policy is based on the potential changes in profit resulting from a change in policy.

1.   An increase in the credit period may increase the quantity of goods sold. This would have the following effects on pre-tax profits:

    a.   An increase in pre-tax profits equal to the profit contribution per dollar of sales times the anticipated increase in sales.

    b.   A cost increase resulting from additional investment in receivables (and inventories in some cases).

    c.   A cost increase resulting from additional bad debts.

2.   Liberalization of cash discount policies may result in the following effects:

    a.   An increase in sales and pretax profit contribution.

    b.   A reduction in the receivables balance resulting in either additional income from alternative investments or a decrease in the cost of funds invested in receivables.

    c.   A reduction in cash revenues resulting from the discount itself.

3.   Increases in collection effort and methods might result in:

    a.   Reduced sales and pretax profit contribution.

    b.   Increased collection expenses.

    c.   Reduced bad-debt losses.

IV.   The evaluation of credit applicants is based on the firm's credit and collection policies. Several main steps are common to most credit evaluation processes:

    A.   Information on the credit worthiness of an applicant is gathered from sources such as financial statements submitted by the applicant, credit reporting organizations, banks, and the firm's prior experience with the customer.

    B.   In analyzing the credit-worthiness of customers, the cost of analysis should be considered.

    C.   The "*five C's of credit*" provide a useful framework for organizing information about an applicant.

        1.   *Character* concerns the applicant's willingness to meet credit obligations.

        2.   *Capacity* refers to the applicant's ability to meet obligations based on his liquidity and projected cash flows.

        3.   *Capital* refers to the applicant's overall financial strength based on net worth.

        4.   *Collateral* refers to assets that may be pledged as security. In trade credit decisions, collateral is seldom a major consideration since foreclosing on the pledged assets is often an expensive and time- consuming process which does not adequately substitute for prompt receipt of cash.

        5.   *Conditions* refer to the general economic climate and outlook that may affect the customer's willingness and ability to pay.

    D.   Numerical scoring systems are sometimes useful, particularly in consumer credit.

V.   Inventories serve as a buffer between the various phases in the procurement-production-sales process. Manufacturing firms usually hold three types of inventories consisting of raw materials, work-in-process and finished goods.

    A.   The raw materials inventory consists of stores of items used in production.

        1.   Raw materials inventories allow firms to take quantity discounts.

        2.   Raw materials inventories assure supply in times of scarcity.

    B.   Work-in-process inventories consist of items currently at some intermediate state of completion.

        1.   Work-in-process occurs naturally as materials are put into production.

        2.   Work-in-process allows for asynchronous schedules among departments.

3.   The size of the work-in-process inventory usually increases with the length and complexity of the firm's production cycle.

C.   Finished goods inventories consist of items ready and available for sale.

   1.   The finished goods inventory permits prompt filling of orders.

   2.   The finished goods inventory allows production runs which are large enough to attain economies of scale by minimizing fixed set-up costs.

VI.   Three distinct types of costs are usually associated with an inventory policy.

   A.   Ordering costs represent the costs of placing and receiving an order of goods.

      1.   For external purchases, ordering costs include the cost of preparing the purchase order, expediting, receiving the goods, and handling payment.

      2.   For internally produced goods, the order costs consist mainly of the production set-up costs.

      3.   While some order costs may vary with the size of the order, most simple inventory control models assume them to be fixed.

   B.   Carrying costs consist of the costs of holding items in inventory for a given period of time.

      1.   Carrying costs include storage and handling costs, obsolescence and deterioration costs, insurance, taxes, and the cost of funds invested in inventory.

      2.   Carrying costs are usually expressed in terms of a cost per unit per period or as a percentage of the inventory value per period.

   C.   Stockout costs are incurred when a firm is unable to fill an order because the item is not available in inventory.   Stockout costs may involve lost sales, costs of rescheduling production, and the costs of placing and expediting special orders.

   D.   Normally, production and marketing managers have primary responsibility for determining specific quantities of the various types of inventories that the firm holds.   Financial managers should see that the funds are invested in a manner consistent with shareholder wealth maximization.

VII.   A number of inventory control models are available that can help in determining the optimal inventory level of each item. Models can be classified into deterministic or probabilistic models.

A. The basic economic order quantity (EOQ) model is a deterministic model that is simple to use. The primary objective of the EOQ model is to find the order quantity, Q, that minimizes total inventory costs.

   1. The basic EOQ model has several assumptions.

      a. Annual demand or usage is known with certainty.

      b. Demand is stationary throughout the year—no seasonality.

      c. Orders to replenish inventory are instantaneously filled.

      d. Given known demand and zero ordering lead times there are no stock outs and no need for safety stocks.

   2. The EOQ equation may be derived in several steps:

      a. The total cost equation is:
         Total costs = ordering costs + carrying costs   or,
         Total carrying costs = (Number of orders per year
                                          x   cost per order) + (Average inventory
                                          x Annual carrying cost per unit)

      b. Algebraically, the total cost equation is expressed as

$$\text{Total costs} = \left(\frac{D}{Q} \times S \right) + \left(\frac{Q}{2} \times C \right)$$

         where

         Q = order quantity in units,
         D = annual demand for the item in units,
         S = cost of placing and receiving an order (or set-up cost),
         C = annual cost of carrying 1 unit of the item in inventory.

      c. The EOQ is the value of Q that minimizes total costs. Using calculus this is equal to:

$$Q^* = \sqrt{\frac{2SD}{C}}$$

      d. Besides the optimal EOQ, another useful item of interest is the optimal length of one inventory cycle, i.e., the optimal time between orders. The optimal time is given by:

$$T^* = \frac{(365 \times Q^*)}{D}$$

B.   Probabilistic inventory control models are more complex models that take into account fluctuations in demand and the possibility of stock outs in modeling the optimal inventory problem.

    1.   The probabilistic model allows for a safety stock to meet unexpectedly high demand and delays in lead time.

    2.   Determining the optimal stock requires balancing the expected costs of stock outs against the cost of carrying additional inventory.

C.   Just-in-time inventory management systems are based on the idea that all required inventory should be supplied to the production process at exactly the right time in the right quantities.

TRUE AND FALSE QUESTIONS

Agree with each of the statements or **reject** it and modify it so that it is acceptable.

1.   Methods used for analyzing the credit-granting decision are highly unique.

2.   A firm should attempt through its credit policy to minimize its bad debt expense.

3.   Default risk refers to the probability that a customer will fail to pay.

4.   Credit terms of 2/10, net 30 means that the customer must pay 2% of the invoice within 10 days and the balance in 30 days.

5.   The average collection period and bad-debt loss ratios are overall measures of the quality of accounts accepted.

6.   The average collection period can be found as (365)(AR)/Credit Sales.

7.   Credit should never be granted until all available sources of information regarding the applicant have been utilized.

8.   Collateral is seldom of major importance in trade credit.

9.   Liberalization of credit terms may result in an increase in the investment in inventory.

10.   Conditions as used in the five C's of credit refers to the terms of credit.

11.   Inventories act as buffers between the segments of the firm's procurement, production, and sales cycles.

12.   Carrying costs constitute all the costs of holding items in inventory for a given period of time.

13.   Stockout costs occur whenever a business is unable to fill customer orders because the item is not currently in inventory.

14.   The EOQ model is a probabilistic model.

15.   The primary objective of the EOQ model is to find the order quantity that minimizes total ordering costs.

16.   Just-in-time inventory systems are based on the idea that all required inventory items should be supplied to the production process at exactly the right time and in the exact right quantities.

17.   Safety stocks refer to inventory that's maintained as a protection against losses due to theft or fire.

Answers to True and False Questions

1.   Credit granting decisions are essentially investment decisions.
2.   Minimizing bad debts may result in credit policies that are overly stringent and result in lost sales. Credit policies should be based on profitability.
3.   True.
4.   Credit terms of 2/10, net 30 mean that the customer may take a discount of 2% of the invoice amount if he pays within 10 days. The net amount of the invoice is due in 30 days.
5.   True.
6.   True.
7.   Credit policies must consider the cost of collecting and evaluating information. Decisions should be based on the least cost analysis which will produce a satisfactory decision.
8.   True.
9.   True.
10.   Conditions refers to the general economic climate and outlook which may affect the customer's willingness and ability to pay.
11.   True.
12.   True.
13.   True.
14.   EOQ is a deterministic model.
15.   The primary objective of the EOQ model is to find the order quantity that minimizes total inventory costs.
16.   True.
17.   Safety stocks serve to meet unexpectedly high demand during the lead time, unexpected delays in lead time, or both.

MULTIPLE CHOICE QUESTIONS

1.   _____ is credit extended by a company to another while _____ is credit extended by a company to its ultimate consumers.
   A.   Investor credit;   consumer credit
   B.   Trade credit;   consumer credit
   C.   Consumer credit;   trade credit
   D.   Trade credit;   marginal credit
   E.   Marginal credit;   investor credit

2.   _____ are the criteria that the firm uses to screen credit applications to determine whether credit should be extended.
   A.   Credit standards
   B.   Credit policy
   C.   Credit terms
   D.   Credit quality
   E.   Quality control

3.   Which of the following would not occur as a firm's credit standards are relaxed?
   A.   Credit sales increase
   B.   Accounts receivable increase
   C.   Bad debt expense increase
   D.   An additional investment in inventory
   E.   All of the above would occur with relaxed credit standards.

4.   Credit terms consist of:
   A.   Credit period and credit standards.
   B.   Credit standards and cash discounts.
   C.   Collection effort and credit period.
   D.   Credit period and cash discounts.
   E.   Cash discount and collection effort.

5.   The collection effort must be a balance between _____ and the _____.
   A.   Credit policy;   credit standards
   B.   Desires of the customers;   desires of the sales staff
   C.   Excessive leniency;   risk of alienating customers
   D.   The size of the firm's accounts receivables;   bad debt ratio
   E.   Management's goals and objectives;   long-term profitability

6.   Of the "five C's of credit", _____ refers to the applicant's ability to meet obligations based on his liquidity and projected cash flows, and _____ refers to the applicant's overall financial strength based on net worth.
   A.   Capacity;   capital
   B.   Capital;   conditions
   C.   Capacity;   conditions
   D.   Conditions;   capital
   E.   Conditions;   capacity

7. An important part of managing accounts receivable is monitoring their status. A useful means of monitoring accounts receivable is _____.
    A. Account classification.
    B. Seasonal datings.
    C. Collection effort.
    D. Aging analysis.
    E. All of the above.

8. Of the three types of costs associated with inventory policy, _____ include storage and handling costs, obsolescence and deterioration costs, insurance, taxes and the costs of funds invested in inventory.
    A. Ordering costs
    B. Holding costs
    C. Carrying costs
    D. Storage costs
    E. Inventory control costs.

9. If the cost of placing and receiving an order increases, then the economic order quantity (EOQ) will:
    A. Remain unchanged.
    B. Increase.
    C. Decrease.

10. _____ are incurred when a firm is unable to fill an order because the item is not available in inventory.
    A. Carrying costs
    B. Marginal costs
    C. Inventory costs
    D. Filling costs
    E. Stockout costs

Answers to Multiple Choice Questions

1.	B	5.	C	9.	B
2.	A	6.	A	10.	E
3.	E	7.	D		
4.	D	8.	C		

PROBLEMS

1.   Universal Steel Products, Inc. distributes wholesale steel. Annual credit sales are $365 million spread evenly throughout the year. Their accounts receivable balance is $10.5 million. Terms of credit are net 30. Determine:

   a.   Average daily credit sales

   b.   Average collection period

Solution:

   a.   Assuming 365 days per year, average daily credit sales are:
         365,000,000/365 = $1,000,000

   b.   Average collection period = accounts receivable/daily credit sales
         = 10,500,000/1,000,000 = 10.5 days

2.   Aim Household Products wishes to speed up collection of its receivables. Aim currently offers credit terms of 1/20, net 40. It is considering changing to terms of 2/15, net 30. The collection period is expected to be reduced from 50 to 25 days. The percentage of customers paying within the discount period is expected to increase from 60% to 80%. Bad debt losses average 5% of sales and are not expected to change under the proposed policy. No change in the inventory level is expected. Annual billings are $25 million. The variable cost ratio is 65%. The pre-tax return on funds made available by this change in policy is 25%. Assuming that the change in terms is made, determine the following:

   a.   The amount of funds released by the decrease in receivables.

   b.   The earnings on the funds released.

   c.   The cost of the additional cash discounts taken.

   d.   The net effect on Aim's pre-tax profits.

Solution:

   a.   AR (Current) = 50 days x $25,000,000/365 = $3,424,658

         AR (Proposed) = 25 days x $25,000,000/365 = $1,712,329
         Funds released = Current AR - Proposed AR = $1,712,329

   b.   Earnings on released funds = 1,712,329 x .25 = $428,082

   c.   Proposed discounts = $25,000,000 x .80 x .02 = $400,000

Current discounts = $25,000,000 x .60 x .01 = $150,000
Increased cost of discounts = $400,000 - $150,000 = $250,000

d.
Earnings on released funds	$1,712,329
-Increased cost of discounts	-250,000
Net pre-tax profit effect	$1,462,329

3. The Chicken Little Company is considering liberalizing its credit standards in order to increase sales. Under the proposed policy, credit will be liberally granted to more buyers. It is anticipated that annual sales of $5.2 million will increase by 25%. Bad debt losses will increase from 4% of sales to 5% of sales and the collection period will increase from 75 days to 110 days. No change in inventory is required. Chicken Little's profit contribution is 40% of sales and its required pre-tax return on receivables is 15%. Determine the net effect of this plan on the company's pre-tax profits.

Solution:

Additional sales = (percent increase)(present sales)
$$= (.25)(5,200,000) = \$1,300,000$$

Profit on additional sales
$$= (\text{contribution})(\text{additional sales})$$
$$= (.40)(1,300,000) = \$520,000 \quad (A)$$

Additional average receivables balance
$$= \text{New balance - old balance}$$

New receivables balance
$$= (\text{average daily sales})(\text{collection period})$$
$$= (6,500,000/365)(110) = \$1,958,904$$

Old receivables balance
$$= (5,200,000/365)(75) = \$1,068,493$$

Additional average receivables balance = $890,411

Cost of additional receivables investment
$$= (\text{additional investment})(\text{required return})$$
$$= (890,411)(.15) = \$133,562 \quad (B)$$

Additional bad debt loss
$$= (\text{new sales})(\text{new ratio}) - (\text{old sales})(\text{old ratio})$$
$$= (6,500,000)(.05) - (5,200,000)(.04) = \$117,000 \quad (C)$$

Cost of additional inventory balance
$$= (\text{additional investment})(\text{required return})$$
$$= (0)(.15) = \$0 \quad (D)$$

Net change in pre-tax profits
= A - (B + C + D) = $269,438

4.   Leisure-Time Retirement World has asked you to perform an aging of their accounts receivable. It is now January 1. The aging is to be in categories of current, 1-30 days past due, 30-90 days past due, and more than 90 days past due. All bills are due net 30. You may assume that all months have 30 days. The accounts are as follows:

Account No.	Invoice Date	Amount Due
1131	Dec. 15	$1,225
3771	Nov. 14	765
7121	Nov. 25	522
9131	Dec. 14	1,204
4181	Aug. 10	469
3171	Dec. 5	1,707
3441	Sep. 8	295
4411	Oct. 28	417
6996	Sep. 5	983
1558	Jul. 5	1,945

Solution:

All accounts billed during December are current.
All accounts billed during November are 1-30 days past due.
All accounts billed during September and October are 30 to 90 days past due.
All accounts billed prior to September are more than 90 days past due.
From the above, we obtain the following schedule:

Current	$4,126
1 - 30 days past due	1,287
30 - 90 days past due	1,695
Over 90 days past due	2,414

5.   The Comp Store sells 5,000 units of a particular model of computer per year. The demand for this computer model is uniform through out the year. Comp Store pays $725.00 to its supplier for each of these computers. Annual inventory carrying costs are 15% of inventory value. The cost of placing and receiving an order are $ 550.00. Assume that inventory replenishment occurs instantaneously. Determine the following:

a. Economic order quantity.
b. Total annual inventory costs of this policy.
c. Optimal ordering frequency.

Solution:

a.   S = \$550.00;   D = 5,000 computers
        C = 0.15 x 725.00 = \$108.75 / computer

$$Q^* = \sqrt{\frac{2(\$550.00)(5,000)}{\$108.75}}$$

$Q^* = 225$ computers

b.

$$\text{Total costs} = \left(\frac{5,000}{225} \times \$550.00\right) + \left(\frac{225}{2} \times \$108.75\right)$$

Total costs = \$24,456.60

c.

$$T^* = \frac{(365 \times 225)}{5,000}$$

$T^* = 16.4$ days

6.   Rework problem 2 using the Excel template for credit term analysis (Credterm). The results should look as follows:

Accounts Receivable Management - Analysis Of Credit Terms

Summary Of Cost Ratios
Variable Cost Ratio   60.00%
Opportunity Cost Of:
  Cash Balances   0.00%
  Accounts Receivable   20.00%
  Inventory Investment   0.00%

Summary Of Current Receivables Policy
Discount Period (Days)   15
Credit Period (Days)   30

Cash Discount (%)	1.00%
Percent Of Customers Taking Cash Discount	60.00%
Annual Level Of Credit Sales	$5,000,000
Average Collection Period (Days)	40
Bad-Debt Loss Ratio	5.00%
Current Cash Balance	$0
Current Inventory Investment	$0

Results Under The Current Credit Policy

Profitability of Sales	$2,000,000

Average Investment In Receivables	$547,945

Cost Of:

Receivables Investment	$109,589
Cash Balance	$0
Inventory Investment	$0
Cash Discounts	$30,000
Bad-Debt Losses	$250,000
Total Cost of Current Credit Policy	$389,589

Impact Of Average Collection Period Differing From The Credit Period:

If Average Collection Period = Credit Period:

Average Investment In Receivables	$416,667
Cost Of Receivables Investment	$83,333

Additional Average Receivables Investment	$131,279

Cost Of Additional Receivables Investment	$26,256

Impact Of The Proposed Change In Credit Terms

Proposed Account Receivable Policy

Discount Period (Days)	10
Credit Period (Days)	30
Cash Discount (%)	2.00%

Percent of Customers Taking Cash Discount   80.00%

Forecasted Impact On Operations

Expected Change In Credit Sales ($) $0

Expected Average Collection Period (Days)   25

Expected Bad-Debt Loss Ratio (%)   5.00%

Additional Cash Balance Required ($) $0

Additional Inventory Required ($) $0

Impact Of Changes On Pre-Tax Profits

Marginal Sales $0

Profitability Of Marginal Sales $0

Decreased Investment In Receivables $205,479

Additional Cash Balance $0

Additional Inventory Investment $0

Earnings on Released Receivables Investment $41,096

Less Cost Of Additional:

    Cash Balance $0

    Inventory Investment $0

    Cash Discounts $50,000

    Bad-Debt Losses $0

Incremental Cost Of Change In Credit Terms   ($8,904)

Net Impact On Pre-Tax Profits   ($8,904)

Chapter

18

Short- and Intermediate-Term Financing Alternatives

Firms usually seek a balance of short-term, intermediate-term, and long-term sources of funds. Short-term credit includes all debt obligations that were originally scheduled for repayment within one year. Short-term debt may be either secured or unsecured and can be obtained from a variety of sources. Some of these sources are spontaneous such as trade credit and accruals while others such as bank credit, commercial paper and loans obtained against receivables or inventories are negotiated. Intermediate-term loans are also covered in this chapter.

I.   Short-term credit can come from several sources, all of which have a cost.

    A.   The *annual financing cost, AFC*, annualizes the cost of short-term borrowing:

$$AFC = \frac{Interest + Fees}{Usable\ funds} \ x \ \frac{365}{Maturity(days)}$$

This is a simple interest rate, not a compound rate.

    B.   The true *annual percentage rate, APR*, that does consider compounding is:

$$APR = \left[1 + \frac{Interest + Fees}{Usable\ funds} \right]^{m} - 1$$

where m is the number of times per year the loan is compounded per year, i.e., m = 365/maturity (days).

II.   The most important source of short-term financing for business firms is trade credit.

    A.   *Trade credit* arises whenever a firm receives merchandise from a supplier and is permitted to wait a specified period of time before paying for it.

        1.   Most trade credit is extended on open account. Open account trade credit is recognized on the books of the firm as accounts payable. No formal debt instrument is created.

        2.   An alternative to open account credit involves issuance of a promissory note carried on the books under notes payable.

        3.   Trade credit is considered a spontaneous source of financing since it tends to expand naturally as the firm's business expands.

    B.   The cost of trade credit can be inferred from the credit terms. Credit terms specify the conditions under which a business is required to repay the credit that a supplier has extended. Credit terms include the length, beginning date of the credit period, and cash discount (if any) for prompt payment.

        1.   When a cash discount is offered, an identifiable expense of trade credit arises in the form of lost discounts if payment is not made within the discount period.

        2.   If a firm does not take the cash discount but pays on the last day of the credit period, the annual financing cost of missing the discount is given by:

$$AFC = \frac{\% \, discount}{100\% - \% \, discount} \times \frac{365}{Credit \, period \, - \, Discount \, period}$$

        3.   The cost of lost cash discounts can be reduced by late payment. This is called stretching accounts payable. Intangible costs in terms of lowered credit rating and ability to obtain future credit may result. Tangible costs of late charges or specific interest may offset the savings.

III.   Accruals and deferred income are additional sources of spontaneous financing.

    A.   Accruals of wages, taxes, and interest increase the firm's short-term liabilities and hence provide short-term financing. Use of these is determined by legal and practical considerations regarding the timing of payment, however.

    B.   Deferred income consists of payments received for goods and services to be delivered at a future date. Until the firm earns these advance payments through the fulfillment of its obligation, they represent a liability on the balance sheet.

IV.   Loans from commercial banks are an important source of negotiated short-term financing.

    A.   Bank loans may be secured or unsecured. Bank loans usually appear as notes payable on the balance sheet.

    B.   Bank credit is commonly available under three different arrangements: single loans, lines of credit, and revolving credit agreements.

        1.   *Single loans* are usually arranged for specific financing needs.

            a.   The interest rate charged on a single loan is usually related to the prime rate.

            b.   The effective annual percentage cost of a bank loan depends on the payment schedule and whether a compensating balance is required.

            c.   If the interest is payable at maturity, the effective cost is equal to the stated interest rate.

            d.   If the loan is discounted, the bank deducts the amount of interest from the loan proceeds. This increases the actual interest rate above the stated rate.

        2.   A *line of credit* is an agreement that permits the firm to borrow up to a predetermined limit at any time during the life of the agreement.

            a.   A line of credit is usually negotiated for a one year period.

            b.   The interest rate on a line of credit is usually stated in terms of the prime rate and varies as the prime rate changes during the year.

            c.   A line of credit may contain restrictive covenants on working capital, allowable debt, and so on.

            d.   A line of credit frequently requires that the firm have no loans outstanding under the agreement for a portion of the year.

            e.   A line of credit does not guarantee that the bank will lend the firm the requested funds. The bank is not legally obligated to make loans if the firm's financial position has deteriorated or the bank lacks sufficient loanable funds to honor all commitments.

        3.   A *revolving credit* agreement legally commits the bank to making loans up to the credit limit specified in the agreement.

            a.   Revolving credit agreements are usually secured.

b.   Revolving credit agreements usually require the firm to pay a commitment fee on the unused portion of the funds.

c.   The effective annual interest cost on a revolving credit agreement contains both actual interest costs and the commitment fee.

$$AFC = \frac{Interest\ costs + Commitment\ fee}{Usable\ funds} \times \frac{365}{Maturity(days)}$$

V.   *Commercial paper* consists of short-term unsecured promissory notes issued by large well-known corporations.

A.   Maturities of commercial paper range from a few days to a maximum of 9 months. Maturity longer than 9 months would require SEC registration.

B.   Commercial paper is sold on a discount basis so that the firm receives less than the stated amount and repays the full amount. The annual financing cost is computed as follows:

$$AFC = \frac{Interest\ costs + Placement\ fee}{Usable\ funds} \times \frac{365}{Maturity(days)}$$

C.   Purchasers of commercial paper include corporations with idle cash, banks, insurance companies, pension funds, money market funds, and other financial institutions.

D.   If a firm's financial position deteriorates, it may be difficult or impossible to sell commercial paper.

VI.   Accounts receivable are one of the most common forms of collateral for secured short-term borrowing.

A.   Accounts receivable are fairly liquid and are easier to handle than physical assets in the event of default.

B.   Accounts receivable financing is subject to fraud if the borrower pledges nonexistent accounts. Administrative costs to the lender may be high.

C.   Accounts receivable financing takes two common forms--*pledging and factoring.*

1.   When accounts receivable are pledged, the firm retains title to them and continues to carry them on its balance sheet.

a.   The firm sends copies of invoices to the lender who determines the amount he will advance depending on the credit-worthiness of the receivable. The borrower signs a note for the amount advanced.

b.   If the loan is on a non-notification basis, the borrower receives payment on the invoices and then pays the lender.

c.   If the loan is on a notification basis, the customer is notified to send payment directly to the lender.

d.   The annual percentage cost of a loan involving pledged receivables consists of both the interest expense on the loan and the service fees charged for processing the receivables.

2.   Factoring receivables involves the outright sale of the receivables to a financial institution known as a factor.

a.   When receivables are factored, title passes to the factor and they no longer appear on the balance sheet of the firm.

b.   Most factoring is on a non-recourse basis; as a result, the factor assumes the risk of default.

c.   The firm may receive proceeds from the receivables from the factor as they are received (which is called maturity factoring) or may obtain an advance which constitutes a loan against the future collections (which is called advance factoring).

d.   Costs of factoring include the fees and charges for the services as well as explicit interest on advances.

e.   The cost of factoring may be offset by a reduction in the firm's own costs of collection, credit administration, etc.

3.   Because domestic banks and lenders may be unfamiliar with foreign customers, special arrangements are used to obtain financing from foreign receivables.

a.   Some factors will finance foreign receivables that are insured by the Export-Import Bank.

b.   A forfait company will finance receivables based on contracts guaranteed by a foreign bank or government.

c.   Trading companies take title to goods and arrange shipment to foreign buyers. Trading companies work with sales contracts guaranteed or insured by programs of U.S. and foreign governments.

VII.   Inventories constitute another common source of collateral for secured loans.

    A.   The suitability of inventory for collateral depends on the nature of the inventory. Particularly important characteristics include perishability, identifiability, marketability, and price stability.

    B.   Inventory loans are available from commercial banks and finance companies.

    C.   A number of arrangements are available with regard to possession of the collateral by the borrower or by a third party.

        1.   A floating lien is a general claim on the firm's entire inventory.

            a.   Floating liens offer the lender little security.

            b.   The loan amount as a percentage of inventory value is usually small.

            c.   Floating liens are used for large-volume, small-value, high-turnover inventory held by turnover.

        2.   A trust receipt is another form of inventory loan with the inventory held by the borrower.

            a.   As the inventory is sold, the proceeds are forwarded to the lender along with notification of the goods sold.

            b.   Trust receipts require specifically identifiable units of inventory.

            c.   Trust receipt arrangements are common for items such as automobiles and appliances. These arrangements are also known as floor planning.

        3.   Terminal warehouse plans require that the inventory be held in a bonded warehouse operated by a public warehouse company.

            a.   The warehouse issues a receipt for the merchandise that then becomes the collateral for the lender.

            b.   As the loan is paid off, the lender authorizes the warehouse to release the inventory.

            c.   In addition to specific interest on the amount advanced, warehouse fees must be paid. These may be offset by reductions in the firm's own handling and storage costs.

4.   Under field warehouse agreements, the goods are kept in a segregated portion of the firm's premises under the control of a warehouse company. Other portions of the operation are similar to those under terminal warehousing.

VIII.   A *term loan*, or intermediate-term credit, is defined as any debt obligation having an initial maturity between one and ten years.

A.   Term loans are available from a wide variety of sources including banks, insurance companies, pension funds, small business investment companies, government agencies and equipment suppliers.

B.   Particularly in smaller amounts, term loans are usually less expensive than issuing bonds or common stock.

C.   Term loans are often better suited for financing than short-term loans because of a reduction of the problems of future interest rate variability and ability to renew the loan. This is particularly true for financing small additions to plant and equipment where the cash flows from the investment often cover the servicing requirements of the debt.

D.   Term loans can also be used to finance moderate increases in working capital if the length of the loan approximately matches the time the working capital will be needed or until the debt can be amortized out of earnings.

E.   Term loans usually require that the principal be amortized over the life of the loan. Amortization requires that the borrower make regular periodic payments of principal and interest.

1.   A common arrangement is for the borrower to make regular equal payments so that the present value of the annuity of payments is equal to the amount of the loan.

2.   Another arrangement calls for equal reductions in principal during the life of the loan together with payment of interest on the outstanding balance.

3.   Partial amortization may be used which results in a lump payment called a "balloon payment" at the maturity of the loan.

4.   Term loans may call for periodic payment of interest with a final balloon payment equal to the amount of the loan (bullet loan).

F.   Interest costs on term loans depend on a number of factors—particularly, the general level of interest rates. Variable rates dependent on the prime rate or another indicator are sometimes used.

G.   Term loan agreements often call for the borrower to keep a percentage of the loan balance on deposit as a compensating balance. This can increase the effective interest rate on the loan.

H.   In the case of higher risk loans to companies with promising growth potential, a term loan agreement may call for issuance to the lender of a warrant giving the lender an option to purchase equity in the company at a future date.

I.   *Security provisions* in term loans are dependent on the credit standing of the borrower. Security provisions can take many forms:

    1.   Assignment of payments due under a particular contract.

    2.   Assignment or pledging of inventories, receivables or securities.

    3.   The use of a floating lien on inventories and receivables.

    4.   A mortgage on property, plant or equipment.

    5.   An assignment of the cash surrender value of a life insurance policy.

    6.   A pledge of marketable securities by the borrower.

J.   *Affirmative covenants* outline actions that a firm agrees to take during the term of the loan. These include such things as providing financial statements and cash budgets, carrying insurance on assets and against insurable business risks, maintaining minimum levels of net working capital, and maintaining personnel acceptable to the lender.

K.   *Negative covenants* outline actions which a firm agrees not to take during the term of the loan. These may include agreements not to merge with other firms, not to pledge assets as security to other lenders, or not to make or guarantee loans to other firms.

L.   *Restrictive covenants* limit the firm's potential actions but do not prohibit them. Restrictions might limit dividends, limit employee compensation, limit additional borrowing and limit investment activities.

M.   Term loan agreements contain *default provisions* which permit the lender to insist on immediate repayment under certain conditions.

IX.   Term loans are available from a number of sources.

A.   Banks prefer loans having relatively short maturities, yet they are a major source of term loans.

B.   Insurance companies and pension funds are a source of term loans.

    1.   Insurance companies and pension funds prefer longer term loans.

    2.   Prepayment of loans from these sources may involve penalties.

3.   Loans from insurance companies and pension funds are usually secured.

4.   Due to the longer maturity and lack of compensating balance arrangements, loans from these institutions tend to have slightly higher stated interest rates than term loans from banks.

C.   The Small Business Administration (SBA), an agency of the Federal government, was established to make credit available to small businesses.

1.   SBA loans are usually secured.

2.   Most SBA loans are participation loans obtained from a bank with the SBA guaranteeing up to 90% of the amount.

3.   Direct loans are available from the SBA on a limited basis.

4.   Economic opportunity loans up to $25,000 and 15 years maturity are available from SBA to assist economically and socially disadvantaged individuals who own their own firms.

D.   Small business investment companies (SBIC's) are licensed by the government to make debt or equity investments in small firms.

1.   SBIC's obtain capital by borrowing from the SBA and other sources.

2.   SBIC's specialize in firms with growth potential.

3.   Because the borrowers tend to have above average risk, these loans tend to be more expensive than bank loans.

E.   Industrial Development Authorities (IDA's), organized by state and local governments, issue bonds and use the proceeds to build facilities which are then leased to a firm. Because the bonds are tax exempt, the financing costs are often lower than on directly issued corporate bonds.

F.   Municipalities issue pollution control revenue bonds. The proceeds are used to assist industry in acquiring pollution control equipment. Because the bonds are tax exempt, the financing costs are lower than if industry raised the funds directly.

G.   *Equipment financing loans* are loans to purchase equipment which then serves as collateral on the loan.

1.   The equipment is usually of a type that is readily marketable such as motor vehicles.

2.   These loans are usually amortized over the expected life of the equipment.

3.   Equipment financing loans are available from the usual financial intermediaries as well as from equipment sellers themselves.

4.   Two legal forms are common for equipment financing loans.

a.   *Conditional sales contracts* are common when financing is from the equipment seller. In a conditional sales contract, the purchaser usually makes a down payment and a series of periodic payments. Title does not pass to the purchaser until the contract is fulfilled.

b.   *Chattel mortgages* are often used by financial intermediaries. A chattel mortgage is a mortgage on property other than real estate.

TRUE AND FALSE QUESTIONS

Agree with each of the statements or **reject** it and modify it so that it is acceptable.

1.   Long-term debt with less than 1 year to maturity is a source of short-term financing.

2.   The cost of lost cash discounts is reduced the longer the firm does not pay.

3.   Accruals are an easily managed source for short-term financing.

4.   A line of credit obligates a bank to make the funds available upon request.

5.   A revolving credit agreement obligates the bank to make the funds available upon request in accordance with the agreement.

6.   Commercial paper has a relatively high risk of inability to renew the loan if money becomes tight or the firm's financial position deteriorates.

7.   Factoring of accounts receivable always involves an interest charge as well as service fees.

8.   A floating lien is a general lien on all the inventory of the borrowing firm.

9.   Terminal warehouse plans are also known as floor planning.

10.   The formula for the cost of short-term credit can be summarized as:
(Total fees and interest paid)/Amount available for use.

11.   A term loan is a long-term debt obtained from sources other than bonds.

12.   Term loans avoid the renewal risk present in short-term loans.

13.   Term loans are usually amortized.

14.   Longer maturity term loans are usually obtained from banks while shorter maturity ones are usually obtained from insurance companies and pension funds.

15.   Most SBA loans are made directly from the SBA to the borrower and provide financing for new businesses with no assets available for security.

16.   Industrial Development Authorities provide a means to channel the proceeds of tax exempt bonds to private industry.

Answers to True and False Questions

1.   Only debt with an initial maturity of less than 1 year is considered short-term financing although longer-term debt which will mature in less than a year is a current liability.
2.   True. (The apparent reduction may be offset by intangible costs in the form of a lowered credit rating, however.)
3.   Accruals are not generally susceptible to discretionary increase and hence are not easily managed.
4.   A line of credit does not obligate a bank to make the funds available.
5.   True.
6.   True.
7.   Factoring does not involve an interest charge unless an advance is drawn against the factored receivables.
8.   True.
9.   Trust receipt inventory financing is also known as floor planning.
10.   False. The number of days credit is extended is relevant.

$$AFC = \frac{Interest + Fees}{Usable\ funds} \times \frac{365}{Maturity(days)}$$

11.   A term loan is intermediate term debt with a maturity of 1-10 years.
12.   True.
13.   True.
14.   Banks prefer to make shorter term loans while insurance companies and pension funds prefer longer term loans.
15.   Most SBA loans are participation loans and require security.
16.   True.

MULTIPLE CHOICE QUESTIONS

1.   _____ is the most important source of short-term financing for business firms.
        A.   Commercial paper
        B.   Deferred income
        C.   Accruals
        D.   Trade credit
        E.   Bank loans

2.   _____ consists of payments received for goods and services to be delivered at a future date. Until the firm earns these advance payments through the fulfillment of its obligation, they represent a liability on the balance sheet.
    A.   Accounts payable
    B.   Deferred income
    C.   Accruals
    D.   Trade credit
    E.   Accounts receivable

3.   _____ consists of short-term unsecured promissory notes issued by large well-known firms.
    A.   Commercial paper
    B.   A line of credit
    C.   A term loan
    D.   Trade credit
    E.   A bank loan

4.   _____ is an agreement that permits the firm to borrow up to a predetermined limit at any time during the life of the agreement.
    A.   Commercial paper
    B.   A line of credit
    C.   A term loan
    D.   A revolving credit agreement
    E.   A bank loan

5.   _____ are one of the most common forms of collateral for secured short-term borrowing.
    A.   Accounts payable
    B.   Common stock
    C.   Fixed assets
    D.   Marketable securities
    E.   Accounts receivable

6.   A _____, or intermediate-term credit, is defined as any debt obligation having an initial maturity between one and ten years.
    A.   mortgage loan
    B.   line of credit
    C.   term loan
    D.   trade credit
    E.   bank loan

7.   A _____ is a general claim on the firm's entire inventory, where a _____ is a loan on specifically identifiable units of inventory.
    A.   floating lien; trust receipt
    B.   trust receipt; field warehouse arrangement
    C.   floating lien, field warehouse arrangement
    D.   field warehouse arrangement; floating lien
    E.   field warehouse arrangement; trust receipt

Solution:
a.   Determine the amount of the equal payments.

$1,000,000 = Payment x PVIFA$_{0.08,5}$ = Payment x 3.993

Payment = $250,438

For an amortization schedule we set up a table showing the balance at the beginning of each year, the payment, the amount of the payment representing interest, and the amount paid toward the principal.   For each year, the interest is 8% of the beginning balance; the principal payment is the difference between the payment and the interest. New balance is old balance less principal.

Year	Payment	Interest	Principal Repayment	Remaining Balance
0	---	---	---	1,000,000
1	250,438	80,000	170,438	829,562
2	250,438	66,365	184,073	645,489
3	250,438	51,639	198,799	446,690
4	250,438	35,735	214,703	231,987
5	250,438	18,559	231,879	108[*]

[*]The remaining balance does not equal zero because of rounding.   A payment of $250,456.45 would be more precise.

b.   In a bullet loan, only the accrued interest is paid during years 1-4. The final payment includes the final interest payment and the entire principal amount.

Year	Payment	Interest	Principal Repayment	Remaining Balance
1	80,000	80,000	0	1,000,000
2	80,000	80,000	0	1,000,000
3	80,000	80,000	0	1,000,000
4	80,000	80,000	0	1,000,000
5	1,080,000	80,000	1,000,000	0

c.   This balloon loan payment scheme can be viewed as a $500,000 loan amortized with equal annual payments together with a $500,000 bullet loan. For years 1-4, the total payment is the amortization payment on $500,000 plus the interest on the remaining $500,000. The Final payment consists of the amortization payment, the interest on the bullet, and the principal payment on the bullet. Once the payments are determined, operations in the table are identical to those for an amortized loan. Interest is 8% of the balance. Principal is payment less interest, the next year's balance is the old balance less the principal payment. The payment for years 1 to 4 on the amortized portion is determined by

$500,000 = Payment x PVIFA$_{.08,5}$ = Payment x 3.993
Payment = $125,219

The payment of the bullet portion is simply
        Payment = .08 x 500,000 = $40,000
The total payment is the sum of the two parts or $165,219.
This final payment is equal to the regular payments plus the $500,000 balloon or $665,219.
A second way to visualize this problem is:

$$1,000,000 = \text{payment} \times \text{PVIFA}_{.08,5} + \text{PVIF}_{.08,5}$$

$$1,000,000 = \text{payment} \times 3.993 + 500,000 \times .681$$
$$1,000,000 = \text{payment} \times 3.993 + 340,500$$
$$\text{payment} \times 3.993 = 659,500$$

$$\text{payment} = 165,164$$

This payment differs from the others due to rounding error in the present value factors. The first four payments are $165,164 and the fifth is $165,164 + $500,000 = $665,164. Using $165,219 as the payment, the amortization table is:

Year	Payment	Interest	Principal Repayment	Remaining Balance
0	---	---	---	1,000,000
1	165,219	80,000	85,219	914,781
2	165,219	73,182	92,037	822,744
3	165,219	65,820	99,399	723,345
4	165,219	57,868	107,351	615,994
5	665,219	49,280	615,939	55*

*A payment of 165,228.23 would reduce this to zero.

d.   In this case, the total payment varies. The payment on the principal amount is always equal to $1,000,000/5 = $200,000. The interest payment is equal to 8% of the beginning balance for the year. The total payment is the sum of the two.

Year	Payment	Interest	Principal Repayment	Remaining Balance
0	---	---	---	1,000,000
1	280,000	80,000	200,000	800,000
2	264,000	64,000	200,000	600,000
3	248,000	48,000	200,000	400,000
4	232,000	32,000	200,000	200,000
5	216,000	16,000	200,000	0

8.   The 29th National Bank of Lubbock will lend you $10,000 for 3 years with a stated interest rate of 8.29% to be paid in advance for the entire three years. What is the effective annual percentage cost?

Solution:

The total interest is given by
Interest = Principal x Rate x Years = 10,000 x .0829 x 3 = 2,487
The net cash flow from the loan at the time it is made is equal to 10,000 - 2,487= 7,513. To find the effective rate we use

$$PV = FV \times PVIF_{i,n}$$
$$7,513 = 10,000 \times PVIF_{i,3}$$
$$i = 10\%$$

9.   Do problem 4(a) using the Excel template accompanying the text (Compbal). The results should look as follows:

Compensating Balance Requirements - Effective Annual Rate Analysis

Total Line of Credit		$1,000,000.00
Commitment Fee on Unused Portion of Credit Line		1.00%
Loan Principal		$250,000.00
Nominal Interest Rate (1 = Discounted Loan)	0	10.00%
Compensating Balance Requirement (%)		15.00%
Funds Available To Meet Compensating Requirement		$0.00

Required Compensating Balance	$37,500.00
Annual Interest	$25,000.00
Commitment Fee	$7,500.00
Total Usable Funds	$212,500.00

Effective Annual Cost Of Compensating Balance	15.29%

10.   Rework problem 5 using the Excel template for accounts receivable factoring analysis (Factorar). The results should look as follows:

	Factoring Accounts Receivables
Summary Of Input	
Average Level of Receivables	$300,000.00
Average Collection Period	30
Factoring Commission	2.50%
Reserve Allowance For Returns	10.00%
Interest On Proceeds Advanced (Annual Rate)	10.00%
Savings In Credit Department Per Collection Period	$500.00
Bad-Debt Losses Per Collection Period	$6,000.00

Analysis Of Factoring Agreement		
Average Level Of Receivables		$300,000
Less: Factoring Comission	2.50%	$7,500
Less: Reserve For Returns	10.00%	$30,000
Amount Available For Advance Before Interest		$262,500
Less: Interest On Proceeds Advanced	10.00%	$2,188
Amount Advanced By Factor		$260,312

Annual Cost Of Factor Agreement		
Factoring Comission	$7,500	
Interest Expense	$2,188	
Gross Factoring Cost	$9,688	
Annual Factoring Cost (Gross)		$116,250
Less: Annual Savings In Credit Department		$6,000
Less: Annual Bad-Debt Losses		$72,000

Net Annual Cost Of Factoring Receivablee	$38,250

Annual Percentage Cost Before Cost Savings and Bad-Debt Losses	44.66%

Effective Annual Percentage Cost Of Factoring Agreement	14.69%

Chapter

19

Lease Financing

Leasing is a means of obtaining use of an asset for a period of time without owning the asset. In the lease contract, the property owner (the lessor) agrees to permit the property user (the lessee) to use the property for a stated period of time in exchange for a series of periodic payments.

I. In a "true lease" (the focus of this chapter), the lessor holds legal title to the asset while the lessee has no ownership interest in the asset.

   A. There are two major classes of true leases

      1. An *operating lease*, sometimes called a service or maintenance lease, is an agreement for period to period use of an asset. Maintenance and insurance are usually included in the lease.

      2. A *financial* or *capital lease* is noncancellable. The lessee is usually responsible for maintenance and possibly for insurance and property taxes.

         a. A financial lease may originate as a *direct lease* in which the lessee acquires use of an asset it has not owned.

         b. A financial lease may originate as a *sale and leaseback* in which the lessor purchases the asset from the lessee and then leases it back to the lessee.

      3. A *leveraged lease* is a three-party financial lease consisting of the lessee who acquires use of the asset, the lessor who holds an equity interest in the asset, and a lender who finances the purchase of the asset by the lessor.

315

II.   There are a number of potential advantages and disadvantages to leasing.

    A.   Advantages:

        1.   Lease agreements tend to be more flexible than loan agreements particularly with regard to restrictive covenants.

        2.   Leasing may effectively allow you to depreciate land.

        3.   Payments may be lower because of the tax benefits to the lessor.

        4.   The lessee may avoid some of the risk of obsolescence.

        5.   For small or marginally profitable firms leasing may be the only source of financing available.

        6.   Earnings are smoother and EPS in the early years is higher under leasing because the accelerated depreciation does not show on the lessee's income statement.

        7.   Leasing provides essentially 100% financing.

        8.   Leasing can reduce pressures on the lessee's liquidity.

        9.   Leasing may permit divisional/plant managers the flexibility in acquiring assets if lease payments are not subject to internal capital budgeting constraints.

    B.   Disadvantages:

        1.   Leasing is often more expensive than ownership.

        2.   The lessee loses the benefit of the salvage value. This is particularly significant in real estate.

        3.   Approval for improvements in leased real estate may be difficult to obtain.

        4.   Financial leases may not be canceled without a substantial penalty.

III.   Leasing assets involves a number of tax and accounting considerations.

    A.   Often one of the advantages of true leases is derived from tax considerations.

        1.   Care must be taken that the arrangement is recognized as a lease rather than an installment purchase plan by the IRS. To meet IRS requirements for a lease, the following guidelines are considered.

          a.   The remaining useful life of the equipment at the end of the lease must be the greater of 1 year or 20% of the cost of the property.

          b.   Leases may not exceed 30 years for tax purposes.

          c.   The lessor must receive a reasonable return of investment.

          d.   Renewal options must be closely related to the economic value of the asset.

          e.   If the agreement contains a purchase option at the end of the lease, the purchase price must be based on the asset's market value at the time.

          f.   For leveraged leases, the lessor must provide at least 20% equity.

          g.   Property valuable only to the lessee may not be leased.

     2.   IRS restrictions are designed to prohibit lease transactions set up purely to speed up tax deductions.

  B.   The Financial Accounting Standards Board requires that financial leases be capitalized.

     1.   A liability equal to the present value of the lease payments discounted at the firm's borrowing rate for a secured loan of similar maturity is shown.

     2.   The asset value of the lease is also reported.

     3.   Further details must be provided in the footnotes to the financial statements.

IV.   Many small firms have sought lease financing as an alternative to traditional bank financing, particularly when credit is tight.

  A.   The entrepreneurial firms cited several reasons for leasing, including (1) less cash required up front, (2) better protection against obsolescence at the end of the lease term, (3) quicker approvals from lessors than from lenders, and (4) fewer restrictive covenants from lessors than from lenders.

  B.   These advantages may be expensive. (1) The effective interest costs of leasing are often quite high compared to borrowing. (2) The lessee must give up the tax benefits of ownership (the asset's depreciation tax shields).

V.   The determination of lease payments from the lessor's perspective consists of present value analysis similar to capital budgeting decisions.

  A.   The lessor's required payment is an annuity payment than can be found with this three-step process:

Step 1: Compute the lessor's amount to be amortized

Initial Outlay
Less: Present value of after-tax salvage
Less: Present value of depreciation tax shelter
Equals: Amount to be amortized

Step 2: Compute after-tax lease income requirement

Amount to be amortized =
Present value of after-tax lease payment

Step 3: Compute before-tax lease payment

$$Lease\ payment\ =\ \frac{After-tax\ lease\ income\ requirements}{1-lessors'\ marginal\ tax\ rate}$$

B.   An example of finding the required lease payment from the lessor's perspective is given in Problem 1. There are a couple of things to keep in mind.

1.   The discount rate is the lessor's after-tax required rate of return.

2.   Lease payments are usually due at the beginning of the period, in which case the computation of the present value of the lease payments must be for an annuity due rather than an ordinary annuity.

VI.   Lease-Buy analysis from the lessee's perspective compares leasing to the alternative to borrowing to buy.

A.   The basic approach of the lease-buy analysis model is to compute the *net advantage to leasing* (NAL):

	Installed cost of the asset
Less:	Present value of the after-tax lease payment
Less:	Present value of the depreciation tax shield
Plus:	Present value of after-tax operating costs incurred if owned but not if leased
Less:	Present value of the after-tax salvage value
Equals:	Net Advantage to Leasing (NAL)

B.   If the NAL is positive, it is cheaper for the lessee to lease the asset than to borrow and buy it. If the NAL is negative, leasing is unattractive. It is easy to see how each of the items above affects the attractiveness of leasing. For example, a larger lease payment reduces the NAL.

C.   Problem 2 illustrates the calculation of the lessee's net advantage of leasing.   There are several things to keep in mind.

    1.   The installed cost is the purchase price plus installation and shipping charges.

    2.   The present value of the after-tax lease payment is found by discounting at the lessee's after- tax marginal cost of borrowing. The lease payment is usually an annuity due.

    3.   The annual depreciation tax shield is the depreciation times the lessee's marginal tax rate. The present value of the depreciation tax shield is found using the lessee's after-tax marginal cost of borrowing.

    4.   If leased, some operating costs (such as property tax payments, insurance, and some maintenance costs) may be paid by the lessor. If so, these savings are discounted at a rate reflecting their relative certainty, frequently the lessee's after-tax marginal cost of borrowing.

    5.   Because the salvage value belongs to the lessor, this amount lost to the lessee is discounted at a rate reflecting its uncertainty, frequently the lessee's weighted cost of capital (which is higher than the after-tax cost of borrowing).

TRUE AND FALSE QUESTIONS

Agree with each of the statements or **reject** it and modify it so that it is acceptable.

1.   A lease is a written agreement that permits the lessee to use a piece of property owned by the lessor in exchange for a series of periodic lease or rental payments.

2.   If certain guidelines are satisfied, firms that lease assets may deduct the full amount of the lease payment for tax purposes.

3.   In bankruptcy, a lender has a stronger claim than a lessor typically does.

4.   A larger lease payment decreases the lessee's net advantage of leasing.

5.   When the Financial Accounting Standards Board require a firm to capitalize its leases, this means that the lease must be disclosed in capital letters in the footnotes to its financial statement.

6.   The Depository Institutions Deregulation and Monetary Control Act of 1980 prohibited commercial banks from participating in leasing markets either as lessors or as lessees.

7.   Operating leases are noncancellable.

8.   In order to qualify as a lease under IRS regulations, a lease agreement must contain a renewal option at the same payment rate as the original lease.

9.   Financial leases provide a means of obtaining assets in exchange for an agreement to make periodic payments without increasing the debt on the balance sheet.

10.   In finding the lessee's net advantage of leasing, the various cash flows are discounted at the firm's cost of capital.

Answers to True and False Questions

1.   True.
2.   True.
3.   In bankruptcy, a lessor has a stronger claim than a lender typically does.
4.   True.
5.   When a firm capitalizes a lease, it recognizes the value of the leased assets on the asset side of the balance sheet and recognizes a similar liability on the liability/equity side of the balance sheet.
6.   Commercial banks are major players in the leasing markets.
7.   Financial leases are noncancellable; operating leases may be cancelled.
8.   Renewal options should reflect the economic value of the asset at the time of renewal.
9.   Generally financial leases must be capitalized so that the present value of the debt is reflected in both the assets and liabilities.
10.   When calculating the lessee's net advantage of leasing, the after-tax lease payment and the depreciation tax shelter are discounted at the lessee's after tax marginal cost of borrowing.

MULTIPLE CHOICE QUESTIONS

1.   In a lease, the property owner, the _____, agrees to permit the property user, the _____, to use the property of a stated period of time in exchange for a series of periodic payments.
        A.   lessee; lessor
        B.   leaser; leasee
        C.   lessor; leasee
        D.   leaser; lessee
        E.   lessor; lessee

2.   _____, sometimes called a service or maintenance lease, are agreements for period to period use of an asset. Maintenance and insurance are usually included in these leases.
        A.   Direct leases
        B.   Operating leases
        C.   Financial leases
        D.   Leveraged leases
        E.   Capital leases

3.   A _____ is a three-party financial lease consisting of the lessee who acquires use of the asset, the lessor who holds an equity interest in the asset, and a lender who finances the purchase of the asset by the lessor.
   A.   sale and leaseback
   B.   operating lease
   C.   leveraged lease
   D.   capital lease
   E.   direct lease

4.   Which of the following is not an advantage of leasing?
   A.   Lease agreements tend to be more flexible than loan agreements.
   B.   Leasing reduces pressures on the lessee's liquidity.
   C.   Leasing avoids some of the risk of obsolescence.
   D.   Leasing provides 100% financing.
   E.   All of the above are advantages of leasing.

5.   Which of the following is disadvantage of leasing?
   A.   Leasing is more expensive than ownership.
   B.   Earnings are more variable and EPS is lower in the early years of a lease.
   C.   Leasing provides not tax advantages over asset ownership.
   D.   Operating leases can not be cancelled without substantial penalty.
   E.   All of the above are disadvantages of leasing.

6.   Which of the following is not a reason that entrepreneurial firms give for lease financing rather than bank financing?
   A.   Less up front cash required
   B.   Lower effective interest cost of leasing over borrowing
   C.   Quicker approvals from lessors than from lenders
   D.   Fewer restrictive covenants from lessors than from lenders
   E.   All of the above are reasons entrepreneurial firms give for lease financing rather than bank financing

7.   The appropriate discount rate that a prospective lessor should use to determine the value of lease is:
   A.   the before-tax required rate of return
   B.   the after-tax cost of debt.
   C.   the after-tax required rate of return.
   D.   the before-tax cost of debt.
   E.   the cost of equity capital.

8.   If the NAL (net advantage to leasing) is positive, then:
   A.   It is cheaper for the lessee to lease an asset than to borrow and buy it.
   B.   It is cheaper for the lessee to borrow and buy an asset than to lease it.
   C.   The lessor will make a profit on the lease.

9.   Which the following would increase the NAL of an asset all other things remaining constant?
   A.   An increase in the expected salvage value of the asset.
   B.   A reduction in the after-tax lease payments.
   C.   A reduction in the initial cost of asset.
   D.   An increase in the present value of the depreciation tax shield.
   E.   All of the above changes would increase the NAL of an asset.

10.   The present value of the after-tax lease payment is computed by discounting these payments at the:
   A.   After-tax marginal cost of capital.
   B.   Cost of equity capital.
   C.   After-tax cost of equity capital.
   D.   After-tax marginal cost of debt.
   E.   After-tax required rate of return.

Answers to Multiple Choice Questions

1.	E	5.	A	9.	C
2.	B	6.	B	10.	D
3.	C	7.	C		
4.	E	8.	A		

PROBLEMS

1.   Heavy Equipment Leasing Corporation wishes to lease some new forging and grinding equipment to the New Mexico Mining Company. What lease payment should Heavy charge? The relevant information is:

   installed cost = $25,000,000.
   20 year lease with lease payments at the beginning of each year.
   straight-line depreciation (of the full $25,000,000) over 20 years to a zero salvage value.
   expected salvage value is $3,000,000 (which will be a taxable gain).
   Heavy's marginal tax rate is 40 percent.
   Heavy wishes a 12% after tax rate of return.

Solution:

Step 1: Compute the lessor's amount to be amortized
   PV of after-tax salvage
$$= 3,000,000(1-0.40)PVIF_{.12,20}$$
$$= 1,800,000(0.1037) = \$186,660$$
   PV of depreciation tax shelter
$$= 1,250,000(0.40)PVIFA_{.12,20}$$
$$= 500,000(7.4694) = \$3,734,700$$

Chapter

20

Financing with Derivatives

Derivatives are securities whose value is derived from the value of another asset. They play an important role in the management of a firm's assets and liabilities. Derivative securities can be classified into several classes including options, forward-type contracts, and swaps.

I.   An *option* is a security that gives its holder the right, but not the obligation, to buy or sell an asset at a set price during a specified time period. A wide array of securities contains option features. Some of these are:

     A.   A *call* option is an option to *buy* a particular asset whereas a *put* option is an option to *sell* it. The set price at which the option holder can buy (or sell) an asset is called the exercise price or strike price. Marketed call options exist for common stocks, Treasury bonds, foreign exchange, and many other instruments. These options are traded on organized exchanges such as the Chicago Board Options Exchange and the Chicago Mercantile Exchange.

     B.   A *convertible security* is a fixed income security with a call option on common stock. Convertible bonds and preferred stock can be exchanged for a set number of shares of common stock.

     C.   A *warrant* is a call option issued by a company on its own securities, usually on its own stock.

     D.   Firms issue *callable bonds* that have a call feature which gives the company the option to buy back the debt issue from the holders if a decline in interest rates would make the call worthwhile.

     E.   Through a *rights offering*, firms sometimes give common shareholders the option to purchase additional shares of their stock, in proportion to the shareholders' current ownership, at a price below the current market price.

II.   There are several variables that affect the value of an option.

    A.   Boundaries or limits exist to the value of a call option.

        1.   At maturity (when the option expires), if the stock price is above the exercise price:
Value of a call option at expiration = Stock price - Exercise price

        2.   Prior to maturity, a call option sells for more than this amount:
Value of a call option prior to expiration > Stock price - Exercise price

        3.   Under no conditions will an investor pay more for an option than the stock price:
Maximum value of call option = Stock price

        4.   An option cannot have negative value (such as if exercising an option when the exercise price is above the stock price) because a rational investor will simply not exercise the right to buy the stock.
Minimum value of a call option = 0

    B.   Specific variables that affect the value of a call option include:

        1.   An increase in the stock price (with the exercise price and everything else constant) will increase the value of a call option.

        2.   A higher exercise price (everything else the same) reduces the value of a call option.

        3.   The longer the time remaining until expiration the higher the option value (all other things being equal).

        4.   The higher the level of interest rates, the higher is the call option's value (all other things being equal).

        5.   The greater the volatility of the stock price, the higher is the call option value (all other things being equal).

    C.   The common stock of any firm with debt outstanding can be viewed as a call option.

        1.   In a firm with debt outstanding, the stockholders can be viewed as having sold the firm to the debtholders. The stockholders have an option to buy back the firm from the debtholders (by paying the promised debt payments).

        2.   At the time the debt is due, if the value of the firm exceeds the debt claim, the stockholders will exercise their option by paying off the debt. On the other hand, if the value of the firm is less than the debt claim, the stockholders will let their option expire by not repaying the debt (i.e., defaulting on the debt).

3.   One implication of this analysis is that risk-increasing investments that may benefit stockholders at the expense of debtholders. High payoffs benefit stockholders and low payoffs increase the probability of defaults on debt.

III.   Both debentures and preferred stock can be convertible into shares of the firm's common stock. Issuance of these securities usually represents a future issuance of common stock since ultimate conversion is anticipated.

A.   The terms of conversion are represented in the conversion price.

1.   At conversion, the convertible security is surrendered for a quantity of common stock which, when priced at the conversion price, has a total value equal to the par value of the convertible.

2.   The number of shares that can be obtained in conversion is called the conversion ratio. The conversion ratio is given by:

Conversion ratio = Par value of security/Conversion price

3.   The conversion price is higher than the stock price at the time the securities are issued. The difference is called the conversion premium.

B.   Many reasons exist for issuing convertibles:

1.   To make the fixed income security more attractive so that lower interest or dividends may be paid.

2.   To "sell" common stock in the future when the price will be higher.

3.   To allow time for investments financed with the funds from issuance of the security to begin to pay benefits before the additional common stock is used in the calculation of EPS.

4.   Relatively small, risky companies whose common stock is publicly traded are the principal issuers of convertibles. Convertibles can lessen the agency conflict between stockholders and debtholders. Since convertible owners have an equity stake in the company, they will be entitled to some of the benefits that stockholders can receive if they invest in high risk projects.

C.   Convertible securities are a cross between fixed income securities and common stock, thus, their valuation is more complex than that of simple securities.

1.   The conversion value is the value of the common stock that could be obtained in conversion. This is given by:

Conversion value = Conversion ratio x Stock price

2.   The straight-bond value or investment value of a convertible is the value it would have if it did not have the conversion feature. This is equal to the present value of its future cash flows discounted at a rate k_d which is the current yield to maturity for similar nonconvertible securities.

$$Straight\text{-}bond\ value = \sum_{t=1}^{m} \frac{Interest}{(1+k_d)^t} + \frac{Principal}{(1+k_d)^m}$$

3.   The market value is the price the security trades for in the market.

a.   The market value is usually slightly above the higher of the conversion value or the investment value.

b.   The difference between the market value and the higher of the conversion value or the investment value is the premium.

D.   Convertible securities can be converted voluntarily by investors or the issuing company can force conversion.

1.   Voluntary conversion can occur at any time prior to expiration of the conversion feature.

2.   Conversion can be forced if the issuer uses the call privilege on the security. If the conversion value is higher than the call price, investors will convert to common stock rather than have the security called.

E.   If a convertible security (or warrant) issue is exchanged for common stock, the number of common shares outstanding will increase and earnings per share usually is reduced (diluted). Companies with convertible securities and warrants outstanding must calculate EPS in two ways, primary earnings per share and fully diluted earnings per share.

IV.   A warrant is an option, issued by the firm, to purchase a specific number of shares at a specified price during the life of the warrant.

A.   Warrants are usually issued in conjunction with an issue of other securities in order to make them more attractive.

B.   Warrants are characterized by the exercise price and the expiration date.

1.   The exercise price is the price at which shares of common stock may be purchased. The exercise price is usually 10% to 30% above the market price of the common stock at the time the warrant is issued.

        2.   The expiration date is the date when the option to purchase the common stock ends. Most warrants have an expiration date 5 to 10 years after the date of issue.

C.   Warrants can usually be traded separately from the security with which they are originally issued.

D.   The exercise or expiration of warrants does not affect the security with which they were issued on the books of the firm.

E.   The primary reason for issuing warrants is to "sweeten" the security with which they are issued by allowing purchasers to participate in increases in the common stock price and to sell common stock in the future.

F.   The valuation of warrants is more complex than that of simple securities.

        1.   The basic value of a warrant is the greater of \$0 or the profit that could be made by exercising the warrant and immediately selling the stock. This is given by:

$$\begin{matrix} Formula \\ value \\ of\ a \\ warrant \end{matrix} = max\left[\$0;\ \left(\begin{matrix} Common\ stock \\ market\ price \\ per\ share \end{matrix} - \begin{matrix} Exercise \\ price \\ per\ share \end{matrix} \right) \times \begin{matrix} No.\ of\ shares \\ obtainable\ with \\ each\ warrant \end{matrix} \right]$$

        2.   The market value of a warrant usually exceeds the formula value. The difference is called the premium.

        3.   Because of the potential for price appreciation of the common stock during the life of the security, warrants carry a premium

G.   Warrants provide leverage to investors because the warrant holder can obtain the benefits of increasing stock prices for an investment in the warrant which is less than would be required for the stock.

H.   There are some similarities and differences between warrants issued as part of a fixed income security offering and convertible securities.

Similarities:

        1.   Both convertibles and warrants tend to lessen potential agency conflicts between fixed-income security holders and stockholders.

        2.   Both can result in the deferred issuance of common stock at a price higher than that prevailing at the time of the convertible or warrant issue.

3.   Both can result in savings of interest expense or preferred dividend expense for the issuing company.

Differences:

1.   The company receives additional funds when warrants are exercised, whereas no funds are received at the time convertibles are converted.

2.   The fixed-income security (with which the warrants were issued) remains on the books after the warrants are exercised. The convertible security is exchanged for common stock and is taken off the company's books.

3.   Because of the call feature, the company has more control over when convertible securities are converted than when warrants are converted.

V.   If a company's charter contains a provision for preemptive rights, then any new common stock must be sold through a rights offering. Other companies may choose to issue new equity through a rights offering rather than the underwriting procedure of a public offering.

A.   A single right attaches to each outstanding share.

B.   The ratio of outstanding shares to shares to be issued determines the number of rights required to purchase one new share.

C.   Possession of the required number of rights allows the holder to purchase one share of stock at the subscription price.

D.   To provide an incentive for stockholders to exercise their rights, the subscription price is less than the current market price.

E.   Stockholders who do not wish to exercise their rights can sell them in the open market.

F.   Like dividends, rights are subject to a shareholder of record date. As in the case of dividends, a purchaser becomes a holder of record five trading days after purchase. A stock trades "rights-on" until it goes "ex- rights." The stock goes ex-rights four days before the holder of record date.

G.   Rights have economic value.

1.   The theoretical value of a right while the stock is selling "rights-on" is given by

$$R = \frac{M_o - S}{N + 1}$$

where M_o is the rights-on price of the stock, S is the subscription price, and N is the number of rights required to purchase one share.

2. The theoretical value of a right after it is detached from the stock is given by

$$R = \frac{M_e - S}{N}$$

where M_e is the ex-rights price of the stock.

H. Rights usually trade in the market for a price greater than the theoretical value because of the potential for the price of the stock to increase before they are exercised.

VI. A financial swap is another type of a derivative security that is a contractual agreement between 2 parties (usually financial institutions or businesses) to make periodic payments to each other. Interest rate swaps and currency swaps are the 2 major types of swaps.

A. Interest rate swaps can be used to protect financial institutions and businesses against fluctuations in interest rates.

B. A basic example of interest rate swap is one in which a party seeks to exchange floating rate interest payments for fixed interest rate payments or vice-versa. Consider an example of a finance company with floating rate debt that wants to protect itself from rising rates. The finance company can reduce its risk by undertaking the following swap:

1. The finance company can enter into a swap contract with another company that agrees to pay interest costs in excess of a specified rate for a given period of time.

2. If interest rate rises, the finance company will rising payments from the swap agreement to cover its losses on the original floating rate debt.

Many financial institutions act as intermediaries in arranging swaps.

TRUE AND FALSE QUESTIONS

Agree with each of the statements or **reject** it and modify it so that it is acceptable.

1. A put option is a security that gives its holder the right to buy an asset at a set price during a specified time period.

2. At expiration, a call option will sell for (1) the excess of the stock price over the exercise price or (2) zero, whichever is greater.

3. Options frequently have negative value.

4. An increase in the stock price increases the value of a call option (all else the same).

5.   An increase in the stock price volatility increases the value of a call option on the stock (all else the same).

6.   Convertible features are available only on corporate bonds.

7.   The number of debentures required to obtain one share of stock is called the conversion ratio.

8.   At the time of issue, the conversion value is usually less than the market price of the stock to ensure that conversion will occur.

9.   The conversion value represents a floor for the price of the convertible security.

10.   A firm often calls a convertible security in order to prevent it from being converted.

11.   The market price of a convertible is usually slightly less than the lesser of the conversion value or the investment value.

12.   When a warrant is exercised, the security with which it was issued is cancelled and removed from the books of the company.

13.   Warrants are attractive to investors because they provide leverage.

14.   Primary earnings per share is the earnings available if the dividend on a convertible preferred is ignored.

15.   Warrants are traded on the Chicago Board Options Exchange.

16.   Other things equal, the value of a right attached to the stock is identical to the value of a right that is detached from the stock.

17.   Swaps are used to protect financial institutions and businesses against fluctuations in interest rates.

Answers to True and False Questions

1.   A <u>call</u> option is a security that gives its holder the right to buy an asset at a set price during a specified time period.
2.   True.
3.   Options can be worthless, but they cannot have negative value because the holder will not exercise options if it is not in the investor's best interests to do so.
4.   True.
5.   True.
6.   Both debentures and preferred stock exist that can be convertible into shares of the firm's common stock.

7.   The number of shares of stock obtainable from one debenture is called the conversion ratio.

8.   At the time of issue, the conversion value is usually less than the investment (bond) value of the security. This ensures that the funds are available for use for a while before the number of c mon shares will increase.

9.   The investment (bond) value represents a floor for the price of the convertible security.

10.   A firm often calls a convertible security in order to force holders to convert it.

11.   The market price of a convertible is usually greater than the higher of the conversion value or the investment value.

12.   Exercise of a warrant has no effect on the security with which it was issued.

13.   True.

14.   Primary earnings per share is the earnings available to common stock after preferred dividends are considered. This ignores the potential increase in the number of shares from exercise of warrants and convertibles.

15.   Warrants are traded on the stock exchanges. Warrants, issued by the firm, are not the same as options traded on the CBOE which are not issued by the firm and cannot result in an increase in the number of common shares outstanding.

16.   True. (The formulas differ because of the fact that the stock price right-on includes the value of the right. Dividing by N+1 prevents double counting of the value of the right.)

17.   True.

MULTIPLE CHOICE QUESTIONS

1.   A call option gives the holder of the option the right to _____ the asset, where a put gives the holder the right to _____ the asset.
        A.   sell; buy
        B.   buy; sell
        C.   buy; buy
        D.   sell; sell

2.   _____ give the issuing company the right to buy back the security issue from the holder.
        A.   Convertible securities
        B.   Warrants
        C.   Callable securities
        D.   Rights offerings
        E.   Call options

3.   At maturity of a call option, if the asset price is greater than the exercise price, then the value of the call option is equal to:
        A: Zero.
        B.   The value of the underlying asset.
        C.   The exercise price of the option.
        D.   The exercise price of the option less the underlying asset value.
        E.   The underlying asset value less the exercise price of the option.

4. Which of the following will reduce the value of a option all other things constant?
   A. An increase in the value of the underlying asset
   B. An increase in time remaining until the option matures.
   C. An increase in the general level of interest rates.
   D. An increase in the exercise price of the option
   E. An increase in the volatility of the underlying asset's value.

5. Which of the following is not a viable motive for issuing convertible securities?
   A. To minimize underwriting costs.
   B. To sell common stock in the future.
   C. To allow time for investments financed with the funds from issuance of the security to begin to pay benefits before the additional common stock is used in the calculation of EPS.
   D. To reduce agency conflicts between stockholders and bondholders.
   E. To lower interest rates and dividends may be paid.

6. The conversion price of a convertible security is higher than the market value of the common stock at the time of original issue. The difference is called the:
   A. Conversion ratio.
   B. Conversion premium.
   C. Conversion value.
   D. Investment value.
   E. Par value.

7. The primary motive for a firm to issue warrants is:
   A. To add liquidity to the market for their common stock.
   B. To provide an additional incentive to the firm's management team.
   C. To avoid potential dilution of EPS by the issuance of other convertible securities.
   D. To make the accompanying securities more attractive to investors.
   E. To reduce the agency conflicts between the debtholders and shareholders.

8. If a convertible security's conversion value exceeds the security's call price, the firm can force conversion by:
   A. Issuing new common stock.
   B. Rendering a tender offer to the security holders.
   C. Exercising the security's call feature.
   D. Converting the outstanding security into subordinated debentures.
   E. Evoking the conversion cause in the security's indenture.

9. Warrants differ from convertible securities in that:
   A. Warrants reduce the agency conflicts between shareholders and debtholders where convertible securities do not.
   B. Warrants reduce the interest or dividend expense associated with a security issue where convertible securities do not.
   C. Warrants defer the ultimate issuance of common stock where convertible securities do not.
   D. The firm receives additional funds when warrants are exercised where no additional funds are received by the firm with convertible securities.

10.   Which of the following statements is not true concerning rights offerings?
    A.   A single right attaches to each outstanding share.
    B.   Rights cannot be sold or transferred from the shareholder of record
    C.   The rights offering's subscription price is less than the current market price.
    D.   Rights have economic value.
    E.   All of the above are true.

Answers to Multiple Choice Questions

1.	B	5.	A	9.	D
2.	C	6.	B	10.	B
3.	E	7.	D		
4.	D	8.	C		

PROBLEMS

1.   Desktop.com has an issue of convertible debentures outstanding. Par value is $1,000 and the conversion price is $50. The coupon interest rate is 6% paid annually. The bonds mature in 10 years and are callable at 106. The company has a tax rate of 40%.

    a.   If the company's stock is selling at $40, calculate the conversion value.

    b.   Assume that similar straight debt yields 9%. Calculate the investment value of the convertible.

    c.   What should the approximate market value of the convertible be?

    d.   What is the minimum stock price at which the company should call the debentures and force conversion?

    Solution:

    a.   Conversion value = stock price x (par value/conversion price)
            Conversion value = 40 x (1000/50) = $800

    b.   Investment value = price as straight bond
            Investment value = 60 x $PVIFA_{0.09,10}$ + 1000 x $PVIF_{0.09,10}$
            Investment value = 50(6.4177) + 1000(0.4224) = $743.29

    c.   The convertible should be selling for slightly more than the higher of the conversion value or the investment value. It should be selling for somewhat more than $800.00.

d.   In order to force conversion, the stock price must be high enough that the conversion value exceeds the call value. Investors are indifferent if conversion value equals call value.

(stock price)(conversion ratio) = call value

(stock price)(par value/conversion price) = call value

(stock price)(1000/50) = $1060

(stock price)(20) = $1060

stock price = $53

If the debenture is called when the stock price is greater than $53 per share, conversion should occur.

2.   The Technology Company has warrants outstanding. Each warrant entitles the holder to purchase two shares of the company's common stock at an exercise price of $25 per share. The current market price of the warrant is $16 and the price of the common is $32. What is the premium on the warrant?

Solution:

The formula value of the warrant is the greater of $0 or

(stock price - exercise price)(shares per warrant) = (32-25)(2) = $14

The premium is the difference between the market price of the warrant and its formula value.

Warrant premium = $16 - $14 = $2

3.   Your firm is considering issuing $20 million of convertible debentures. The conversion price is $50 per share. The present capital structure appears as follows.

Long-term debt	$100 million
Common stock ($5 par)	50 million
Additional paid-in capital	100 million
Retained earnings	200 million

a.   Show the capital structure if the convertibles are issued.

b.   Show the capital structure after conversion takes place.

Solution:

a.

Long-term debt	$120 million
Common stock ($5 par) (10 million shares)	50 million
Additional paid-in capital	100 million
Retained Earnings	200 million

b.

Long-term debt	$100 million
Common stock ($5 par) (10.4 million shares)	52 million
Additional paid-in capital	118 million
Retained earnings	200 million

When the convertible debentures have been converted to common stock, the par value is added to the common stock account and the remainder to the additional paid-in capital. The debt is cancelled.

4. When a company's stock was trading at $12, outstanding warrants on the stock were trading at $3. When the stock was trading at $15, the warrants were trading at $6. Calculate the percentage returns to an investor who bought the stock at $12 and sold at $15 and the returns to another investor who traded in the warrants at the same time.

Solution:

The percentage return on the stock is $(15 - 12)/12 = 25\%$.

The percentage return on the warrants is $(6 - 3)/3 = 100\%$.

5. An issue of 8% convertible debentures is issued at par and will mature in 30 years. The conversion ratio is 10. Conversion is expected to occur in 10 years when the stock price is $130. The company has a 40% tax rate. Find the component cost of capital. (Hint: Try 7%.)

Solution:

The after-tax cost of capital associated with a convertible is found by using the relation:

$$\text{Issue price} = (\text{coupon interest})(1 - T)(PVIFA_{r,n}) + (CV_n)(PVIF_{r,n})$$

where r is the after-tax cost of capital, n is the expected number of years until conversion, and CV_n is the expected conversion value in n years. r is found by trial and error. In the present problem we have:

$$1000 = (80)(.6)(PVIFA_{r,10}) + (10)(130)(PVIF_{r,10})$$

Trying 7% we get

$$\$998 = (80)(.6)(7.024) + (10)(130)(.508)$$

6.   The Dawson Trail Gold Company is issuing new common stock through a rights offering. The stock is selling for $45 per share. The subscription price is $42. Five rights are needed to purchase one share.

    a.   Calculate the theoretical value of the right while the stock is selling rights-on.

    b.   Other things equal, what should the price of the stock be immediately after going ex-rights?

    c.   Calculate the value of the right after the stock goes ex- rights.

    d.   If the stock goes back to $45, find the ex-rights value.

Solution:

a.

$$R = \frac{M_o - S}{N + 1} = \frac{45 - 42}{5 + 1} = \$.50$$

b.   Other things equal, the price of the stock should decline by the value of the right. The new price should be $44.50.

c.

$$R = \frac{M_e - S}{N} = \frac{44.50 - 42}{5} = \$.50$$

d.   The formula is the same as in part c, but the numbers are:

$$R = \frac{M_e - S}{N} = \frac{45 - 42}{5} = \$.60$$

7.   Rework problem 1(a),(b) using the Excel template for convertible bond valuation (Convsec). The results are as follows:

Valuation Of Convertible Bonds	
Par Value Of Bond	$1,000.00
Call or Sale Value of Bond	$1,000.00
Annual Coupon Rate	5.00%
Coupon Periods Per Year	1
Years To Maturity	10
Required Rate Of Return	8.00%
Conversion Price	$40.00
Market Value Of Firm's Common Stock	$30.00
Current Market Price Of Convertible Bond	$0.00
Stock/Bond Conversion Ratio	25
Conversion Value	$750.00
Straight Bond Value	$798.70
Minimum Market Value Of Convertible Bond	$798.70

Chapter

21

International Financial Management

This chapter continues the discussion of international finance introduced in Chapter 2. In this chapter we discuss factors that determine exchange rates, look at ways to forecast future exchange rates, and consider different aspects of foreign exchange risk and how to manage it.

I.   Exchange rates between currencies fluctuate over time, reflecting supply and demand considerations for the currencies.

   A.   The demand for a currency (like the British pound) comes from foreign buyers who must pay for their purchases from Britain, foreign investors who desire to make investments in Britain, and from speculators. The supply of a currency (like the pound) comes from British importers who must sell pounds to pay for their imports, Britains who wish to invest abroad, and speculators.

      1.   Exchange rates are affected by economic and political conditions that affect the demand and supply for a country's currency.

      2.   Government policies that limit imports (tariffs and quotas) and restrictions on foreign exchange transactions tend to reduce the supply of that country's currency on the foreign exchange market.

      3.   Political stability affects the risks perceived by foreign investors and companies that do business in a country.

   B.   There is a close relationship between the interest rates in two countries and the forward exchange rate premium or discount. This is due to *covered interest arbitrage* and *interest rate parity*.

      1.   Suppose that the interest rate is 5% in the US and 10% in Britain. As long as the forward premium, (F-S)/S, is less than 5%, you can make risk-free profits by borrowing in the US at 5%, buying pounds in the spot market, investing at 10% in

341

Britain, and selling pounds in the forward market. This process is called covered interest arbitrage.

2.   The effect of these covered arbitrage transactions is to create a relationship called *interest rate parity* (IRP). The theory of IRP states that the annual percentage forward premium for a currency is equal to the approximate difference in interest rates prevailing between the two countries. The exact relationship is:

$$\left(\frac{F - S_0}{S_0} \right) = \left(\frac{i_h - i_f}{1 + i_f} \right)$$

where i_h is the home (U.S) interest rate, i_f is the comparable foreign (British) interest rate, F is the direct quote forward rate, and S_0 is the direct quote spot rate. The interest rate must be for the same number of days as the forward rate. If interest rate parity does not hold, arbitrage opportunities exist.

The equation above can be rewritten as:

$$\frac{F}{S_0} = \left(\frac{1 + i_h}{1 + i_f} \right).$$

An approximation of the IRP relationship is:

$$\left(\frac{F - S_0}{S_0} \right) \approx \left(i_h - i_f \right)$$

When interest rate parity exists, differences in interest rates between two countries will be offset by the difference in forward and spot exchange rates.

C.   If there are no significant costs or other barriers associated with moving goods and services between markets, the price of each product should be the same in each market. In economics, this is known as the *law of one price*. Across countries, the law of one price says that prices should be the same across countries, after making an appropriate exchange rate conversion. This condition is called purchasing power parity.

1.   Absolute purchasing power parity does not hold because of the costs of moving goods and services and because of tariffs and other trade barriers.

2.   Relative purchasing power parity (PPP) states that changes in the differential rates of inflation between two countries will be offset by equal, but opposite changes in the expected future spot exchange rate. The algebraic relationship is:

$$\left(\frac{S_1 - S_0}{S_0}\right) = \left(\frac{\pi_h - \pi_f}{1 + \pi_f}\right)$$

where S_1 is the expected future spot rate (direct quote), S_0 is the current spot rate (direct quote), p_h is the expected home country (U.S.) inflation rate, and p_f is the expected foreign country inflation rate.

This equation can also be written as

$$\left(\frac{S_1}{S_0}\right) = \left(\frac{1 + \pi_h}{1 + \pi_f}\right).$$

3. PPP infers that if a country (such as the U.S.) has a lower inflation rate than its trading partners, then its currency (the dollar) should increase in value relative to its trading partners.

4. Empirical tests of PPP indicate that PPP holds up fairly well over long periods, but is a mediocre predictor of short-term currency value changes.

D. The expectations theory of forward exchange rates indicates that the forward rate should be an unbiased estimate of expected future spot rates.

$$F = S_1$$

The theory does not mean that the forward rate will always equal the future spot rate, but simply that it is an unbiased estimate that is good on average. The theory also does not incorporate risk.

E. The final relationship covered is the international Fisher effect, which states that differences in interest rates between two countries should be offset by equal but opposite changes in the future spot exchange rate.

1. The Fisher effect (domestic) says that nominal interest rates are based on the real interest rate plus the effect of expected inflation:
$$(1 + i) = (1 + i_R)(1 + \pi)$$
where i is the nominal rate of interest, i_R is the real rate of return, and p is the expected inflation rate. This equation is also written as
$$i = i_R + \pi + i_R \pi$$

2. If real rates of return vary across countries, capital should flow to those countries with the highest real returns. In the absence of government interference and holding risk constant, the process of arbitrage should eventually cause equal real rates of return across countries.

3.   If real rates of return are equal across countries, the international Fisher effect states that differences in interest rates between two countries should be offset by equal but opposite changes in the future spot exchange rate:

$$\left(\frac{S_1 - S_0}{S_0}\right) = \left(\frac{i_h - i_f}{1 + i_f}\right)$$

or

$$\left(\frac{S_1}{S_0}\right) = \left(\frac{1 + i_h}{1 + i_f}\right).$$

E.   In general, exchange rates fluctuate over time in response to changing supply and demand. Economic and political conditions change the supply and demand for a country's currency. Differential inflation rates and interest rates affect both spot rates and forward rates.

II.   Foreign exchange risk occurs whenever a portion of the cash flows expected to be received by a company are denominated in foreign currencies. There are three primary categories of foreign exchange risk that multinational firms must consider. These are (1) transaction exposure (short-term), (2) economic (or operating) exposure (long-term), and (3) translation (accounting) exposure. The value of a contract denominated in a foreign currency (either a future inflow or outflow) changes due to a change in the exchange rate. International companies can manage foreign exchange risk by hedging.

A.   In foreign trade, firms have transaction exposure. For example, a U.S. business may purchase goods from a Japanese supplier and the transaction is stated in Japanese Yen. The U.S. firm is exposed to exchange rate risk if the value of the Yen changes. For short-term contracts, the firm can protect itself in two ways:

1.   Executing a contract in the forward exchange market or in the foreign exchange futures market is the first method to manage exchange rate risk. In the example, the U. S. business could buy Japanese Yen in the forward exchange market. In contrast to forward contracts, futures contracts are standardized with respect to size and delivery dates and traded on organized exchanges.

2.   The second technique is called a money market hedge. The U.S. firm could borrow funds from its bank, exchange them for Japanese yen in the spot market, and invest the Yen in interest-bearing Japanese securities that mature on the date payment is due to the Japanese supplier.

B.   Economic (or operating) exposure refers to changes in a firm's operating cash flows (and hence the firm's value) that happens because of *real* rather than *nominal* changes in exchange rates.

1. Changes in real exchange rates change the competitiveness of firms in different countries.

2. Multinational firms can manage the impact of real changes in exchange rates in several ways:
    - Shift production from high-cost plants to low-cost plants.
    - Increase productivity (with new labor saving technologies, flexible manufacturing systems, etc.).
    - Outsource the supply of many of the components needed to produce your product to lower-cost locations.
    - Increase product differentiation to reduce the price sensitivity of your customers.
    - Enter markets with strong currencies and reduce involvement in competitive markets with weak currencies.

C. Firms with direct investments in foreign subsidiaries face exchange rate risk in the form of translation exposure.

    1. Accounting procedures define how the balance sheets of foreign subsidiaries are translated into the parent company's balance sheet. Current accounting standards are set forth in *Statement of Financial Accounting Standards Number 52.* Its main provisions are:

        a. Current assets (unless covered by forward exchange contracts) and fixed assets are translated into dollars at the rate of exchange prevailing on the date of the balance sheet.

        b. Current and long-term liabilities payable in a foreign currency are translated into dollars at the rate of exchange prevailing on the date of the balance sheet.

        c. Income statement items are translated at either the rate of exchange on the date of each transaction or at a weighted average of the exchange rates for the period of the income statement.

        d. Equity accounts, including common stock and contributed capital in excess of par value, are translated at historical rates.

        e. Gains and losses are reported on the balance sheet as a separate adjustment to parent's stockholders' equity in an account called "cumulative foreign currency translation adjustments." Gains and losses are not recognized on the income statement until the parent's investment in the foreign subsidiary is sold or liquidated.

    2. If a foreign subsidiary's assets are greater than its liabilities, foreign currency translation losses will occur if the exchange rate decreases.

3. A hedge is an offsetting transaction designed to reduce or avoid risk. A company can hedge against economic and translation exposure by financing its foreign assets with debt denominated in the same currency.

4. A multinational company can also reduce its exchange risk (as well as the risk of expropriation or nationalization of its assets by a foreign country) by developing a diversified portfolio of foreign investments.

III. An ethical issue confronts U.S. firms that are prohibited from paying bribes to obtain business abroad. The Foreign Corrupt Practices Act makes bribes in many forms illegal. However, in many countries, bribes are not only permitted, but expected.

TRUE AND FALSE QUESTIONS

Agree with each of the statements or **reject** it and modify it so that it is acceptable.

1. If the interest rate is greater in the United States than in Switzerland, the spot rate will be greater than the forward rate (in dollars per Swiss franc).

2. If you owe a debt in a foreign currency (such as Canadian dollars) in three months, you can protect yourself from exchange rate risk by buying Canadian dollars in the forward exchange market.

3. Borrowing in a foreign country to help finance an investment in that country is one way a multinational company can reduce exchange rate risk.

4. Assume a U.S. company has a subsidiary in a foreign country. If the foreign subsidiary has more foreign denominated assets than liabilities, a decrease in the exchange rate (the direct quote, dollars per unit of the foreign currency) will result in translation losses.

5. The theory of interest rate parity states that the percentage differential between the spot and forward rate for a currency is equal to the approximate difference in the interest rates in the two countries over the same time horizon.

6. The current spot rate is considered to be an unbiased estimator of the future spot currency rate.

7. The theory of relative purchasing power parity states that in comparison to a period when exchange rates between two countries are in equilibrium, changes in differential rates of inflation between the countries will be offset by equal, but opposite changes in the future spot currency rate.

8. The Fisher effect states that real interest rates are approximately equal to the sum of the nominal interest rate and the expected inflation rate.

9.   The international Fisher effect theory states that differences in interest rates between two countries should be offset by equal, but opposite changes in the future spot rate.

10.   A hedge is a special international transaction that often is referred to as "greenmail."

11.   In the Eurocurrency market, Eurodollar loans are priced against a benchmark called the American Regulated Bank Offer Rate, or ARBOR.

Answers to True and False Questions

1.   If the interest rate is greater in the United States than in Switzerland, the spot rate will be <u>less</u> than the forward rate (in dollars per Swiss franc).
2.   True.
3.   True.
4.   True.
5.   True.
6.   True.
7.   True.
8.   The Fisher effect states that the nominal interest rate is approximately equal to the sum of the real interest rate and the expected inflation rate.
9.   True.
10.   A hedge is simply an offsetting transaction designed to reduce or avoid risk.
11.   In the Eurocurrency market, Eurocurrency loans are priced against a benchmark called the London interbank offer rate, or LIBOR.

MULTIPLE CHOICE QUESTIONS

1.   The demand for a currency arises from _____ where the supply of currency comes from _____.

A.   The rate of growth in the country's GDP; the rate of monetary expansion.
B.   The demand for the country's exports; the rate of monetary expansion.
C.   The demand for the country's imports; the rate of growth in the country's GDP.
D.   The demand for the country's imports; the demand for the country's exports.
E.   The demand for the country's exports; the demand for the country's imports.

2.   Interest Rate Parity (IRP) suggests that the interest rate differential between two countries should be appropriately equal to the:
A.   Inflation rate differential.
B.   Forward discount or premium on the exchange rate.
C.   Expected change in the exchange rate value.
D.   Real exchange rate differential.
E.   Real exchange rate.

3.   If there are no significant costs or other barriers associated with moving goods and services between markets, the price of each product should be the same in each market. In economics, this is known as _____.

A.   The law of one price.
B.   The Same Price Principle.
C.   The International Fisher Effect.
D.   Covered interest arbitrage.
E.   The Price Equalization Principle.

4.   If real rates of return are equal across countries, the international Fisher effect states that differences in interest rates between two countries should be offset by changes in:

A.   The current spot exchange rate.
B.   The future spot exchange rate
C.   The expected inflation rate differentials.
D.   The current interest rate differentials.
E.   The forward exchange rate.

5.   A U.S. computer manufacturer faces stiff competition from Thai competition. If the Thai Bhat depreciates, the dollar price of the foreign producer's merchandise will be significantly lower. This is an example of _____ exposure.

A.   Transaction
B.   Translation
C.   Economic

6.   According to relative purchasing power parity, if Country A experiences higher inflation than does Country B, then:

A.   Country A should have higher interest rates than Country B.
B.   Country A's currency should sell at a forward discount to Country B's currency.
C.   Country A's currency should depreciate relative to Country B's currency.
D.   Country A should have a lower real rate of return on investments than Country B.
E.   Country A should expect slower economic growth than Country B.

7.   The management of multinational manufacturer is concerned about a real depreciation in the US dollar. Which of the following would <u>not</u> be an effective means of hedging this exposure?

A.   Shift production out of the US.
B.   Increase productivity of existing production facilities.
C.   Outsource the supply of components to low-cost producers.
D.   Increase product differentiation.

8.   A U.S. steel producer has a direct investment in a steel mill in Zaire. The entire output of the mill in Zaire is sold in Zaire. Local markets provide all raw material and labor. All profits are reinvested in new plant and equipment; yet, the firm has _____ exposure.

A.   Transaction
B.   Translation
C.   Economic

9. Under FASB 52, current assets and fixed assets of non-domestic operations must be translated into the parent's financial statements at:
   A. The historical exchange rate.
   B. The weighted average exchange rate.
   C. The current exchange rate.

10. Under FASB 52, exchange rate losses arising from translation of foreign operations into the home currency are:
    A. ignored.
    B. deducted from net income.
    C. not recognized until disposal of the asset.
    D. reported in the equity section of the balance sheet.
    E. offset by other income.

Answers to Multiple Choice Questions

1.	E	5.	C	9.	C
2.	B	6.	C	10.	D
3.	A	7.	A		
4.	B	8	B		

PROBLEMS

1. The annualized interest rate in the U.S. is 5.5% and the interest rate in Switzerland is 3.5%. The spot rate is $0.6247 per Swiss Franc. If interest rate parity holds, what should be the 90-day forward rate for Swiss Francs?

Solution:

Use the formula

$$\left(\frac{F - S_0}{S_0}\right) = \left(\frac{i_h - i_f}{1 + i_f}\right)$$

The 90-day interest rate in the U.S. is 5.5%(90/360) = 1.375% and the 90-day rate in Switzerland is 3.5%(90/360) = 0.875%. Substituting into the interest rate parity equation :

$$\frac{F - 0.6247}{0.6247} = \frac{.01375 - .00875}{1 + .00875}$$

Solve this for the Forward rate to get:

Forward rate = $0.6278 per Swiss Franc.

The forward rate is above the spot rate because the U.S. interest rate exceeds the interest rate in Switzerland.
The IRPT equation was also stated in another form:

$$\frac{F}{S_0} = \left(\frac{1 + i_h}{1 + i_f}\right).$$

Using this equation for the forward rate gives us:

$$\frac{F}{0.6247} = \frac{1.01375}{1.00875}$$

This gives the same answer, the forward rate F = 0.6278.

2.   Ace Technologies has sold some computer chips to a Japanese firm and will be paid 400,000,000 yen in 90 days. The spot rate is 105.65 yen per dollar and the 90-day forward rate is 104.10 yen per dollar.

a.   If Paul sells the yen in the forward exchange market, how many dollars will he receive?

b.   On the other hand, suppose Paul waits and sells the yen in the spot market 90 days from now. What will his receipt be worth in dollars if the spot rate increases 3%? Decreases 3%?

Solution:

a.   Receipt in dollars = 400,000,000 yen/104.10 yen per dollar
               = $3,842,459

b.   3% increase in spot rate: 105.65(1.03) = 108.82

Receipt in dollars = 400,000,000 yen/108.82 yen per dollar
               = $3,675,795

3% decrease in spot rate: 105.65(.97) = 102.48

Receipt in dollars = 400,000,000 yen/102.48 yen per dollar
               = $3,903.201

3.   The spot rate on Swiss Francs is 0.6073 dollars per franc and the 180-day futures exchange rate is 0.6280 dollars per franc. Suppose you can earn 5% in 180 days in the United States and 3% in 180 days in Switzerland. With $1,000,000, should you invest in the U.S. or in Switzerland (ignore taxes and any applicable laws)?

Solution:

In the U.S. in 180 days, your investment earns 5%.

Terminal wealth = 1,000,000(1 + .05) = $1,050,000

In Switzerland, sell your dollars for francs in the spot market, calculate your terminal wealth in francs at 3%, and sell your francs for dollars in the futures market.

In the spot market, the price per franc is .6073, so buy 1,000,000/.6073 = 1,646,633 francs

Terminal value (francs) = 1,646,633(1 + .03) = 1,696,032 francs

Convert to dollars in 180-day futures.

Terminal wealth = 1,696,032(.6280) = $1,065,108

Even though the interest rate is lower in Switzerland, you earn more there because the Swiss Franc is expected to grow in value at an annual rate of about 3.4% relative to the dollar, which more than offsets the 2% interest rate differential.

4.   In Sweden, the real interest rate is 2.0% and the expected inflation rate is 4.8%. What should be the nominal interest rate according to the Fisher effect?

Solution:

$$(1 + i) = (1 + i_R)(1 + \pi)$$

$$(1 + i) = (1.02)(1.048) = 1.06896$$

Solve this relationship for i, the nominal interest rate.
The nominal interest rate is 6.896%.

The alternate equation for i is

$$i = i_R + \pi + i_R \pi$$

$$i = .02 + .048 + .02(.048) = .06896 = 6.896\%$$

5.   The spot rate for Brazilian Real is now $0.9123 per Real. The expected inflation rate for the U.S. over the next year is 3.5% and the expected inflation rate in Brazil is 9% over the same period. Use the concept of relative purchasing power parity (PPP) to forecast the expected spot rate in one year.

Solution:

There are two equivalent equations that will give us an exact forecast. The first is:

$$\left(\frac{S_1 - S_0}{S_0} \right) = \left(\frac{\pi_h - \pi_f}{1 + \pi_f} \right)$$

Substituting into this equation:

$$\left(\frac{S_1 - 0.9123}{0.9123} \right) = \left(\frac{0.035 - 0.09}{1.09} \right)$$

which gives an expected spot rate of $S_1 = \$.86627$ per Real.

The other equation for PPP is

$$\left(\frac{S_1}{S_0} \right) = \left(\frac{1 + \pi_h}{1 + \pi_f} \right).$$

Putting the values for the current spot rate and inflation rates into this equation gives us:

$$\left(\frac{S_1}{0.9123} \right) = \left(\frac{1.035}{1.09} \right).$$

The expected spot rate is $0.86627 per Real.

6.   The current spot rate for Canadian dollars is $0.7200 per Canadian dollar. If the one year interest rate in the U.S. is 6% and in Canada is 8%, what is the expected spot rate one year from now. Use the concept of the international Fisher effect (IFE) to obtain your answer.

Solution:

There are two equivalent formulas that will give an exact answer. The first is:

$$\left(\frac{S_1 - S_0}{S_0} \right) = \left(\frac{i_h - i_f}{1 + i_f} \right)$$

Substituting in the values for this problem gives us

$$\left(\frac{S_1 - 0.7200}{0.7200}\right) = \left(\frac{.06 - .08}{1.08}\right)$$

Solving for S_1 results in an expected spot rate of $0.7067.

The other equation you can use is

$$\left(\frac{S_1}{S_0}\right) = \left(\frac{1 + i_h}{1 + i_f}\right).$$

Substituting into this equation gives us

$$\left(\frac{S_1}{0.7200}\right) = \left(\frac{1.06}{1.08}\right).$$

This gives us the same expected spot rate of $0.7067 per Canadian dollar.

Chapter

22

Corporate Restructuring

Corporate restructuring covers a broad array of activities that include changes in ownership, asset structure and/or capital structure of a company. This chapter covers two types of restructurings—mergers and business failures.

I.   Businesses may grow externally by acquiring or combining with other businesses. When two companies combine, the shares of the acquired company are purchased by the acquiring company.

     A.   There are several legal types of combinations.

          1.   A *merger* is a combination of two (or more) companies in which the surviving company continues to operate under its own name and the other company (or companies) legally ceases to exist.

          2.   A *consolidation* is a combination in which the combining companies are dissolved legally and a new company is formed.

          3.   The term acquisition is synonymous with merger.

     B.   Mergers can also be categorized as vertical, horizontal, or conglomerate mergers.

          1.   A *vertical merger* is between companies that may have a buyer-seller relationship with each other.

          2.   A *horizontal merger* is a combination between companies that compete directly with each other.

          3.   A *conglomerate merger* is a combination in which the companies neither compete with each other nor have a buyer-seller relationship.

C.   A merger may be completed through a stock purchase or an asset purchase.

    1.   In a stock purchase, the acquiring company buys the stock of the target company and assumes its liabilities.

    2.   In an asset purchase, the acquiring company buys some (or all) of the assets of the target company and does not assume any of its liabilities.

D.   One form of business combination is the *holding company* in which the acquiring company purchases all or a controlling block of another company's shares. The companies then become affiliated, with the acquiring company becoming the holding company in a parent-subsidiary relationship.

E.   A *joint venture* is a business combination in which two unaffiliated companies contribute to a company formed to engage in some business activity.

F.   In a *leveraged buyout* (LBO), a buyer borrows a large amount of the purchase price to buy a company or division of a company. The LBO of a publicly held company is sometimes referred to as *going private* because the entire equity of the company is purchased by a small group of investors and is no longer publicly traded.

G.   Divestitures and restructurings often accompany mergers.

    1.   In a *divestiture*, part of the company can be sold for cash. Or, part of the company can be divested through a *spinoff* where shares in the divested company are distributed on a pro rata basis to the shareholders of the parent company. Another technique is an *equity carve-out* where shares in a subsidiary or division are sold directly to the public, with the parent company usually retaining a controlling interest in the shares outstanding.

    2.   In an *operational restructuring*, the company changes the asset side of the balance sheet. In a *financial restructuring*, the company changes its capital structure.

H.   There may be a friendly agreement between two merging companies. If not, the acquiring company may make a *tender offer* to purchase the common stock of the merger candidate. The tender offer price must offer a premium over the target's market price to induce the target's shareholders to sell.

I.   Several reasons have been advanced for the increased corporate restructuring in recent years.

    1.   The failure of internal control mechanisms to prevent unproductive investment and organizational inefficiencies allows acquirers to pay large premiums over the current market values of firms.

2.   Large investors have taken an active role in setting the strategic direction and monitoring the performance of companies. In some cases, they have given an equity position to managers to encourage these changes.

3.   There was ready availability of credit (junk bonds) to finance restructurings.

4.   A long economic expansion increased the revenues and asset values of acquired companies, allowing acquirers to sell off unwanted assets and to meet their debt obligations.

J.   Many companies have undertaken anti-takeover measures (also known as shark repellents) to discourage unfriendly takeover attempts.

1.   One such measure is staggering the terms of the board of directors so that it may take several years to replace the entire board.

2.   Key executives may be given "golden parachute" contracts in which they receive expensive benefits in the event of a merger.

3.   A supermajority rule requires a supermajority of the shares (e.g., 80%) to approve a takeover proposal.

4.   Firms may issue "poison pill" securities that become exercisable when an unfriendly bidder obtains control of a certain percentage of the company's shares. Exercising the poison pill may make the acquisition very expensive to the bidder.

5.   In an unfriendly takeover attempt, the management of the target company might attempt a friendly merger with another company (the "white knight").

K.   Once an unfriendly takeover attempt has been initiated, the target company's management has other anti-takeover measures that it can employ to deter the takeover.

1.   The target firm management can find another more friendly company ("White Knight"), to make a counter offer for the firm.

2.   The target management can attempt to negotiate with the bidding party for a "standstill" agreement limiting the bidder's holdings in the target firm, usually in exchange for some concessions.

3.   The target management can undertake a "pac-man" defense and make a bid for the bidder.

4.   Engage in litigation to delay the takeover attempt.

5.   The target management can engage in asset and/or liability restructuring such as selling important assets or loading up on debt to repurchase stock and make itself less desirable to the bidder.

6.   The target firm can engage in "greenmail" by buying back the bidder's shares in the target firm at a premium.

L.   There are several reasons a company might seek external growth through mergers.

    1.   It may be less expensive to buy needed assets by acquiring a firm that has them than to purchase the assets directly.

    2.   Economies of scale sometimes result from a horizontal merger. Synergy exists if the net income of the combined firms exceeds the sum of the net incomes before merger.

    3.   The acquiring firm in a vertical merger may wish to assure the availability of raw materials or end-product markets.

    4.   More rapid growth is frequently possible through acquisitions than through internal growth.

    5.   The firm's management may desire greater diversification.

    6.   A firm that has suffered losses and has a tax-loss carryforward may wish to merge with a profitable firm to use the tax-loss carryforwards.

M.   Two different methods of accounting for mergers are employed: the purchase method and the pooling-of-interests method.

    1.   In the purchase method, the total value paid or exchanged by the acquiring firm is recorded on the books. Tangible assets are recorded at their fair market value and any excess paid beyond this is recorded as goodwill ("investment in consolidated subsidiaries in excess of net assets at date of acquisition, less amortization").

    2.   In the pooling-of-interests, the acquired company's assets are recorded in the acquiring company's books at their former book value. Thus, no goodwill accounts are created.

    3.   Since goodwill must be amortized (like a depreciation charge), reported net income is higher using the pooling-of-interests method. Furthermore, since amortization of goodwill is not a tax-deductible expense, it is deducted from net income after taxes.

N.   Taxes are affected by how an acquired company's shareholders are paid for their shares.

    1.   Merger transactions that are effected through the use of voting equity securities are tax-free.

    2.   If the acquired company's shareholders are paid cash or non-voting securities in exchange for their shares, any gains are taxable at the time of the merger.

II.   The valuation of a merger candidate is an application of capital budgeting principles.

    A.   Valuation of a merger candidate is necessary to determine the price to be paid. Three major methods are used.

        1.   The *comparative price-earnings ratio method* examines prices and associated price-earnings ratios in recent acquisitions of similar companies.

        2.   The *adjusted book value method* attempts to determine the market value of the company's assets.

        3.   The *discounted cash flow method* applies usual capital budgeting techniques by discounting expected future free cash flows at an appropriate risk-adjusted rate. The free cash flow is computed as follows:

$$FCF = CF - I(1-T) - D_p - P_f - B - Y$$

where

FCF	=	free cash flow,
CF	=	after-tax operating cash flow,
I	=	before-tax interest payment,
T	=	corporate tax rate,
D_p	=	preferred dividends
P_f	=	required redemption of preferred stock,
B	=	required redemption of debt, and
Y	=	investment in property, plant, and equipment needed to maintain cash flow

    B.   The terms of a merger may involve almost any combination of cash, stock, or other financial instruments.

        1.   In a stock-for-stock exchange, the exchange ratio (ER) is the ratio of shares in the surviving company received to the number of shares surrendered in the acquired company.

        2.   The current earnings per share of the surviving company will increase (or decrease) if the price-earnings ratio of the surviving firm is greater than (or less than) the price-earnings ratio (using acquisition price) of the acquired firm. The post-merger price of the firm's stock may go up or down depending on the post-merger price-earnings ratio determined in the marketplace. Normally, the post-merger price-earnings ratio determined in the marketplace. Normally, the post-merger price- earnings ratio is a weighted average of the pre-merger price-earnings ratios. Earnings per share growth through mergers may be more fantasmic than real.

        The earnings per share for the combined companies, EPS_c, is:

$$EPS_c = \frac{E_1 + E_2 + E_{12}}{NS_1 + NS_2 (ER)}$$

where

E_1	=	earnings of the acquiring company,
E_2	=	earnings of the acquired,
E_{12}	=	synergistic earnings for the merger (if any),
NS_1	=	number of outstanding shares for acquirer,
NS_2	=	number of outstanding shares for acquired company, and
ER	=	exchange ratio

If an acquirer suffers immediate EPS dilution, EPS may eventually be increased if the target is predicted to have fairly rapid earnings growth.

3.   The maximum price an acquiring company should pay for a target firm is given by:

$$P_{max} = (P/E)_1 (EPS_2)$$

where:

P_{max}	=	maximum offering price without incurring an initial EPS dilution,
$(P/E)_1$	=	P/E ratio of acquiting company, and
EPS_2	=	P/E ratio of acquiring company.

From P_{max}, the exchange ratio can be easily computed.

C.   LBO financing can be fairly complex

1.   The equity portion of the financing is known as "ground floor" financing.

2.   The "second floor" or "top floor" financing consists of short term financing usually from commercial banks using accounts receivable and inventory as collateral.

3.   A substantial portion of financing comes from "mezzanine" financing consisting of high risk subordinated debentures often called junk bonds.

4.   LBOs are accompanied by significant cost-cutting programs to improve efficiency.

5.   LBO assets are typically written-up to market value that can be substantially greater than book value resulting in significant tax shelters from high depreciation charges.

III.   There are different legal types of failures.

    A.   A firm is *technically insolvent* if it is unable to meet its current obligations as they come due, but the firm's assets have greater value than its liabilities.

    B.   A firm is *legally insolvent* if the recorded value of its assets is less than the recorded value of its liabilities.

    C.   A firm is not actually *bankrupt* unless it is unable to pay its debts and it files a bankruptcy petition in accordance with Federal bankruptcy laws.

IV.   There are a variety of reasons why businesses fail.

    A.   Economic factors such as industry weakness and low profitability result in business failures.

    B.   Financial factors such as heavy operating expenses and too little capital.

    C.   Experience factors such as poor management.

    D.   Other factors such as fraud, neglect, poor strategies, and disasters.

V.   A failing firm has two alternatives.

    A.   The failing company can (1) attempt to resolve its difficulties with its creditors on a *voluntary* or *informal* basis, or (2) petition the courts and formally declare *bankruptcy*. A company's creditors may also petition the courts to declare the company bankrupt.

    B.   Regardless of whether the firm deals with its difficulties informally or formally, the company must decide whether to reorganize or liquidate the business.

        1.   The company should reorganize if its *going-concern value* exceeds its *liquidation value* and the company should liquidate if its liquidation value is more than its going-concern value.

        2.   Liquidation value is the proceeds that would be received from the sale of the firm's assets minus its liabilities.

        3.   The going-concern value is the capitalized value of the company's operating earnings minus its liabilities.

VI.   When a company has cash flow problems, there are informal alternatives besides formal bankruptcy.

    A.   One of the first things a troubled firm may do is to stretch its payables, which may buy a few weeks of time.

B.   Debt restructuring is one alternative available to a failing firm in which it attempts to resolve its difficulties with creditors on a voluntary basis through an extension or a composition.

    1.   In an *extension*, the failing firm gets its creditors to agree to extend the time it has to pay its debts.

    2.   In a *composition*, the creditors agree to settle for less than 100% of the amount owed and accept this as full discharge of their original claims.

    3.   Before lenders agree to a debt restructuring, they may also require the firm's suppliers to make concessions. The lenders may demand warrants in return for their concessions.

C.   A troubled company can sell off real estate or operating divisions to raise cash.

D.   Another method of raising cash is a sale and leaseback of land and buildings.

E.   A *creditors' committee* may be formed to represent the company's creditors. The creditors' committee meets and negotiates with the company's management on appropriate actions to take. If successful, the legal and administrative expenses associated with formal bankruptcy may be avoided.

F.   An *assignment* is the process of liquidation outside of the bankruptcy courts. A trustee is assigned the assets, and then the trustee is responsible for selling the assets and distributing the proceeds in the best interests of the creditors.

VII.   Formal U. S. bankruptcy procedures are codified in the Bankruptcy Reform Act of 1978. *Reorganization*, which should be attempted when a company's going-concern value exceeds its liquidation value, is covered in *Chapter 11* of the Bankruptcy Reform Act.

A.   In a Chapter 11 proceeding, the failing company seeks protection from its creditors while it attempts to work out a plan of reorganization.

B.   The court may appoint a trustee to run the business and protect the creditors' interests.

C.   Chapter 11 bankruptcy proceedings may be initiated voluntarily by the company (voluntary petition) or by a group of three or more unsecured creditors with aggregate claims of at least $500 (involuntary petition).

D.   After working out a plan of reorganization, the plan must be approved first by the bankruptcy court and then by the company's creditors. If the court and creditors approve, the company can leave Chapter 11.

E.   The bankruptcy court and the Securities and Exchange Commission (SEC) review the plan of reorganization on the basis of its *fairness* and its *feasibility*. Fairness means that claims are settled in order of their priority. Feasibility means that the business has a good chance of reestablishing successful operations.

F.   Following the SEC review for fairness and feasibility, the bankruptcy court submits the plan of reorganization to the company's security holders. Before the court can finally approve the plan, two- thirds of each group of debtholders and a simple majority of stockholders must vote in favor of the plan. Dissenters may appeal to a higher court.

G.   A new alternative for firms considering bankruptcy is the pre-packaged bankruptcy. A pre-packaged bankruptcy must be agreed upon by at least 51% of creditors who hold at least two-thirds of the debt before a filing can be made. Pre-packaged bankruptcy has the advantage of shortening the bankruptcy process by a few months.

VIII.   *Liquidation*, which should be attempted when the company's going-concern value is less than its liquidation value, is covered in *Chapter 7* of the Bankruptcy Reform Act of 1978.

A.   The court selects a referee to handle the administrative procedures. The referee arranges a meeting of the creditors who, in turn, select a trustee to liquidate the business and distribute the proceeds according to the priorities in Chapter 7 of the Bankruptcy Reform Act.

B.   Secured debts are satisfied first from the sale of the secured assets. Then the following order of priority is used to pay unsecured debts:

1.   expenses involved in administration of the bankruptcy;

2.   business expenses incurred after an involuntary petition is filed, but before a trustee is appointed;

3.   wages owed for services performed during the three months prior to bankruptcy proceedings, not to exceed $2,000 per employee;

4.   certain unpaid contributions to employee benefit plans (limited to $2,000 per employee);

5.   certain customer lay-away deposits, not to exceed $900 per individual;

6.   taxes owed to Federal, state, and local governments;

7.   claims of general or unsecured creditors;

8.   preferred stockholders; and

9.   common stockholders.

TRUE AND FALSE QUESTIONS

Agree with each of the statements or **reject** it and modify it so that it is acceptable.

1.   In a merger of two companies, both companies continue to exist and to operate under their own names.

2.   A consolidation is a form of business combination in which a company (the parent) purchases 100% or a controlling interest in another firm (the subsidiary). Both firms legally continue to exist.

3.   A *vertical merger* is between companies that may have a buyer-seller relationship with each other where a *horizontal merger* is a combination between companies that compete directly with each other.

4.   One possible motive for mergers is to get assets cheaply when the acquired firm's securities are selling for substantially less than the value of its assets.

5.   When a high price-earnings ratio business acquires a low price-earnings ratio business, the earnings per share and market price per share of the surviving firm will increase.

6.   When a merger is accomplished by a pure exchange of shares (specified in the exchange ratio), the selling firm's stockholders are liable for capital gains taxes at the time of the merger.

7.   A leveraged buyout is a transaction in which the buyer of a company borrows a large portion of the purchase price, using the purchased asset as partial collateral for the loans.

8.   Shark repellants refers to measures firms use to discourage unfriendly takeover attempts.

9.   "White Knight" refers to the situation where the target firm turns around and makes a bid for the bidder.

10.   "Mezzanine" financing consists of equity financing usually associated with leveraged buyouts.

11.   An acquiring firm is legally obligated to pay book value for any company it wishes to buy.

12.   In the purchase method of accounting for mergers, acquired assets are recorded at their fair market values, and any additional amount paid is listed as goodwill, which must then be amortized.

13.   A tender offer is a public announcement by a company (or individual) indicating that it will pay a price above the current market price for the shares "tendered" of a company it wishes to acquire.

14.   A firm is technically insolvent when it is unable to meet its current obligations as they come due, but the firm's assets are worth more than its liabilities.

15.   One thing a firm with cash flow problems may do to buy time is to stretch its accounts receivable.

16.   In an extension, the failing company gets its creditors to extend the time it has to pay its debts.

17.   In a composition, the creditors agree to accept less than 100 percent of the amount owed and discharge the balance of their claims.

18.   When the going-concern value of a bankrupt business exceeds the liquidation value, the firm should be liquidated and the proceeds distributed to various creditors.

19.   An assignment is the process of informally liquidating a business outside of the jurisdiction of the bankruptcy court.

20.   In a bankruptcy, secured creditors (such as mortgage holders) have top priority in liquidation.

21.   When the SEC evaluates a plan or reorganization for fairness, the SEC tries to predict whether the business has a good chance for reestablishing successful operations.

22.   Frequently, failing firms have too much financial leverage, too much short-term debt relative to long-term debt, and poor management of receivables and payables.

23.   A business cannot be forced into bankruptcy involuntarily.

24.   An advantage of "prepackaged bankruptcy" is that it can speed up the bankruptcy process by several months.

Answers to True and False Questions

1.   In a merger of two companies, the surviving company continues to operate under its own name and the other company legally ceases to exist.
2.   The statement applies to a holding company. In a consolidation, the combining companies are dissolved legally and another new company is formed.
3.   True.
4.   True.
5.   Earnings per share will increase, but the behavior of the share price is much more complicated (it may go in any direction).
6.   Stock-for-stock exchanges are tax-free.
7.   True.
8.   True.
9.   "White Knight" refers to the situation where the target firm facing the prospect of an unfriendly takeover finds another more friendly company (the "white knight") to make a counter offer for the firm.
10.   "Mezzanine" financing consists of high risk subordinated debentures, often called junk bonds, associated with leverage buyouts.

11.   There is no legal reason to pay book value for anything.
12.   True.
13.   True.
14.   True.
15.   This would make their cash flow problems worse. The company could stretch its payables.
16.   True.
17.   True.
18.   In this situation, a reorganization should be attempted.
19.   True.
20.   Secured creditors have top priority in liquidation only to the extent that their claims are satisfied by the secured property. Any amount left over is considered a general claim, which is behind several categories on the priority for paying unsecured claims (ahead of preferred and common stockholders).
21.   Fairness means that claims are settled in priority and feasibility means that the firm has some prospect of operating profitably.
22.   True.
23.   A company's creditors can petition the courts to have a company declared bankrupt.
24.   True.

MULTIPLE CHOICE QUESTIONS

1.   The difference between a merger and a consolidation is that:
   A.   Consolidations involve nondomestic firms and mergers include only domestic ones.
   B.   Mergers involve larger firms than do consolidations.
   C.   With a consolidation, the combining companies are dissolved and an entirely new company is formed.
   D.   With a merger, the combining companies are dissolved and an entirely new company is formed.
   E.   A merger involves the issuance of common stock and no new security issues are included in a consolidation.

2.   _____ mergers are combinations of companies that compete directly with each other.
   A.   Vertical
   B.   Horizontal
   C.   Conglomerate
   D.   Competitive
   E.   Operational

3.   The management team of Company A borrows a large amount of money and buys the outstanding equity shares in the company. This is an example of:
   A.   A joint venture.
   B.   An equity carve-out.
   C.   An operational restructuring.
   D.   A leveraged buyout.
   E.   A financial restructuring.

4.   An anti-takeover measure that makes outstanding securities exercisable when an unfriendly bidder obtains control of a specified number of outstanding shares is known as a:
        A.   Poison pill.
        B.   Golden parachute.
        C.   Pac-man defense.
        D.   Self-destruction device.
        E.   White knight.

5.   Which of the following is not a valid reason for a company to seek external growth through mergers?
        A.   To maintain availability of raw materials.
        B.   To achieve greater diversification.
        C.   To take advantage of its tax-loss carryforwards.
        D.   To achieve economies of scale.
        E.   To avoid paying a dividend.

6.   In the _____ method of accounting for mergers, the acquired company's assets are recorded on the acquiring company's books at their former book value and no goodwill is created.
        A.   Purchase
        B.   Pooling-of-interests

7.   Which of the following will increase the free cash flow of a firm al other things unchanged?
        A.   A reduction in the after-tax operating cash flow
        B.   An increase in the annual interest payment on outstanding debt.
        C.   A reduction in the preferred dividend payment.
        D.   An increase in the corporate tax rate.
        E.   An increase in the required annual investment in property, plant and equipment.

8.   In a stock-for-stock exchange, the _____ is the ratio of shares in the surviving company received to the number of shares surrendered in the acquired company.
        A.   Swap ratio
        B.   Purchase ratio
        C.   Acquisition ratio
        D.   Merger ratio
        E.   Exchange ratio

9.   In the event of financial difficulties and bankruptcy, a firm should reorganize if its _____ exceeds its _____.
        A.   Going-concern value; liquidation value.
        B.   Assets' value; liabilities value.
        C.   Market value; asset value.
        D.   Market value; liquidation value
        E.   Going-concern value; liabilities value.

10.   If a firm files for bankruptcy under Chapter 7 of the Bankruptcy Reform Act of 1978, which of the
following claims is paid first?
   A.   Taxes owed the Federal, state and local governments
   B.   Preferred stockholders
   C.   Common stockholders
   D.   Wages owed for services performed
   E.   Customer lay-away deposits

Answers to Multiple Choice Questions

1.	C	5.	E	9.	A
2.	B	6.	B	10.	D
3.	D	7.	C		
4.	A	8.	E		

PROBLEMS

1.   Abbott Industries has negotiated the acquisition of The Castello Corporation. Under the terms of
the merger, Castello shareholders will receive 0.700 shares of Abbott for each of their old shares.
The pre-merger data for the two firms is

	Abbott	Castello
Sales	$200,000,000	$30,000,000
Net income	23,100,000	4,000,000
Common share outstanding	3,500,000	1,000,000
Earnings per share	6.60	4.00
Stock price	77.25	28.00
Price/earnings ratio	11.7x	7x

Assume there is no synergism.

a.   What is the post-merger earnings per share?

b.   If the post-merger price/earnings ratio drops to 10x, what is the premium received by
Castello shareholders (using the new price of Abbott)?

c.   Was this a successful merger for Abbott shareholders?

Solution:

a.   Net income = $23,100,000 + $4,000,000 = $27,100,000

Outstanding shares = 3,500,000 + 0.7(1,000,000) = 4,200,000

Earnings per share = 27,100,000/4,200,000 = $6.452

b.   Price = $6.452(10) = $64.52

Premium = [0.7(64.52) - 28]/28 = (45.164 - 28)/28

Premium = 17.164/28 = 0.613 or 61.3%

c.   No. Their shares dropped from $77.25 to $64.52, a decrease of $12.73 per share (about 16.5%). On the other hand, Castello shareholders realized a 61.3 percent gain.

2.   The president of Texas Conglomerated Inc., blindly seeks mergers without regard to anything except the effect on current earnings per share. TCI's current net income and outstanding shares are $125,000,000 and 25,0000,000, respectively, the EPS is $5.00, and the price per share is $57.50. Billy Bob Smith, TCI's president, wants to buy out Kansas Knitting which has net income of $8,000,000, a price of $40.00, EPS of $8.00, and 1,000,000 outstanding shares.

a.   What is the maximum number of new shares Billy Bob can offer for Kansas and keep his EPS at its current level?

b.   Billy Bob can float a bond paying 12% interest and use the proceeds to purchase Kansas stock for cash. How much can he offer and maintain his EPS? The tax rate = 0.40.

Solution:

a.   5.00 = net income/number of shares

5.00 = (125,000,000 + 8,000,000)/(25,000,000 + X)

X = 1.6 million shares

b.   5.00 = net income/number of shares

5.00 = [(125,000,000+8,000,000-0.12(B)(1-.40)]/25,000,000

B = $111,111,111

Billy Bob could offer $111,111,111 total or $13.89 per share for Kansas if he used a leveraged buyout and his EPS would still be $5.00.

3.   Princeton Products, Inc., is being liquidated following bankruptcy. The liabilities and capital of the firm prior to bankruptcy were:

Accounts payable	$10,000,000
Short-term bank loan (secured by accounts receivable)	3,500,000
Accrued wages (all less than $2,000 per person and earned in the last three months)	1,500,000
Accrued taxes	2,000,000
Mortgage (secured by property)	10,000,000
Debenture	5,000,000
Subordinated debenture (subordinated to debenture)	3,000,000
Preferred stock	2,000,000
Common stock	8,000,000
Retained earnings	(4,500,000)
Total Liabilities and Capital	$40,500,000

The trustee has liquidated the firm's assets for $30,000,000, which includes $4,500,000 for the accounts receivable and $6,000,000 for the property which was security for the mortgage. Court costs and legal fees are $4,000,000. There are no customer lay-away deposits, no unpaid business expenses incurred after filing bankruptcy. Indicate the money each class of creditors or owners should receive from the liquidation proceeds following the priorities in Chapter 7 of the Bankruptcy Reform Act of 1978.

Solution:

Total liquidation proceeds	$30,000,000
Less distributions to secured creditors:	
Short-term bank loan	3,500,000
Mortgage bond	6,000,000
Funds available after secured claims	$20,500,000
Less priority claims:	
Bankruptcy administration costs	4,000,000
Wages due employees	1,500,000
Taxes	2,000,000
Funds available for general creditors	$13,000,000

$$\begin{array}{c} \textit{Settlement percentage} \\ \textit{for general and} \\ \textit{unsecured creditors} \end{array} = \dfrac{\begin{array}{c} \textit{Funds available for general} \\ \textit{and unsecured creditors} \end{array}}{\begin{array}{c} \textit{Total claims of general} \\ \textit{and unsecured creditors} \end{array}}$$

$$\frac{13,000,000}{22,000,000} = .590909$$

Claimant	Total Claim	Settlement (59%) Before Adjustment for Subordination	Settlement (59%) After Adjustment for Subordination
Accounts Payable	$10,000,000	$ 5,909,091	$ 5,909,091
Mortgage	4,000,000	2,363,636	2,363,636
Debenture	5,000,000	2,954,546	4,727,273
Subordinated debenture	3,000,000	1,772,727	0
	$22,000,000	$13,000,000	$13,000,000

Funds available for preferred and common shareholders: $0

After payment of secured claims, $20,500,000 remains. The short-term bank loan secured by accounts receivable is paid off 100% and the $6,000,000 proceeds of the sale of property are applied to the mortgage bonds, which leaves the mortgage bondholders as general creditors for the $4,000,000 unsatisfied balance of their bond. A total of $7,500,000 now is used for the priority claims for bankruptcy administration costs, wages payable, and taxes payable. Since only $13,000,000 are available for general creditor claims of $22,000,000, general creditors received approximately 59 cents on the dollar. The funds due to the subordinated debentures are transferred to the debenture holders, and, since the debentures were not fully paid, the subordinated debenture owners receive nothing. Preferred and common stockholders get nothing.